ABZZ

ALPHA BETA ZERO TO ZILLION WORD CODES FOR NUMBERS

by

Dr Godwin Lekwuwa

authorHOUSE®

AuthorHouse™ UK
1663 Liberty Drive
Bloomington, IN 47403 USA
www.authorhouse.co.uk
Phone: 0800.197.4150

Published by AuthorHouse   01/15/2016

ISBN: 978-1-5049-9508-5 (sc)
ISBN: 978-1-5049-9509-2 (hc)
ISBN: 978-1-5049-9507-8 (e)

Print information available on the last page.

DEDICATION

Dedicated to all mental Athletes

CONTENTS

ABOUT THE AUTHOR

Godwin Lekwuwa is a Consultant Clinical Neurophysiologist based in the United Kingdom. He graduated as a medical doctor in 1981. During his medical school days he developed special interest in the neurological sciences, the human mind and the nature of man. To enhance his understanding of the human mental mechanisms, he took a master's degree in psychology and a PhD degree in Neurology from the Institute of Neurology, Queen square London. The ideas used in this book have been nurtured, incubated and refined since his medical school days. The memory aspects of these techniques were quite handy for examinations and won him almost all the prizes available in his medical school graduation year. The methods elaborated in this book are the basis for his encyclopedic knowledge of medical literature which surprises most people who know him. As the saying goes, "when a man appears to have specially developed faculties, ask him what books he reads". A book is a machine to think with.

SHORT SUMMARY

The ABZZ word code system is a method which can be used to convert any given number to word code equivalents. With this method, any given number from zero to zillion can be converted to word codes. The principles of this method are explained in this book. This book also contains a thesaurus which gives two examples of easily derivable and meaningful word-code equivalents of every number from "0 – 9999". It is a forerunner to a proposed online thesaurus which would list word code alternatives of every number from zero to one billion (0 – 1,000,000,000).

For centuries, people have been attracted to the idea of converting numbers to words. One of the major advantages of this is that people would be able find meaningful word names for phone numbers, passwords, pin numbers, log-in numbers, access codes etc. Other advantages include the ability to generate prospective number codes based on any words of your choice. Numerous other advantages and uses are elaborated in this book.

Word-code systems for numbers devised over the centuries have been cumbersome and difficult to use. This has limited their use in everyday life. The ABZZ word code system introduces a new, simpler and user friendly system of converting any given numbers to words and vice versa. The principles of the system can be mastered in a few minutes. Regular usage would engrain it as one of our basic thinking processes.

INTRODUCTION

ABZZ stands for Alpha Beta Zero to Zillion. The idea contained within this book is a method which can be used to convert any given number to its word code equivalent. With this method, any given number from zero to zillion can be converted to alphabet word-code equivalent. This book contains a thesaurus which gives two examples of easily derivable and meaningful word-code equivalents of every number from "0 – 9999". It is a forerunner to a proposed online thesaurus or database which would show many word code alternatives of every number from "0 – 1,000,000,000".

One of the major advantages of this is that people would be able find a word name for their phone numbers, or any memorable numbers. Other advantages include the ability to generate prospective number codes based on any words of your choice. There are numerous other advantages and uses enumerated in this book.

For centuries, people have been attracted to the idea of converting numbers to words. One major reason for this is the desire to use words as memory aids for numbers. In modern times, the average person has needs to remember phone numbers, registration numbers, passwords, pin numbers, log-in numbers, car numbers, house numbers, passport numbers, dates, access codes, and credit card numbers etc. Numbers can be long, but memory span is short. Numbers are abstract, dry, dull, and dreary. The brain is not usually excited by numbers unless they are associated with exciting consequences, meanings or results. When numbers are converted to words, the imagination comes to life. Imagination helps to transform simple, dull, bland and non-stimulating numbers into vibrant, colourful and attractive images which stick to the mind.

Fortunately, mankind has discovered that external memory aids such as written words, digital memories in computers, mobile phones and electronic tablets are far more reliable and robust than the human memory. However, there are still hosts of benefits we can derive by being able to convert numbers to words and vice versa. These benefits we shall see in the course of this book.

The desire to use words as memory aids can be traced back to Adam. Adam did not try to use word-codes for numbers but he obviously used words to aid memory when God told him to name the animals of the fields. Adam sat in his throne room as the animals trundled past in the plains below:

"And I shall call this a Rhinoceros"

Eve: "why call it such an awkward name darling?"

Adam: "Can't you see it looks like a Rhinoceros, stupid?" Adam could see it. Rhino means nose, and Ceros means horn; horn on the nose! This is the beginning of word-code mnemonic systems.

People have wittingly or unwittingly used word-code mnemonics to remember at every age. Most scientific nomenclature is based on word-code mnemonic systems. Science uses Latin, Greek and other ancient language prefixes and suffixes to cobble new meaningful words and compound words together. The nomenclature systems used in many sciences have made it easy to cobble root words into new compound words which are easily understood without need to consult a dictionary. As a Clinical Neurophysiologist, I have to remember most of the 640 skeletal muscles in the human body. I have to remember their attachments and their functions. But this has been made easy by the use of word codes in the nomenclature of the Neuromuscular System. For instance, if somebody says "examine the Flexor Pollicis Longus"; I know he is saying "examine the long flexor muscle of the thumb". Likewise, "Abductor Digiti Minimi Manus" will be the abductor muscle of the little finger of the hand. The muscles of the human body are named such that if you understand Latin, you could accurately come up with the same names without having studied anatomy.

Converting numbers to words, and words back to numbers is a further step in the bid to use familiar meaningful words as memory aids. Unfortunately, many word-code systems for numbers devised over the centuries have been cumbersome and difficult to use. This has limited their use in everyday life. According to a Wikipedia review the idea of converting alphabets to numbers was said to have started with Pierre Herigone (1580 – 1643) who devised the earliest version of the Major Memory System. This system was further developed by Stanislaus Mink Von Wennsshein. The objective of this system was to create a memory system that could convert numbers into letters and letters into numbers. In 1730, Richard Grey devised a system that used both consonants and vowels to represent digits. This system was said to be complicated and was improved upon in 1808 by Gregor Von Feinaigle who introduced the method of representing the digits with consonant sounds. The method of using consonant sounds to represent number digits has continued to evolve over the years to the present day Mnemonic Major System which is widely used, but cumbersome. Authors who have added to this system over the years include Francis Fauvel Gouraud[1], Harry Lorayne[2] and Tony Buzan[3]. Other modifications of the alphabet-number system include the works of Dominic O'Brien[4].

Herigone's Major Memory System is also recognised as the phonetic system because it works by converting numbers to consonant sounds. The determinant of the number translation of a word is not the spelling of the word but the consonant sounds. Each number is encoded to consonants with similar sounds, pronounced with similar mouth and tongue positions. Thus j, sh, ch, dg, zh, and soft "g", encode the number 6. Double letters of the same consonant are disregarded and retain the sound and number encoded by one consonant. The letters s, z and soft c encode the number "0". But hard "C" encodes the number 7.

The new ABZZ word code system

The ABZZ word code system for numbers described in this book aims to introduce a new, simpler and user friendly system of converting any given numbers to words and vice versa. One difficulty which has existed over the centuries with trying to devise word-codes for numbers has been the finite number of words available in the human vocabulary. Numbers are unlimited, but words are limited. Rapidly expanding developments in many sciences, arts and digital literature, have given rise to exponential increase in the number of words available in the human vocabulary. Before the arrival of the internet, the availability of words and their meanings were limited. One would have needed large libraries with tomes of encyclopedias to have access to the sizable number of words available today for human usage. With the internet, myriads of words are now at our finger tips. The ABZZ is an idea whose time has come. The next chapter will discuss the principles of the ABZZ word-code system for numbers.

1) Gouraud, Francis Fauvel; Phreno-Mnemotechny or The Art of Memory, Wiley and Putnam, 1845.

2) Lorayne, Harry and Lucas, Jerry; The Memory Book: The classic guide to improving your Memory at work, at School, at Play. Ballantine Books; Reissue edition 1996.

3) Buzan, Tony; Master your Memory. BBC Worldwide Limited, Millennium edition 2000.

4) O'Brien Dominic, You Can Have Amazing Memory; learn life changing techniques and tips from the memory maestro: Watkins Publishing, London 2011.

PRINCIPLES OF THE ABZZ NUMBER WORD-CODE SYSTEM

The ABZZ system works by converting numbers into consonants and vice versa.

There are 26 letters in the Latin-English Alphabet system. The 26 letters are made of 20 consonants, five vowels (a, e, I, o, u) and "y" which frequently acts as a vowel but can also act as a consonant. In the ABZZ system, "y" is always treated as a vowel. This means there are 6 vowels and 20 consonants in the ABZZ alphabet system.

There are 10 single integer numbers in the decimal numbering system. These numbers are 0, 1, 2, 3, 4, 5, 6, 7, 8, 9.

Given that there are 20 consonants and 10 integer numbers, 2 consonants are assigned to code for each number in the ABZZ system. The numbers and the consonants that code for each of them can easily be remembered using the following verse:

ZERO WON HOBO QUIT MAFIA; LIVE SIX KICK JADED PIGGY

Each number from 0 - 9 is represented by two consonants as listed in the table below.

Number Digit	Consonant equivalents of number digits	Memory Verse
0	Z, R	ZERO
1	W, N	WON
2	H, B	HOBO
3	Q, T	QUIT
4	M, F	MAFIA
5	L, V	LIVE
6	S, X	SIX
7	K, C	KICK
8	J, D	JADED
9	P, G	PIGGY

Table 1 showing the number equivalent of each consonant

To use the system, all you need is the ability to know the consonants which encode each of the digits from 0 – 9. The short verse above is to help remember what consonants code for what digits. This verse which can be memorised in less than a minute lays the foundation for using the ABZZ system. The verse contains all letters of the alphabet.

An alternative but similar verse would be: ZERO WON HOBO QUIT FAME; LIVELY SIX KICK JADED PIGGY.

The consonants act as bricks in which numbers are inscribed. The vowels act as mortar which bond the bricks together. The vowels are just fillers and do not have any numbers inscribed on them. No consonants are neglected as long as they have appeared in the spelling of a word. With these bricks and mortar, any combination of numbers, from zero to zillion, can be constructed into meaningful word, words, phrases or texts. This is number masonry and graffiti.

Every consonant in the ABZZ system has a number encoded in it. This means that every word with a consonant has a number equivalent. Double letters of the same consonant are not regarded as one letter unlike the phonetic number coding systems. Simple words, compound words, short words and long words can all be used. Number codes are often easier to remember when all the number-digits can be captured into one word. The fewer the number of word chunks that make up the memory code, the easier it is to handle. Most numbers in everyday use can be encoded with 1 – 3 chunks of words.

There are no phonetic components in the ABZZ system. For instance "C" will always remain 7 whether it is a hard C or a soft C. Likewise; "G" is always 9 whether it is a soft "G" or a hard "G". Each letter retains its status independent of associated letters and sound alterations. Thus "H" will always encode 2 regardless of whether it changes phonation as in "CH", "SH" or "GH".

The main sources of words used in the ABZZ system are English grammar and names of people, places and events. Every word in any language could be used as long as it is spelt with English-Latin alphabets and has a meaning to the user. Meaning to the user is the most important consideration in word-codes in the ABZZ system. When words have a meaning, we can readily form mental pictures and associations. Mental images and associations act as essential hooks to anchor memory items to our knowledge substratum and prevent them from sinking into the uncharted oblivion of the unconscious brain. No words are discriminated against whether they are nouns, pronouns, verbs, adverbs, present tense, past tense or plurals etc.

GUIDELINES AND USES OF THE ABZZ WORD-CODE SYSTEM

Name-codes, Nametags, Number-codes, Number-tags

The ABZZ system can be used prospectively to generate a new number-code from words which have special meanings to the user. It can also be used retrospectively to generate a name-code for any given number, short or long.

Prospective nametags

The ABZZ nametag system is excellent when it comes to generating new memorable numbers. In self- generated memorable numbers, it is better to generate the numbers from our own words; words which are meaningful and memorable to us. For instance, you may desire to generate a new pass-code for the combination lock of the "Coffee Room" in your workplace. The desire is to generate a number which is easily remembered by all the office workers who use the coffee room. The memorable number could be encoded as "coffee room" (74404). You might also encode it in the word "Nescafe" (1674). Another prospective example of using the ABZZ is changing your pin number at the ATM machine. If your name is Casper, you can change your password to "7690". For self- generated memorable numbers, it is advisable to use the prospective method and the number of available words you can use is only limited by your vocabulary.

Retrospective Use of ABZZ nametags

Externally generated memory numbers are usually made up by others and given to us to use. This is usually the case with access codes, telephone numbers, and registration numbers. In these cases, you may need to generate your own word-codes or check the word-code thesaurus to find the word equivalents of your memorable numbers. This volume of the ABZZ has been written with tables showing two representative word-codes for all the numbers ranging from "0" to "9999". As a sequel to this publication, it is intended to publish online a thesaurus of all the numbers of up to 10 digits and their lists of word-codes using universally understood vocabulary.

Some numbers in the ABZZ thesaurus have only a few word code options, but other numbers could have word code options reaching several hundreds. This is good and gives people the choice to select words most appealing to them. For each of the numbers 1-9999 represented in this volume, I have chosen just two words which I found immediately appealing. The users are entitled to use alternative words which are more appealing to them. I am not always sure why I have chosen particular words to represent each of the numbers in this volume of ABZZ. It is possible if I have to write this volume again, I will choose different words depending on the momentary reasoning swirling around in my head. For instance, the number "9551" has many word code options as detailed below, but I have chosen to include only "pollen and pillow" in this volume of ABZZ. The following word code options are available for the number 9551:

Apollonia, Apollyon, Argyle-Avenue, Eagle-Lane, Eagle-view, Epyllion, Galilaean, Galilean, Gallane, Gallein, Galleon, Gallian, Galliano, Gallin, Gallina, Gallinae, Galline, Gallon, Galloon, Gallow, Galloway, Galvani, Galvano, Gillian, Gillion, Gluvian, Glylin, Goal-line, Goal-vine, Guillain, Gullion, Paillon, Pallini, Pallone, Paullinia, Paullone, Pavilion, Pavulon, Peel-avenue, Pellionia, Pellow, Pial-vein, Pillion, Pillow, Pillowy, Playline, Pleven, Plevin, Plevna, Pluvian, Pole-lane, Pole-line, Pole-view, Pollan, Pollen, Pollinia, Polyline, Polyvin, Pull-away, Pullen, Pullin, Pull-in, Pull-on, Regal-Lane, Regal-line, Repeal-law, Replevin, and Replevin.

Addition of familiar names and their variants from many languages greatly expands the number of words available in the ABZZ system. When human names are added to the lists of word-code options, the list of available word options get even longer. The word-code options for "9551" will thus elongate to include:

Aguillian, Aguillion, Aguillon, Agullion, Agullon, Aiguillon, Apellonia, Apolline, Apollinia, Apollon, Apollona, Apollone, Apolloni, Apollonia, Apollonio, Auguillon, Egllona, Gaalloway, Gaillani, Gaillon, Galavan, Galaven, Galavin, Galileoin, Galivan, Galivn, Gallain, Gallan, Gallaneau, Gallani, Gallano, Gallaway, Gallawaye, Galleani, Galleano, Galleen, Gallein, Gallen, Gallena, Galleni, Galleno, Galleon, Galleyn, Gallian, Galliani, Galliano, Gallien, Galliena, Galliene, Gallieni, Gallieno, Gallin, Gallina, Galline, Gallineau, Gallini, Gallino, Gallion, Gallione, Gallioni, Galliway, Gallno, Gallon, Gallone, Galloni, Gallow, Gallowa, Galloway, Galloweay, Gallowey, Gallowy, Gallun, Gallway, Gallwey, Gallyean, Gallyeon, Gallyon, Galovan, Galvain, Galvan, Galvani,Galvano, Galvean,Galven, Galvin, Galvina, Galvine, Galvon, Galylean, Gavelin, Gavlin, Geeleven, Gellan, Gellean, Gellein, Gellen, Gelleny, Gellian, Gellin, Gellineau, Gellion, Gellon, Gellone, Gellow, Gelvan, Gelven, Gelvin, Gelvon, Gilalin, Gililan, Gillain, Gillan, Gillane, Gillaney, Gillani, Gillaway, Gillean, Gilleeny, Gilleiien, Gillein, Gillen, Gilleoin, Gilleon, Gilleyian, Gilleyn, Gillian, Gilliana, Gilliane, Gilliean, Gillien, Gillin, Gillino, Gillioen, Gillion, Gillon, Gilloon, Gillow, Gilloway, Gillun, Gillyean, Gillyn,Gillyon, Gilvan,Gilven, Gilvin, Giullian, Giulliano, Givilian, Givvin, Glavan, Glaviano, Glavin, Glavina, Glavine, Glavon, Gleven, Glloway, Glovan, Gloven, Goellen, Goillon, Golivane, Gollain, Gollan, Gollaway, Gollen, Gollin, Gollino, Gollion, Golliway, Gollon, Gollow, Golloway, Golloyn, Gollway, Golovin, Golovina, Golovine, Golovnia, Golvin, Gouillion, Gouillon, Gouliilon, Goullion, Goullow, Guellow, Guillain, Guillan, Guillani, Guillen, Guillian, Guilliani, Guillien, Guillin, Guillion, Guillon, Guilloneau, Guillow, Guillun, Gulielini, Gulilino, Gullain, Gullan, Gullane, Gullen, Gullian, Gulliani, Gulliano, Gullien, Gullin, Gulline, Gullion, Gullon, Gullow, Gullyan, Gulvin, Guuillien, Gyllian, Gyllin, Gyllion, Pallin, Pallini, Pallino, Pallone; Palyulin, Paullin, Pavelin, Pavlina, Pavolini, Pelevin, Pellew, Pellina, Pellini, Pellino, Pellion, Pelyovin, Pillon, Pillone, Pilloni, Pleavin, Plevani, Plevano, Pleven, Plevin, Plouvin, Pollen, Pollin, Pollina, Pollini, Pollino, Polloni, Pollonio, Pullan, Pullano, Pullen, Pullin, Pullini, Pullino, Pulvini, Pulvino, Repellin, Repellini, Yrigollen.

I have endeavoured to use mainly the English language in the word-code options in this edition of ABZZ because of wide universal usage of the English language. The proposed online word-code thesaurus associated with this book would increase its spectrum of word-code options by adding people's names from other languages worldwide. People's names are the best handles we have to most of the world languages. It is up to the user to choose which of these word codes has a meaning to him. If you live in England, the compound word "Hang-hoe" for 2192 would make more meaning whereas the word "Huang-He" would be preferable in China. For a medical doctor, the word "Nocturia" for 1730 would be more attractive whereas a lawyer is more likely to prefer the word "Enactor".

Alpha-numeric memorable codes; Storing and Concealing Passwords

The ABZZ system allows for generation of very strong alpha-numeric passwords which are unique to us. Using the ABZZ coding system a person named Daffy Duck could write his pass-code as "daffy877", or "844duck". Different variations of this could be generated using the same basic technique. You can also partially convert number digits into ABZZ. Given a phone number like 0800250008, you can remember it by partially changing it to ABZZ. In this case 0800250008 could then become 0800Blizzard where Blizzard represents the 250008 component of the number. You can decide on a new password called "Open Sesame" which in alpha-numeric format can become "Open664".

You can also use the ABZZ to code and conceal pin numbers. Tear the original pin number given to you by the bank and save the number as an ABZZ word-code in a diary or other book. The word-code can be buried among other words in a sentence or alphabet soup. You don't necessarily even have to remember the name-code. You just write the name code in a place of choice and anytime you look it up, you convert it back to numbers.

Sentence Option variations in the ABZZ system

One variant use of the ABZZ is to utilise only the numbers encoded by the first consonant in every word of a sentence, catch-phrase, quotation, song, poem or other verse. The following quotations are examples: "Life is too short to be little"; the initial consonants of each word are LSTSTBL or number-code equivalent of 5636325. "A book is a machine to think with"; the initial consonants are BSMTTW or number-code equivalent of 264331. These numbers could well be somebody's memorable codes. Similarly, one may decide to use only the last consonant in each word. In the catch phrase "repeal the law of gravity", the last consonants of each word will form "LHWT" or number-code equivalent of 5213.

Abbreviations

Every consonant in a word code counts. Familiar abbreviations, titles, acronyms and initials of names could all be used to complement words. For instance "CT scanner" would have number-code equivalent of 7367110; "CNN.com" would be 71174; Mini.co.uk would be 4177, and "Mr DJ Sidebottom" would be 4088682334.

Chunking and creating known or new compound words

The working memory of man is known to have a limited capacity. A common measure of the working memory is the memory span, which is said to have around seven elements (plus or minus two). These elements are called chunks. A memory element or chunk could be made of digits, letters, words or other verbal contents. The number of elements in a normal memory span is said to be around 7 for digits, 6 for letters and 5 for words. The number of elements or chunks in a memory span is said to depend on the category and characteristic of the chunks used. A number with 7 digits will thus have 7 chunks. Numbers with more than 9 digits or chunks are difficult to remember off-hand unless a memory technique is used either knowingly or unknowingly. A number composed of 3 digits is easier to remember than a number composed of 7 digits. For words, the memory span is longer when the words are short and more familiar. With or without explicit knowledge of how this system operates, humans have instinctively learnt to increase their memory span by organising memory items into easily remembered chunks. Using the ABZZ system, a single word chunk can be used to code multiple number digit chunks e.g. the single word chunk 'childishness' would code the number '725862166' which is composed of 9 digit chunks.

Most numbers below 100,000 will have single word code equivalents. When single word codes cannot be found for a long multi-digit number, it is advisable to break the number into batches of 1- 4 digits that can easily be coded using 2, 3 or 4 consonant words. The word codes for the number batches are then combined to form meaningful compound words or phrases. As an example, there may not be an easily available meaningful simple word code for the number 2469. You can form a new compound word such as "bum-sag" to code for 2469; the first 2 digits will form "bum" and the last two will form "sag". It is not difficult to imagine the meaning of the new compound word "bum-sag". As an alternative, you can also form the compound word "beef-soup" which also codes for the same number.

Precision in spellings

Numbers are digital and very precise. Word spellings can be altered without changing the meaning of a word. But numbers or number groups cannot be altered without changing what the number stands for. Changing the vowel component of a word does not change the number equivalent; but any change in the consonant component of a word changes its number equivalent. The implication of this is that when converting numbers to words, we have to be precise about the spelling we have in mind. The ABZZ number equivalent of a word depends strictly on the letters that form the word and not the sound of the word. It is important to remember which spelling you have used when words having the same meaning can be spelt in different ways e.g. jail/gaol, hiccough/hiccup, cosy/cozy, Odesa/Odessa, enrol/enroll. It may be important in some cases to be clear whether you are using British spellings or American spellings. The words polarize and polarise have the same meaning but they are spelt differently by the Americans and the British. If you spell the word polarize, the number-code equivalent would be 9500; but if spelt as polarise, the number-code equivalent changes to 9506.

The sound may be similar, but the spellings, meanings and the number equivalents may be very different. In the ABZZ word code system, there is a huge difference between "gracias" and "grassy ass". The number equivalents are 9076 and 906666. It should be remembered that words may even have the same alphabets but have differing meanings e.g. capsize and cap-size; kidnap and kid-nap; inform and in-form; resign and re-sign; godown and go-down.

The meaning of a word and sound may remain unchanged but people often adopt different styles of spelling representation. The following words largely mean the same thing but the spellings are represented differently by different people:

St. Pete	6393
St. Peter	63930
St. Peters	639306
Saint Pete	61393
Saint Peter	613930
Saint Peters	6139306

The Peg memory system

The Peg memory system teaches the use of known items, objects or words to peg or anchor new items to be remembered sequentially. To use the peg system, the user will need to pre-memorize a list of items which will serve as the peg. Once peg lists are formed and memorized, they can be used over and over again in different memory tasks. When there is a need to memorize a list of objects, each new item is anchored to an existing or pre-memorized peg. Peg lists are often generated from groups of items with known sequential positions, words that are easy to associate with numbers, rhymes, and the phonetic major memory system. The ABZZ system can be easily used to generate peg lists as shown by the simple example of words representing the numbers 0 – 9:

0) Zee (as a person's name)

1) Wee

2) Bee

3) Tea

4) Fee

5) Lee (as in the leeward side)

6) Sea

7) Key

8) Dee (as in River Dee)

9) Pea

Mental Training

The brain is like a muscle; the more it is used, the more efficient it becomes. An inherent property of the ABZZ system is that regular usage would improve cogitation, concentration, attention span, vocabulary, spelling abilities and memory. The ABZZ Thesaurus contains thousands of words and names in current use. Usage of the ABZZ system brings to your attention many words which you may not have encountered before. The ABZZ would be a boost for all mental athletes.

Treasury of rhymes

The ABZZ thesaurus is a rich source of rhyming words and sounds. As an illustration, you may be looking for rhymes ending in "ance". Knowing that "ance" in the ABZZ system codes for 17, you could check the thesaurus for word codes ending in "17". Going serially, these would include: 17, 117, 217, 317, 417, 517, etc. By the time you have gone through most of the numbers ending in 17, you would have found a sizeable number of rhyming words like: lance, dance, annoyance, enhance, nuisance, balance, obeisance, trance, finance, affiance, variance, alliance, avoidance, elegance, stance, chance, durance, ordinance, defiance, advance, deviance, penance, glance and guidance. If instead of words ending in "ance", you are interested in words ending in "nic", going through the same word-codes would yield rhymes like: cynic, panic, hunnic, bubonic, botanic, beatnik, hymnic, hygienic, biogenic, teutonic, titanic, taconic, autogenic, myotonic, metonic, masonic, myogenic, laconic, Canonic, actinic, cationic, Ecumenic, clinic, diatonic, phonic, psionic, picnic, peacenik, pyogenic, and geoponic.

Games

The ABZZ thesaurus can be used as a game. Families, groups, or friends travelling together can play challenge games on the ability to generate as many words as possible coding for the number plate of the car ahead, or any other number in sight. This can be a good form of mental athletics among friends.

Pangram

The memory verse for ABZZ can be used as a pangram. The best known English language pangram is "The quick brown fox jumps over a lazy dog". This short sentence contains all the letters of the alphabet and it is commonly used for touch typing practice. Similarly, the Memory verse for ABZZ contains all the letters of the alphabet "Zero won hobo, quit mafia; live six kick jaded piggy".

Naming phones

The ABZZ word-code can be used to convert any phone number into words or alphabet nametag. You can name your phone "Recalcitrant Bully" if the number is 07573013255.

One of the ultimate aims of the ABZZ is to have a thesaurus with words, representing all the numbers from zero to one billion (0 – 1,000,000,000). This would mean that the last 10 digits of phone numbers could be looked up in the thesaurus and converted into worded name-codes for the phone. There are not many single words with up to 10 digits in the English literature. However, compound words, descriptive words, catchphrases, slangs, clauses, clichés, verses and short sentences could all be used to capture long numbers. The use of catchwords and catchphrases is very familiar to those who name horses for horse racing. Eye catching race horse names such as "passing-wind" could become handy if your memorable number is 96619118; "masters-decree" would be appealing if your memorable number is 46306870; and "botox-detox" if your memorable number is 236836. Descriptive names such as "Golden Delicious" would represent 95818576. Combinations of people's first names, middle names and surnames can be used in coding long number digits like phone numbers. A name like "Ludwig Von Drake" would represent 581951807. Phones could have first names, middle names and surnames. Phones could have male or female names. The names of phones could be in any language just like human names. Indeed, hidden and encoded in everybody's name is someone else's memorable number, or phone number waiting to be discovered. Name tags do not need to be proper nouns. They could be descriptive. They could be funny. Indeed, the more funny and weird the name tag sounds, the easier it is for your friends to remember (Von Restorff effect).

ABZZ THESAURUS

The chapters below show two representative word codes for each number from "0 – 9999". As elaborated in the previous chapter, some numbers in the ABZZ thesaurus have only a few word code options, but other numbers could have word code options reaching several hundreds. This is good and gives people the choice to select words most appealing to them. For each of the numbers 0 - 9999 represented in this volume, I have chosen just two words which I found immediately appealing. The users are entitled to use alternative words which are more appealing to them. I am not always sure why I have chosen particular words to represent each of the numbers in this volume of ABZZ. It is possible if I have to write this volume again, I would choose different words depending on the momentary reasoning swirling around in my head. For instance, the number "9551" has many word code options as detailed in the previous chapter, but I have chosen to include only "pollen and pillow" in this volume of ABZZ thesaurus

ALPHA BETA 0 – 999

0	1	2	3	4
Air	No	Bee	Tea	Aim
Zoo	Woe	Hay	Toy	Foe
5	6	7	8	9
Oil	Sea	Key	Day	Ape
Ivy	Ox	Ice	Joy	Age
10	11	12	13	14
War	Nun	Web	Ant	Name
Wire	Wine	Nob	Wet	Wife
15	16	17	18	19
Nail	Nose	Ink	Need	Wig
Wool	Wax	Week	Wood	Nap
20	21	22	23	24
Bear	Bone	Baby	Bat	Beef
Hero	Hen	Hobo	Hut	Home
25	26	27	28	29
Blue	House	Bike	Bed	Bag
Heel	Bus	Hook	Hood	Hoop
30	31	32	33	34
Tyre	Tin	Tibia	Tout	Team
Quiz	Queen	Tube	Quote	Time
35	36	37	38	39
Tail	Tax	Teak	Toad	Tape
Tool	Taxi	Tyke	Quid	Tag
40	41	42	43	44
Maze	Man	Fib	Foot	Memo
Fire	Money	Mob	Mat	Fume
45	46	47	48	49
Fly	Fox	Face	Food	Map
Movie	Mouse	Mike	Mud	Fog
50	51	52	53	54
Layer	Lion	Lab	Loot	Leaf
Ivory	Vine	Vibe	Vote	Life
55	56	57	58	59
Love	Lease	Lake	Lead	Leg
Evil	Visa	Vice	Video	Voyage
60	61	62	63	64
Sore	Sun	Shoe	Suite	Safe
Size	Saw	Ash	Exit	Exam
65	66	67	68	69
Soil	Sex	Sky	Seed	Spy
Exile	Ass	Ski	Side	Soup
70	71	72	73	74
Car	Cow	Cab	Cot	Café
Cry	Coin	Cube	City	Coma

75	76	77	78	79
Cave	Case	Cake	Kid	Cap
Koala	Cox	Cook	Code	Cage
80	81	82	83	84
Door	Jaw	Job	Diet	Dam
Jury	Den	Jab	Jet	Dime
85	86	87	88	89
Dial	Daisy	Joke	Dad	Dog
Jail	Days	Juice	Judo	Jug
90	91	92	93	94
Pear	Pin	Pub	Goat	Game
Guru	Gene	Pooh	Pot	Poem
95	96	97	98	99
Pool	Goose	Peace	Pad	Egg
Glue	Pixie	Geek	Guide	Pipe
100	101	102	103	104
Worry	Neuron	Anaerobe	Wart	Enzyme
Nearer	Norway	Nairobi	Write	Worm
105	106	107	108	109
Nerve	Nurse	Work	Award	Energy
Nearly	Worse	Wreak	Word	Wrap
110	111	112	113	114
Owner	Nanny	New-boy	Newt	Anonym
Winery	Winona	Newby	Annuity	Nanomia
115	116	117	118	119
Annual	Annex	Wink	Wand	Wing
Annul	Onions	Wonky	Wind	Nonage
120	121	122	123	124
Wheeze	Whine	Nubby	White	Whim
Whore	When	Nabob	Whot	Whom
125	126	127	128	129
Whale	Nibs	Unhook	Anybody	Whip
Noble	Whose	Web-key	Nobody	Whoop
130	131	132	133	134
Nature	Nation	With	Antique	Anatomy
Enquiry	Notion	Wythe	Entity	Intima
135	136	137	138	139
Native	Nuts	Notice	United	Antigua
Natal	Ants	Antic	Noted	Net-pay
140	141	142	143	144
Wafer	Woman	Womb	Inmate	Infamy
Woofer	Anemone	Numb	Enmity	Niffy
145	146	147	148	149
Animal	Names	Anaemic	Nomad	Wimp
Anomaly	Animus	Anomic	Numidia	Wampee

150 Never Weaver	151 In-law Nylon	152 Navaho Wilby	153 Invite Wilt	154 Wolf Wolof
155 Novel Navel	156 Waves Wives	157 Invoice Novice	158 Wild Weld	159 Analogue Neology
160 Insure Ensure	161 Insane Unison	162 Wash Wish	163 Waste Nest	164 Awesome Anosmia
165 Weasel Insole	166 Noises Anxious	167 Anoxic Waseca	168 Inside Onside	169 Wasp Wisp
170 Ankara Inker	171 Niacin Weaken	172 Inch Eunuch	173 Nicety Incite	174 Income Wakayama
175 Ankle Weekly	176 Weeks Incus	177 Neck Wacky	178 Naked Unicode	179 Encage Wake-up
180 Indoor Injury	181 Widow Widen	182 Wood-hay Wood-bay	183 Nudity Weed-out	184 Random Najaf
185 Needle Nodule	186 Woods Index	187 Induce Anodic	188 Indeed Undead	189 Indigo Wedge
190 Anger Wager	191 Wagon Weapon	192 Enough Weigh	193 Ingot Inept	194 Angioma Enigma
195 Angel Angle	196 Wages Anopsia	197 No-peace Waupaca	198 Uniped Unpaid	199 Nappy Nippy
200 Breeze Hurry	201 Barn Horn	202 Herb Bribe	203 Brat Heart	204 Broom Harm
205 Bravo Hazel	206 Bruise Horse	207 Brace Brook	208 Bread Bride	209 Barge Harp
210 Benz Honour	211 Banana Bunny	212 Honey-Bee Bonobo	213 Bounty Hint	214 Byname Bionomy
215 Bowl Bowel	216 Beans Bones	217 Bank Hawk	218 Band Hound	219 Bang Bingo
220 Abhor Bohr	221 Baboon Bohn	222 Baobab Hubby	223 Abbot Habit	224 Behoof Bohemia

225	226	227	228	229
Bible	Babies	Abbacy	Behead	Boobage
Babel	Hubs	Boobook	Boyhood	Bob-up
230	231	232	233	234
Heater	Baton	Bath	Bouquet	Beatify
Obituary	Botany	Heath	Butty	Buy-time
235	236	237	238	239
Beetle	Bats	Batik	Hated	Biotype
Hotel	Botox	Abiotic	Heated	Boatage
240	241	242	243	244
Humour	Human	Bomb	Hamate	Buff
Before	Hymn	Bombay	Hefty	Huff
245	246	247	248	249
Bee-fly	Homes	Biface	Bifid	Hump
Homily	Humus	Bamako	Humid	Hemp
250	251	252	253	254
Blaze	Heaven	Bulb	Belt	Half
Boiler	Baloney	Blob	Bolt	Bloom
255	256	257	258	259
Ball	Bolus	Bloke	Blood	Bleep
Bell	Helix	Havoc	Blade	Help
260	261	262	263	264
Boxer	Basin	Bush	Beast	Bosom
Hoaxer	Bison	Bash	Host	Buxom
265	266	267	268	269
Biaxial	Abyss	Husk	Beside	Besiege
Basel	Boss	Basic	Hayseed	Housage
270	271	272	273	274
Baker	Bacon	Beach	Bay-cat	Become
Beaker	Beacon	Beech	Bay-city	Yahoo.com
275	276	277	278	279
Bacule	Abacus	Back	Hooked	Bicep
Boucle	Books	Buck	Booked	Hook-up
280	281	282	283	284
Hydra	Headway	Hijab	Bidet	Hedeoma
Header	Houdini	Head-boy	Hideout	Bodiam
285	286	287	288	289
Beadle	Beads	Bodice	Baddie	Badge
Boodle	Beds	Bed-key	Buddy	Budgie
290	291	292	293	294
Hooper	Bygone	High	Bigot	Bigamy
Beeper	Hygiene	Bough	He-goat	By-gum
295	296	297	298	299
Bagel	Biopsy	Biopic	Biped	Happy
Beagle	Hoops	Bi-peak	Bug-eyed	Hippy

300 Quarry Truro	301 Train Turin	302 Tribe Turbo	303 Tarot Treaty	304 Term Tram
305 Trail Trial	306 Tears Taurus	307 Trace Truce	308 Trade Triad	309 Trip Troop
310 Tenure Tower	311 Town Twin	312 Queen-bee Towhee	313 Tent Tweet	314 Autonomy Autonym
315 Towel Toe-nail	316 Queens Tunes	317 Tank Quincy	318 Tweed Tend	319 Tango Tongue
320 Author Theory	321 Athena Thin	322 Tabby Tubby	323 Tibet Theta	324 Thief Thyme
325 Table Tubule	326 Teahouse Outbox	327 Quebec Tab-key	328 Auto-hide Thud	329 Thug Teabag
330 Otter Tutor	331 Titan Tetany	332 Tooth Tithe	333 Tattoo Tatty	334 Totem Tea-time
335 Title Total	336 Otitis Quits	337 Attic Attica	338 Quietude Tooted	339 Autotype Outtop
340 Timer Tumour	341 Autumn Atman	342 Tomb Tomboy	343 Tomato Tuft	344 Toffee Tummy
345 Oatmeal Tamil	346 Times Items	347 Atomic Outface	348 Timid Tumid	349 Tempo Tea-mug
350 Tailor Tiler	351 Talon Italian	352 Tail-bay Toil-boy	353 Quality Utility	354 Tea-leaf Qualm
355 Atoll Tally	356 Atlas Tales	357 Talk Talc	358 Told Auto-load	359 Tulip Aetiology
360 Taser Tsar	361 Toxin Tyson	362 Quash Tosh	363 Text Toast	364 Autism Toxaemia
365 Outsole Tesla	366 Tissue Texas	367 Task Texaco	368 Tuesday Tuxedo	369 Toe-up Tausug
370 Quaker Outcry	371 Token Tycoon	372 Teach Touch	373 Tact Tacit	374 Tacoma Outcome

375	376	377	378	379
Article	Takes	Tack	Autacoid	Teacup
Takeley	Tics	Quack	Autocide	Toecap
380	381	382	383	384
Outdoor	Tideway	Toe-job	Outdate	Tedium
Tudor	Otodynia	Tudhoe	Tea-date	Tadoma
385	386	387	388	389
Tidal	Tedious	Tajik	Teddy	Tedge
Tidily	Toadies	Toy-decoy	Toddy	Tidy-up
390	391	392	393	394
Tiger	Utopian	Tough	Teapot	Autogamy
Tapir	Tigon	Tophi	Tiptoe	Typify
395	396	397	398	399
Auto-play	Taps	Topic	Tepid	Tippy
Tupelo	Tips	Tapioca	Tea-pad	Quagga
400	401	402	403	404
Ferry	Amazon	Freebie	Fart	Farm
Furry	Marine	Forebay	Fort	Form
405	406	407	408	409
Morale	Mars	Africa	Ford	Frog
Mural	Fries	America	Fraud	Mirage
410	411	412	413	414
Manor	Funny	Fan-boy	Mint	Manama
Minor	Minion	Money-boy	Fanta	Minima
415	416	417	418	419
Final	Means	Monk	Mind	Fang
Fowl	Minus	Fence	Fund	Mango
420	421	422	423	424
Amber	Fabian	Fubby	Ambit	Mayhem
Fibre	Mahayana	Imbibe	Moabite	Ameboma
425	426	427	428	429
Fable	Embase	Emu-beak	Embody	Maybug
Mobile	Mobius	Fee-hike	Embed	Mahagua
430	431	432	433	434
Future	Motion	Myth	Fatty	Motif
Meter	Mutiny	Faith	Motto	Myotome
435	436	437	438	439
Metal	Foetus	Emetic	Maytide	Fatigue
Motel	Mates	Miotic	Fetid	Footage
440	441	442	443	444
Offer	Famine	Mamba	Mufti	Mummy
Memory	Immune	Mumbai	Fomite	Muff
445	446	447	448	449
Family	Famous	Office	Famed	Effigy
Female	Mimosa	Mimic	Fumed	Fumage

450 Fever Malaria	451 Melon Felon	452 Flab Malibu	453 Flat Flute	454 Flame Film
455 Fall Folly	456 False Flies	457 Flake Fluke	458 Field Flood	459 Flag Flog
460 Miser Mixer	461 Fusion Mason	462 Fish Mesh	463 Feast Fist	464 Maxim Museum
465 Mislay Measly	466 Mass Moss	467 Mask Music	468 Fixed Mixed	469 Fixup Mix-up
470 Maker Faker	471 Macaw Mucin	472 Macho Mooch	473 Fact Facet	474 Myokymia McAfee
475 Facial Focal	476 Focus Mucus	477 Muck Mecca	478 Façade Mucoid	479 Make-up Face-up
480 Major Feeder	481 Maiden Median	482 Mad-boy My-job	483 Fadeout Mediate	484 Madam Medium
485 Medal Model	486 Modes Medusa	487 Medic Mediacy	488 Midday Muddy	489 Fudge Midge
490 Empire Imagery	491 Feign Imagine	492 Imphee Faugh	493 Amputee Empty	494 Empyema Magma
495 Maple Ampule	496 Maps Magus	497 Magic Myopic	498 Moped Impede	499 Magpie Magog
500 Lorry Lazier	501 Learn Ovarian	502 Verb Lazy-boy	503 Virtue Variety	504 Alarm Viraemia
505 Larva Laurel	506 Oversea Virus	507 Avarice Lyric	508 Lord Lurid	509 Large Virgo
510 Lawyer Loner	511 Lawn Linen	512 Lowboy Ivanhoe	513 Vent Vanity	514 Venom Alewife
515 Vowel Vinyl	516 Aliens Laws	517 Lance Link	518 Land Lend	519 Lung Lineage
520 Labour Libra	521 Albania Albino	522 Lobby Ali-baba	523 Albeit Layabout	524 Album Alabama

525 Label Libel	526 Vibes Alehouse	527 Oil-bake Eel-hook	528 Libido Lobed	529 Liebig Albugo
530 Altar Voter	531 Latin Ovation	532 Lathe Loathe	533 Aliquot Lotto	534 Liquefy Luteoma
535 Vital Latvia	536 Latex Lotus	537 Lytic Vatic	538 Liquid Yuletide	539 Let-up Latigo
540 Loafer Lemur	541 Lemon Alimony	542 Lamb Limb	543 Limit Vomit	544 Lay-off Luffa
545 Oil-meal Lamely	546 Alms Vamoose	547 Vomica Lamaic	548 Leafed Limeade	549 Lamp Lump
550 Lover Valour	551 Violin Yellow	552 Allah Lavabo	553 Vault Valet	554 Valium Volume
555 Valley Valve	556 Olives Values	557 Lilac Oil-leak	558 Valid Vivid	559 Lavage Allege
560 Elixir Luxury	561 Vision Lesion	562 Leash Lash	563 Least Last	564 Elysium Lexeme
565 Voxel Visual	566 Lasso Lexis	567 Alaska Lusaka	568 Oilseed Leased	569 Visage Lisp
570 Vicar Lycra	571 Alkane Leucine	572 Leech Lochia	573 Elect Vacate	574 Locum Vacuum
575 Alkali Vocal	576 Locus Looks	577 Lack Luck	578 Avocado Lucid	579 Leakage Oil-cup
580 Leader Loader	581 Leaden Lydian	582 Elijah Old-boy	583 Avidity Viduity	584 Ladyfy Vadium
585 Loudly Avidly	586 Leeds Loads	587 Vodka Vedic	588 Lady-day Loaded	589 Ledge Lodge
590 Lager Vapour	591 Lagoon Legion	592 Alpha Laugh	593 Ligate Log-out	594 Legume Lipoma
595 Lapel Legal	596 Legs Lips	597 Alopecia Legacy	598 Lipid Vapid	599 Veggie Leggy

600 Sorry Seizure	601 Siren Serene	602 Sarah Serbia	603 Sort Surety	604 Surf Serum
605 Survey Serial	606 Serious Xerox	607 Source Suzuki	608 Seized Surd	609 Syrup Surge
610 Senior Sneeze	611 Swan Snow	612 Snob Swab	613 Sanity Senate	614 Swim Sonoma
615 Senile Snail	616 Sense Sinus	617 Sink Snake	618 Sand Sound	619 Song Sewage
620 Sahara Shore	621 Shin Show	622 Shah Sheba	623 Sheet Shoot	624 Shame Sebum
625 Shale Shave	626 Shoes Ashes	627 Shake Sheik	628 Shade Shed	629 Shape Ship
630 Star Suitor	631 Satan Stain	632 South Stab	633 State Statue	634 Steam Stem
635 Steal Stool	636 Seats Sites	637 Stake Steak	638 Studio Squad	639 Stag Stage
640 Smear Isomer	641 Safeway Semen	642 Samba Simba	643 Safety Soft	644 Sea-foam Oxfam
645 Smile Simile	646 Siamese Xmas	647 Smoke Safe-key	648 Seafood Same-day	649 Smog Sump
650 Salary Saviour	651 Saloon Saline	652 Slab Slob	653 Salt Slate	654 Asylum Slum
655 Slave Saliva	656 Sales Seals	657 Silk Slice	658 Salad Solid	659 Sleep Slug
660 Assize Assure	661 Saxon Season	662 Sash Sushi	663 Asset Siesta	664 Assume Sesame
665 Sexual Assail	666 Issues Essex	667 Soy-sauce Issue-key	668 Seaside Soused	669 Sausage Assuage
670 Scar Secure	671 Scan Scene	672 Scab Scuba	673 Society Scout	674 Scam Scum

675 Scale Social	676 Excuse Excise	677 Sack Sock	678 Suicide Scud	679 Scoop Skype
680 Oxidize Exedra	681 Sydney Sedan	682 Side-boy Easy-job	683 Exudate Easy-jet	684 Sodium Sodomy
685 Sadly Seed-oil	686 Seeds Exodus	687 Seduce Sudoku	688 Seeded Sided	689 Sea-dog Sedge
690 Sugar Spray	691 Oxygen Spain	692 Sigh Sophia	693 Spit Spout	694 Sigma Spoof
695 Spoil Spool	696 Spouse Spies	697 Space Spike	698 Spade Speed	699 Soggy Seepage
700 Career Crazy	701 Corn Crow	702 Crab Kerb	703 Court Crate	704 Cream Crime
705 Carol Cereal	706 Cars Cruise	707 Creek Crook	708 Card Cord	709 Cargo Courage
710 Canary Cowry	711 Canine Canon	712 Cowboy Knob	713 Cent Knot	714 Cinema Knife
715 Canal Convoy	716 Coins Cows	717 Cynic Kinky	718 Kind Candy	719 King Canopy
720 Chair Chore	721 Chain China	722 Cabby Kebab	723 Cheat Cheque	724 Chef Chum
725 Cable Cabal	726 Aches Cheese	727 Choice Choke	728 Cuboid Chad	729 Chip Cheap
730 Actor Actuary	731 Action Auction	732 Kith Couth	733 Kitty Acetate	734 Citify Katayama
735 Active Actual	736 Cats Coats	737 Arctic Ice-quake	738 Coated Cited	739 Ecotype Key-tag
740 Camera Comer	741 Acumen Iceman	742 Comb Akimbo	743 Comet Comity	744 Coffee Comma
745 Camel Comely	746 Comes Cameos	747 Comic Comice	748 Comedy Comedo	749 Camp Ice-fog

750 Calorie Colour	751 Clan Clone	752 Club Celeb	753 Cavity Cult	754 Calm Claim
755 Call Cell	756 Calyx Clause	757 Civic Cloak	758 Cold Cloud	759 Clap Ecology
760 Caesar Coaxer	761 Cousin Casino	762 Cash Cosh	763 Cast Cyst	764 Caesium Aksum
765 Casual Coaxial	766 Kiss Cyesis	767 Cask Kiosk	768 Ceased Coaxed	769 Cusp Cosy-up
770 Cooker Accrue	771 Cocaine Cocoon	772 Coach Couch	773 Cacti Rocket	774 Cecum Cocoyam
775 Cycle Icicle	776 Cookies Cakes	777 Cock Kick	778 Accede Cycad	779 Occupy Ice-cap
780 Cider Cedar	781 Kidney Codeine	782 Key-job Cudahy	783 Cadet Acidity	784 Academy Acidify
785 Cajole Caudal	786 Codes Kudos	787 Acidic Kodak	788 Caddy Cuddy	789 Coydog Cadge
790 Keeper Cigar	791 Coupon Keep-away	792 Cough Copyboy	793 Caput Capita	794 Key-game Cape-May
795 Couple Cupola	796 Cups Copse	797 Kapok Kopek	798 Cupid Keypad	799 Cuppa Kappa
800 Dizzy Juror	801 Drain Drone	802 Derby Drub	803 Dart Dirt	804 Drama Dream
805 Drive Drool	806 Doors Jars	807 Dark Jerk	808 Dread Druid	809 Drip Drug
810 Donor Junior	811 Down Dawn	812 Dan-buoy Dweeb	813 Dent Junta	814 Dynamo Denim
815 Jewel Jowl	816 Jaws Jinx	817 Dance Donkey	818 Adenoid Dandy	819 Dingo Dung
820 Adhere Daubery	821 Debone John	822 Jobbie Jabby	823 Debit Debate	824 Day-beam Audio-boom

825	826	827	828	829
Double	Jobs	Ad-hoc	Daybed	Debug
Jubilee	Dubious	Day-book	Jihad	Debag
830	831	832	833	834
Editor	Audition	Death	Adequate	Daytime
Auditor	Edition	Edith	Jetty	Diatom
835	836	837	838	839
Detail	Dates	Adequacy	Dated	Audiotape
Dotal	Jets	Idiotic	Edited	Dotage
840	841	842	843	844
Admire	Demon	Dumb	Daft	Dummy
Defer	Domain	Jumbo	Deft	Daffy
845	846	847	848	849
Defile	Defuse	Deface	Doomed	Damage
Joyful	Demise	Edifice	Audio-feed	Jump
850	851	852	853	854
Dealer	Divine	Dolby	Adult	Adolf
Diver	Divan	Delhi	Duvet	Day-life
855	856	857	858	859
Devil	Deluxe	Advice	Divide	Deluge
Doll	Jealous	Device	Devoid	Dialog
860	861	862	863	864
Desire	Disney	Dish	Dust	Dismay
Dysuria	Dixon	Dash	Jest	Audism
865	866	867	868	869
Diesel	Disease	Desk	Dioxide	Dosage
Joyously	Jesus	Disc	Roadside	Dysopia
870	871	872	873	874
Decree	Deacon	Douche	Duct	Decaf
Joker	Jacana	Jacob	Edict	Decima
875	876	877	878	879
Deceive	Diocese	Duck	Decade	Juice-up
Docile	Jokes	Jockey	Decode	Diacope
880	881	882	883	884
Udder	Add-on	Judah	Oddity	Diadem
Adder	Deaden	Day-job	Jadeite	Dodoma
885	886	887	888	889
Doodle	Adidas	Deduce	Daddy	Judge
Deadly	Deeds	Adduce	Jaded	Dodge
890	891	892	893	894
Degree	Deepen	Dough	Depot	Dogma
Diaper	Japan	Dog-bee	Deputy	Adipoma
895	896	897	898	899
Deploy	Dogs	Audio-pace	Do-good	Doggie
Dipole	Jugs	Day-peak	Doped	Jaggy

900 Prayer Pizza	901 Apron Green	902 Probe Grub	903 Great Party	904 Grief Proof
905 Girl April	906 Grease Praise	907 Grace Park	908 Grade Pride	909 Garage Grape
910 Power Penury	911 Gown Opinion	912 Pony-hay Gun-boy	913 Agent Paint	914 Genome Panama
915 Panel Geneva	916 Genius Pins	917 Panic Gunk	918 Agenda Pound	919 Gang Ping
920 Euphoria Giber	921 Phone Phoney	922 Phobia Gabby	923 Photo Upbeat	924 Euphemia Go-home
925 Gable Ghoul	926 Phase Pubis	927 Aphakia Pubic	928 Go-ahead Peabody	929 Phage Pea-bug
930 Guitar Poetry	931 Option Potion	932 Apathy Pith	933 Potato Potty	934 Epitome Uptime
935 Petal Petiole	936 Guts Pets	937 Optic Uptake	938 Gated Agua-toad	939 Potage Potpie
940 Gamer Goofer	941 Gemini Egomania	942 Gameboy Gambia	943 Gamete Gift	944 Gaffe Puffy
945 Gamely Gmail	946 Games Poems	947 Pumice Pomace	948 Pomade Go-mad	949 Pimp Pump
950 Glory Polar	951 Plan Glow	952 Globe Playboy	953 Plate Pilot	954 Plum Golf
955 Glove Pill	956 Galaxy Pulse	957 Palace Police	958 Gold Glad	959 Apology Plug
960 Geyser Poser	961 Poison Epson	962 Gash Push	963 Guest Post	964 Ageism Epsom
965 Pixel Piously	966 Pass Piss	967 Pause-key Pesky	968 Episode Upside	969 Gasp Pea-soup
970 Poker Pacer	971 Epicene Geo-coin	972 Peach Pouch	973 Opacity Pact	974 Pacify Opacify

975	976	977	978	979
Apical	Pieces	Pack	Peaked	Upkeep
Epical	Apices	Peck	Paced	Pay-cap
980	981	982	983	984
Goodyear	Guide-way	Goodbye	Update	Podium
Guider	Gideon	Good-boy	Pedate	Pyjama
985	986	987	988	989
Pedal	Goods	Updike	Giddy	Pudgy
Poodle	Pads	Padauk	Paddy	Good-guy
990	991	992	993	994
Pager	Pagan	Pageboy	Egypt	Pygmy
Paper	Pigeon	Gay-pub	Uppity	Apogamy
995	996	997	998	999
Apple	Eggs	Papacy	Pagoda	Poppy
People	Gypsy	Pig-yoke	Pea-pod	Puppy

ALPHA BETA 1000 – 1999

1000 Warrior Worrier	1001 Narrow War-zone	1002 War-robe Wire-rib	1003 Narrate Nazarite	1004 War-room Nazi-army
1005 Nozzle Wire-reel	1006 Worries War-years	1007 Wire-arc War-race	1008 Wizard Worried	1009 Wire-rope Wear-rag
1010 War-weary Nazi-war	1011 War-win War-union	1012 Wire-web War-nab	1013 Worn-out War-unit	1014 Wary-wife Wear-name
1015 Neuronal War-envoy	1016 Neurons Wrens	1017 War-week Worn-key	1018 Wizened Warned	1019 Wiring Wrong
1020 Wear-bra War-hero	1021 Inurbane War-ban	1022 War-baby Wear-bib	1023 War-heat Wear-hat	1024 Near-home Wareham
1025 Wearable War-haul	1026 Warehouse Wire-box	1027 Anaerobic Wire-hook	1028 Warhead Woozy-head	1029 War-hope War-hype
1030 Writer Nurture	1031 Norton Ionization	1032 North Worthy	1033 Write-out War-rite	1034 War-time Neurotome
1035 Inertial Inertly	1036 Warts Writs	1037 Neurotic Enuretic	1038 Unrated War-tide	1039 Wire-tap Write-up
1040 Warfare Warmer	1041 Norman Wireman	1042 War-fib Warm-boy	1043 Enormity Warm-tea	1044 Wear-off Warm-May
1045 Normal Warmly	1046 Worms Norms	1047 Weary-face War-mace	1048 War-mood Unarmed	1049 Warm-up Neuro-image
1050 War-over War-liar	1051 Wireline Nirvana	1052 War-vibe Wire-lube	1053 Enervate War-vote	1054 War-loom War-life
1055 Unroll Unravel	1056 Nerves No-rules	1057 Warlike Wire-like	1058 World Wire-lead	1059 Neurology Neuralgia
1060 Nursery Wire-size	1061 Warsaw Worsen	1062 Nourish Onrush	1063 Worst Wrist	1064 Aneurysm Wearisome
1065 Onerously War-exile	1066 Neurosis Nurses	1067 Anorexic Run-risk	1068 Nearside Wearside	1069 War-spy Nazi-siege
1070 Worker Wreaker	1071 Narceine Wrekin	1072 Anarchy Anorchia	1073 Workout War-act	1074 War-café Narcoma

1075	1076	1077	1078	1079
Wire-coil	Works	Wreck	Workday	Work-up
War-cave	Anoraks	Wrick	Wreaked	War-cup
1080	1081	1082	1083	1084
Warder	Warden	War-jibe	Near-date	War-doom
War-diary	Worden	Ward-bay	War-jet	Ware-demo
1085	1086	1087	1088	1089
War-dial	Words	Nordic	War-dead	War-dog
Weirdly	Wards	Word-cue	Worded	Wire-edge
1090	1091	1092	1093	1094
Energize	War-gun	Near-pub	Enrapt	War-game
Wire-gauze	Wire-gun	War-gab	Wire-gate	Wear-gem
1095	1096	1097	1098	1099
Neuroglia	Wraps	Wire-poke	Wire-guide	Wrap-up
War-ploy	Energise	War-epic	War-god	Wire-gauge
1100	1101	1102	1103	1104
Inner-ear	Win-run	New-robe	New-rate	New-room
Wee-worry	Non-iron	Non-ruby	Win-rate	Union-army
1105	1106	1107	1108	1109
Unnerve	Owners	New-York	Inward	Enwrap
New-rule	Unawares	Newark	Wayward	Unwarp
1110	1111	1112	1113	1114
Nunnery	Non-union	Wannabe	Winnet	New-wife
Winner	New-wine	Wenonah	Newent	New-name
1115	1116	1117	1118	1119
New-wave	Nannies	Announce	Innuendo	Annoying
Non-wool	New-ways	Annoyance	Unwind	Inning
1120	1121	1122	1123	1124
Anywhere	Inion-bone	New-baby	New-bout	New-home
Wine-bar	New-bin	Wine-hub	Nanobot	Newham
1125	1126	1127	1128	1129
Ennoble	Winehouse	New-book	Nun-hood	Onion-bag
One-whole	Union-base	Wine-hook	New-body	Win-big
1130	1131	1132	1133	1134
Winter	Wanton	New-tab	Annotate	Noon-time
No-entry	Newton	Neon-tube	Unwitty	New-item
1135	1136	1137	1138	1139
Neonatal	Annuities	Noon-quake	Wanted	New-tag
New-tool	Inanities	No-notice	Anointed	Wine-tap
1140	1141	1142	1143	1144
Anonymize	New-moon	Union-mob	Anonymity	Win-fame
Wine-free	Newman	New-fob	Unanimity	Wean-off
1145	1146	1147	1148	1149
New-movie	Anonymous	New-face	New-fad	New-image
New-move	Unanimous	Union-mace	Non-food	Wine-mug

1150 Annular Win-over	1151 New-line New-loan	1152 Nineveh Win-vibe	1153 Innovate Wine-vat	1154 New-life New-leaf
1155 Annually Unwell	1156 Annals Annulus	1157 New-look New-leak	1158 Unwieldy Annual-due	1159 Non-league New-loop
1160 New-user Non-user	1161 In-unison New-sin	1162 Newish Newsboy	1163 Unionist Newest	1164 Unionism Onanism
1165 Unwisely Non-axial	1166 Oneness Nonissue	1167 Wine-sauce Noon-sky	1168 Newsday Annexed	1169 Wine-sip Onion-soup
1170 Winker New-car	1171 New-coin Wine-can	1172 Wench Winch	1173 Enunciate New-kit	1174 New-café Wine-coma
1175 Winkle Wonkily	1176 Winks Innocuous	1177 Wine-cake New-cook	1178 Winked Winced	1179 Wine-keg New-copy
1180 Wonder Wander	1181 Window Wind-way	1182 New-job Inane-jibe	1183 Inundate New-date	1184 Union-demo Windom
1185 Windily New-deal	1186 Winds Nowadays	1187 Wine-juice Inane-joke	1188 Wounded Winded	1189 Wind-up Wine-jug
1190 Winger Wenger	1191 Nonagon New-Guinea	1192 Wine-pub Inane-gab	1193 Wingate Wine-pot	1194 Wine-gum New-game
1195 Wangle Win-ugly	1196 Wings Neon-gas	1197 Win-peace Noon-peak	1198 Winged Wine-god	1199 Anion-gap New-page
1200 Whizz Whirr	1201 Unborn Wherein	1202 Whereby Wheezy-boy	1203 Inherit Inebriate	1204 Wharf In-brief
1205 Whirl Whorl	1206 Whereas Wee-hours	1207 Unheroic Noah-ark	1208 Inbred On-board	1209 Web-rage Nab-rope
1210 Whiner Webinar	1211 Whinny Why-now	1212 Whiny-boy Rainbow-hue	1213 Unbent Why-not	1214 Web-info Nab-enemy
1215 Why-yowl Web-weave	1216 Web-noise Rainbows	1217 Enhance Whence	1218 Unbound Way-beyond	1219 Unhinge Whinge
1220 Wahoo-beer Nubber	1221 Inhibin Web-ban	1222 Wahhabi Web-hub	1223 Inhabit Inhibit	1224 Web-beam Why-him

1225	1226	1227	1228	1229
Nibble	Web-base	Web-book	Nabbed	Web-bug
Wobbly	Web-abuse	Nib-hook	Webbed	Web-hype
1230	1231	1232	1233	1234
Wahoo-tree	Unbeaten	White-boy	Whiteout	What-if
Why-try	Whiten	White-hue	White-tie	Web-team
1235	1236	1237	1238	1239
White-lie	Whites	White-ice	Unabated	Wheat-pie
Whitely	White-sea	White-oak	Unheated	Nib-tip
1240	1241	1242	1243	1244
One-before	Inhumane	Nehemiah	Web-foot	Whiff
Web-maze	Unhuman	N-bomb	Wheft	Whammy
1245	1246	1247	1248	1249
Web-mail	Whims	Noob-face	Whey-feed	Web-map
Unhomely	Whimsy	Web-make	Web-feed	Whump
1250	1251	1252	1253	1254
Inhaler	Wheel-away	Noble-boy	Nobility	One-half
Nebulize	While-away	Whale-bay	Unbolt	Wahoo-leaf
1255	1256	1257	1258	1259
Waybill	Nebulous	Anabolic	Enabled	Weblog
Wholly	Wheels	Whelk	Whole-day	Whelp
1260	1261	1262	1263	1264
Web-user	Inhesion	Whoosh	Website	Web-safe
Nob-size	Anabasine	Wabash	Whist	Unbosom
1265	1266	1267	1268	1269
Web-sale	Inboxes	Whiskey	Unbiased	Web-spy
Nab-soul	Anabiosis	Whisk	Unhoused	Wahoo-sap
1270	1271	1272	1273	1274
Why-care	Web-icon	Which	Web-act	Webcam
Why-cry	Whey-cow	Wheech	Web-city	Web-café
1275	1276	1277	1278	1279
Web-clue	No-hooks	Whacky	Unhooked	Web-copy
Nab-cave	Web-case	Way-back	Unbaked	Whey-cup
1280	1281	1282	1283	1284
Web-diary	Anhedonia	Whydah	Web-data	Web-demo
Whey-jar	Nab-den	Web-job	Whey-diet	Nob-dome
1285	1286	1287	1288	1289
Wheedle	Any-bodies	Web-joke	Unheeded	Nib-edge
Web-idol	No-bodies	Wahoo-juice	Web-dude	Whey-jug
1290	1291	1292	1293	1294
Whip-ray	Woebegone	Web-gab	Unbeget	Web-game
Whooper	Nib-pen	Nob-pub	Whey-pot	Noob-goof
1295	1296	1297	1298	1299
Web-pal	Whips	Nib-poke	Web-guide	Unhappy
Noob-play	Whoops	Web-geek	Whooped	Web-page

1300 Anterior Interior	1301 Neutron Intern	1302 Water-bay Wet-robe	1303 Entirety Nitrate	1304 Interim Anteroom
1305 Natural Neutral	1306 Waters Entries	1307 Enteric Nitric	1308 Intrude Neutered	1309 Entourage Intrigue
1310 Netware Anti-war	1311 Antenna Entwine	1312 Wet-nib Ant-web	1313 Intent Nitwit	1314 Antonym Wet-room
1315 National Notional	1316 Intense Nations	1317 Wet-ink Anti-nuke	1318 Intend Antinode	1319 Waiting Untying
1320 Another Neither	1321 Anthony Within	1322 Entebbe Wet-baby	1323 Without Intubate	1324 Anthem Anathema
1325 Notable Withal	1326 Antabuse Nut-house	1327 Notebook Netbook	1328 Antibody Ant-body	1329 Wet-hug Nut-bag
1330 Nutter Anteater	1331 Initiation Intuition	1332 One-tooth Witty-boy	1333 Antiquity Wet-tout	1334 Unit-item Wait-time
1335 Nettle Intuitive	1336 Entities Iniquitous	1337 Anti-quake Note-take	1338 Initiated Unquoted	1339 Antitype Wattage
1340 Nit-free Antimere	1341 Antimony Note-money	1342 Entomb Entamoeba	1343 Intimate Wet-foot	1344 Unique-fame Nit-foam
1345 Untimely Intimal	1346 Anatomise Antefix	1347 Intimacy Anatomic	1448 Notified Untimed	1349 Nutmeg Anti-fog
1350 Antler Initialize	1351 Antlion Anatolian	1352 Unity-vibe Wet-labia	1353 Nativity Inequality	1354 Initial-fee Antilife
1355 Initially Nutella	1356 Initials Natives	1357 Anti-vice Netlike	1358 Untold Entailed	1359 Antelope Ontology
1360 Nut-size Ant-size	1361 Watson Antisana	1362 Wet-shoe Natasha	1363 Inquest Wet-suit	1364 Wet-sofa Neat-sum
1365 Net-sale Wet-soil	1366 Unity-axis Anti-sex	1367 Nut-sauce Wet-sky	1368 Untaxed Nut-seed	1369 Wet-soap Nut-soup
1370 Enticer Wet-core	1371 Ant-cow Untaken	1372 Watch Witch	1373 Intact Wet-coat	1374 Net-café Ant-coma

1375	1376	1377	1378	1379
Nautical	Antics	Nut-cake	Antacid	Wet-cap
Ant-cave	Nut-case	Untack	Noticed	Net-cage
1380	1381	1382	1383	1384
Nut-jar	Wet-June	Unique-job	Antedate	Nut-jam
Anti-deer	United-way	Neat-jab	Antidote	Wet-dam
1385	1386	1387	1388	1389
Untidily	Wet-days	Anti-decay	Awaited-day	Wet-jug
Wet-July	Wait-days	Nut-juice	Neat-dude	Unique-dog
1390	1391	1392	1393	1394
Integer	Antigen	Unity-pub	Anti-pot	Wit-game
Net-gear	Ontogeny	Ant-pooh	Ant-pet	Neat-opium
1395	1396	1397	1398	1399
Wet-play	Wait-ages	Entopic	Notepad	Ant-egg
Neat-pile	Wet-goose	Neat-poke	Antipode	Note-page
1400	1401	1402	1403	1404
Inferior	Inferno	Wife-robe	Enumerate	Inform
Numerary	Wifi-zone	Enemy-rib	Infuriate	Uniform
1405	1406	1407	1408	1409
Numeral	Nefarious	Enforce	Nimrod	Wife-rage
Unfurl	Numerous	Numeracy	Unafraid	Unmerge
1410	1411	1412	1413	1414
Womanize	Unfunny	Info-web	Infant	Wife-name
Info-war	Unmown	Wife-nab	Infinity	Enemy-info
1415	1416	1417	1418	1419
Nominal	Numinous	Infancy	Unfound	Naming
Womanly	Womanise	Unfence	Unmined	Unifying
1420	1421	1422	1423	1424
Number	Namibian	Name-baby	Info-bot	Info-boom
Numb-area	Name-ban	Enemy-hub	Wombat	Enemy-home
1425	1426	1427	1428	1429
Nimble	Wife-abuse	Info-book	Wifehood	Wife-hug
Womble	Info-box	Enemy-hook	Numbed	Info-bag
1430	1431	1432	1433	1434
Animator	Animation	Name-tab	Infatuate	Info-time
Nimitz	In-motion	Weymouth	Info-tout	Enemy-team
1435	1436	1437	1438	1439
Niftily	Inmates	Animatic	Animated	Name-tag
Nu-metal	Wefts	Enemy-quake	Nematode	Onomatopoeia
1440	1441	1442	1443	1444
Enemy-fire	Info-mania	Enemy-mob	Enemy-fate	Name-memo
Wife-fury	Name-omen	Info-fib	Name-fit	Wife-fame
1445	1446	1447	1448	1449
Waffle	Infamous	In-office	Info-media	Wife-image
Name-file	Name-fix	Enemy-face	Enemy-feud	Info-map

1450 Animal-zoo Owe-favour	1451 Inflow Name-line	1452 Info-lab Enemy-vibe	1453 Unifoliate Inflate	1454 Inflame On-film
1455 Awfully Woefully	1456 Animals Influx	1457 Wife-like Info-leak	1458 Unfold Unmoved	1459 Anemology Animal-ego
1460 Infuser Name-user	1461 Infusion Ion-fusion	1462 Enmesh Waifish	1463 Animosity Infest	1464 Animism Wife-safe
1465 Infusive Enemy-soil	1466 Nemesis Unfussy	1467 Namesake Unmask	1468 Unfixed Infused	1469 Enemy-spy Name-usage
1470 Unmaker Wife-care	1471 Neomycin Name-icon	1472 Name-echo Anaemic-boy	1473 In-fact Infect	1474 Info-café Wife-cameo
1475 Inimical Name-clue	1476 In-focus Enemy-case	1477 Neem-cake Enemy-cookie	1478 Name-code Waif-kid	1479 Name-copy Info-coup
1480 Name-jury Name-diary	1481 Numidian Enemy-den	1482 Name-jibe Enemy-jab	1483 Info-audit Wife-date	1484 Enemy-doom Named-foe
1485 Infidel Unimodal	1486 Nomads Enema-dose	1487 Nomadic Enemy-decoy	1488 Named-day Unified-idea	1489 Enema-jug Unified-pay
1490 Info-guru Enemy-prey	1491 Enemy-gun Anaemia-gene	1492 Nymph Nympho	1493 Numpty Wimp-out	1494 Name-game Wife-poem
1495 Wimple Wimpole	1496 Wimps Waif-guise	1497 Info-geek Wife-epic	1498 Info-guide Name-guide	1499 Name-page Wife-gag
1500 Waverer Navarre	1501 Environ Unlearn	1502 Owl-rib Wool-robe	1503 Invert Univariate	1504 Navy-room Wave-arm
1505 Waverly Nil-oral	1506 Walrus Inverse	1507 Navy-rookie Nile-race	1508 Navy-yard Wave-ride	1509 Enlarge On-average
1510 One-liner Navy-war	1511 Envoy-inn Navy-union	1512 Wivenhoe Weave-web	1513 Invent Walnut	1514 Envenom Naïve-enemy
1515 Unevenly Aniline-oil	1516 In-laws Nylons	1517 Unlink Only-once	1518 Inland Wayland	1519 Waving Weaving
1520 Navy-hero Anal-hair	1521 Navy-bean Owl-bone	1522 Noel-baby Wool-bib	1523 Nail-bite Owl-hoot	1524 Wool-boom Naïve-bum

1525 Enviable Unviable	1526 Navy-base Wool-house	1527 Nail-hook Owl-beak	1528 Nailbed Owl-head	1529 Wool-bag Only-hope
1530 In-vitro Walter	1531 Walton Novation	1532 Wealth Neolith	1533 Novitiate Invite-out	1534 Navy-team Wool-tam
1535 Weave-tale Wave-tail	1536 Owlets Invites	1537 Analytic Naïve-tyke	1538 Invited Wilted	1539 Anal-tag Nail-tip
1540 Welfare Woolmer	1541 Anal-fin Navy-man	1542 Wolf-boy In-limbo	1543 Owl-foot No-limit	1544 Wave-off Navy-fame
1545 Wilful Nail-file	1546 Wool-mix Nail-fix	1547 Envy-face Nail-mace	1548 Owl-food Nile-mud	1549 Weave-image Wily-imp
1550 Unilever Waller	1551 Willow Wallow	1552 Wallaby Well-boy	1553 Wallet Novelty	1554 Nullify William
1555 Involve Neville	1556 Novels Wolves	1557 Wallace Inviolacy	1558 Invalid Unvalued	1559 Envelope Wallop
1560 Analyser Anal-sore	1561 Envision Invasion	1562 Welsh Unleash	1563 Analyst Invest	1564 Navy-exam Envoy-sofa
1565 Enviously Invasive	1566 Analysis Unless	1567 Navy-sky Wave-ski	1568 Wave-aside Unleased	1569 Envisage Navy-spy
1570 Onlooker Walker	1571 Walkway Novocaine	1572 Wave-echo Welch	1573 Invocate Walk-out	1574 Welcome Navy-café
1575 Unlikely Univocal	1576 Novices Invoices	1577 Unlock Unlucky	1578 Invoiced Invoked	1579 Wool-cap Navy-coup
1580 Invader Welder	1581 Nevadan Waved-away	1582 Wild-boy Wild-bee	1583 Wild-oat Navy-jet	1584 Wild-yam Nile-dam
1585 Wildly Owl-dive	1586 Invidious Wilds	1587 Navy-decoy Naïve-joke	1588 Welded Invaded	1589 Wild-pea Wool-dog
1590 Anal-pore Analogize	1591 Anlagen Nail-gun	1592 Navy-pub One-alpha	1593 Navigate Anal-pit	1594 Navy-game Navy-gym
1595 Walpole Anal-pile	1596 Analgesia Analogous	1597 Wave-peak Analogic	1598 Wave-guide Wool-pad	1599 Nail-pop Owl-egg

1600 Insurer Noisy-roar	1601 Noisy-row Anserine	1602 Nose-rub Noisy-rube	1603 Insert Wax-art	1604 Noxzema Noisy-room
1605 On-serve Unsurely	1606 Unserious In-series	1607 Anasarca Wise-rookie	1608 Insured Nose-ride	1609 Noisy-rage Noose-rope
1610 Answer Ensnare	1611 Unsewn Unsown	1612 Wise-nob Insane-boy	1613 Insanity Insinuate	1614 Wise-name Insane-aim
1615 Wise-owl Insanely	1616 Nexins Unisonous	1617 Nuisance Nixie-nook	1618 Unsound Weasand	1619 Waxing Unsung
1620 Washer Wisher	1621 Wash-away Wish-away	1622 Noisy-baby Nosy-hobo	1623 Washout Nose-about	1624 Noise-boom Noisy-home
1625 Unusable Nose-hole	1626 Wishes Wax-base	1627 Wish-key Nose-hook	1628 Wise-head Wax-body	1629 Wash-up Nosh-up
1630 Nestor Waster	1631 Einstein Ionisation	1632 West-bay Nasty-boy	1633 Instate Insatiate	1634 Wise-team Uneasy-time
1635 Instil Nestle	1636 Wastes Anxieties	1637 Noisy-tyke Nose-tic	1638 Instead Unsteady	1639 Instep Wastage
1640 Noise-free Wax-fire	1641 Insomnia Wiseman	1642 Noisy-mob Awesome-boy	1643 Noise-mute Wax-foot	1644 Wise-mum Nose-fume
1645 Wise-move Awesomely	1646 Wise-muse Noisy-mix	1647 Wise-face No-smoke	1648 Awesome-day Noise-mode	1649 Wise-image Awesome-guy
1650 Insular Unsavoury	1651 Insulin Wise-law	1652 Noise-vibe Wise-alibi	1653 Insulate Insult	1654 Oneself Nixie-elf
1655 Enslave Unusually	1656 Insoles Nasalise	1657 Waxy-look Wise-look	1658 Unsaved Unsold	1659 Nosology Wax-leg
1660 Neisseria Nose-size	1661 Nissan In-season	1662 Wax-shoe Noisy-sob	1663 Insist Wisest	1664 Wise-axiom Nose-exam
1665 Anxiously Unisexual	1666 Wise-ass Wessex	1667 Wax-soak Noise-seek	1668 Unsexed Unissued	1669 Wise-sage Noose-sag
1670 Insecure Wiseacre	1671 Nose-cone Nose-acne	1672 Noise-echo Wax-cube	1673 Insect Weskit	1674 Nescafe Noisy-café

1675	1676	1677	1678	1679
Unsocial	Wise-case	Wax-cake	Unasked	Inscape
Noise-clue	No-excuse	Noisy-Kaka	Noisy-kid	Wax-copy
1680	1681	1682	1683	1684
Insider	Wise-doyen	Nose-job	Inside-out	Wisdom
Wise-jury	Noisy-den	Wax-job	Noisy-data	Wise-idiom
1685	1686	1687	1688	1689
Nose-dive	Insidious	Wise-joke	Unseeded	Wise-adage
Wise-deal	Insides	Wise-duke	One-sided	Wax-edge
1690	1691	1692	1693	1694
Inspire	Insignia	Noisy-pub	In-spite	Anisogamy
Wise-guru	Unspin	Noisy-gab	Wise-poet	Wise-game
1695	1696	1697	1698	1699
Wispily	Wasps	Wise-geek	Insipid	Wise-pope
Unspool	Waxy-pose	Nose-poke	Wisped	Noisy-pig
1700	1701	1702	1703	1704
Week-zero	Unicorn	Iowa-crab	Increate	Weak-army
Weak-rear	Einkorn	Weak-rib	On-court	Weak-arm
1705	1706	1707	1708	1709
Incurve	Increase	Uncork	Encored	Encourage
Uncurl	Yonkers	Nice-rice	Uncured	Nicaragua
1710	1711	1712	1713	1714
Awakener	Uncanny	Nice-nob	Ancient	Weak-enemy
Nuke-war	Nice-wine	Ink-nib	Incant	Nice-name
1715	1716	1717	1718	1719
Once-only	Incense	Nuke-nook	Anaconda	Waking
Weak-wave	Neo-cons	Unkink	Weekend	Woking
1720	1721	1722	1723	1724
Anchor	Unchain	Nice-baby	Incubate	In-chief
Nicobar	Incheon	Weak-hobo	Wichita	Wykeham
1725	1726	1727	1728	1729
Anchovy	Incubus	Anechoic	Inched	Nuke-bag
Nuchal	Enchase	No-choice	Niched	Weak-hip
1730	1731	1732	1733	1734
Nectar	Nicotine	Uncouth	Nice-tot	Wake-time
Nocturia	Inaction	Ink-tube	Weak-equity	Weak-team
1735	1736	1737	1738	1739
Inactive	Unctuous	Oncotic	Uncoated	Weak-top
Enactive	Niceties	Nice-tyke	Incited	Nice-tape
1740	1741	1742	1743	1744
Incomer	Nice-man	Weak-mob	Weak-foot	Encomium
Once-more	Weak-money	Wycombe	Nice-meat	Yank-off
1745	1746	1747	1748	1749
Wakeful	Incomes	Nice-face	Nice-food	Encamp
Nice-movie	Weak-aims	Weak-mice	Wikimedia	Nou-camp

1750 Nuclear Unclear	1751 Incline Unclean	1752 Nice-vibe Weak-alibi	1753 Anklet Inoculate	1754 Inoculum Nice-life
1755 Enclave Nucleoli	1756 Nucleus Uncles	1757 Uncloak Nucleic	1758 Include Nuclide	1759 Oncology Unclog
1760 Incisor Incisura	1761 Incision Weak-sin	1762 In-cash Waukesha	1763 Encyst Incest	1764 Yankeeism Nice-sum
1765 Incisive Nice-soul	1766 Anacusis Weak-axis	1767 Weak-sauce Ink-soak	1768 Encased Incised	1769 Nice-soup Ink-usage
1770 Wicker Necker	1771 Wiccan Weak-knee	1772 Wacky-boy Wacko-bay	1773 Wicket Necktie	1774 Nice-cameo Yankee-café
1775 Nickel Unicycle	1776 Necks Wicks	1777 Neck-yoke Nice-cake	1778 Wicked Uncooked	1779 Wickiup Nice-cap
1780 Encoder Nice-jury	1781 Weak-jaw Nice-dean	1782 Naked-boy Weak-jab	1783 Anecdote Inkjet	1784 Nice-dame Nuke-doom
1785 Once-daily Nuke-deal	1786 Week-days Naked-eyes	1787 Nice-joke Weak-duke	1788 Nice-dad Weak-dude	1789 Ink-dip Naked-ape
1790 Weak-gaze Nike-gear	1791 Oncogene Ink-pen	1792 Nice-pub Weak-gibe	1793 Inkpot Incipit	1794 Nuke-game Nice-gym
1795 Uncouple Ink-pool	1796 Nice-guys Nuke-gas	1797 Weak-peak Nice-piece	1798 Inkpad Wikipedia	1799 Oink-pig Weak-peg
1800 Andorra Injurer	1801 Andrew Underway	1802 Wide-robe Indoor-bay	1803 Indurate Wood-rot	1804 Wide-room Wood-roof
1805 Inderal Underlay	1806 Endorse Indoors	1807 Endozoic Indoor-ice	1898 Android Injured	1809 Undergo Underage
1810 Widower Widener	1811 Way-down Indianan	1812 Wide-web Wide-nib	1813 Indent End-note	1814 Wed-wife Awed-enemy
1815 Wood-nail Indianola	1816 Indians Widows	1817 Wide-awake Weed-nook	1818 Endowed Widowed	1819 Ending Undoing
1820 Wide-bore Wood-bar	1821 Woodbine Wood-hen	1822 Needy-baby Wide-hub	1823 Indebt Nude-beauty	1824 Wood-beam Needham

1825	1826	1827	1828	1829
Enjoyable	Woodhouse	Wood-hook	Nude-body	Wood-bug
Inaudible	Wide-base	Wide-book	Nod-head	Wide-hip
1830	1831	1832	1833	1834
Wood-tar	Nidation	Width	Inadequate	End-time
Wide-tyre	Nudation	End-tab	End-quote	Need-item
1835	1836	1837	1838	1839
In-detail	Nudities	Inadequacy	Undated	End-tag
Wood-tile	Wide-toes	Weed-toke	Unedited	Wide-tip
1840	1841	1842	1843	1844
Need-more	Woodman	Endameba	Wood-mite	Neodymium
Wood-fire	Andaman	Wood-fob	Wide-fit	Nod-off
1845	1846	1847	1848	1849
Needful	Wood-mouse	Endemic	Weed-feed	Nude-image
End-file	Wide-mix	Wood-mace	End-feud	Wood-fag
1850	1851	1852	1853	1854
Endeavour	Wood-lane	End-lab	Undulate	Wide-leaf
Nodular	Wide-line	Wide-labia	Undelete	End-life
1855	1856	1857	1858	1859
Woodall	Needles	Wide-leak	Wide-load	Indulge
Enjoy-love	Noodles	Weed-like	Needled	Wood-log
1860	1861	1862	1863	1864
End-user	Wood-saw	Wood-ash	Nudist	Endosome
Wide-size	End-soon	Wide-shoe	Unjust	Nudism
1865	1866	1867	1868	1869
Indusial	Wide-issue	Wood-ski	Woodside	Wood-sage
Wood-seal	Indexes	Index-key	Indexed	Wide-usage
1870	1871	1872	1873	1874
Inducer	Indican	Wood-cube	Inject	Indicium
Indy-car	Wide-ocean	Wood-echo	Indict	Nude-cameo
1875	1876	1877	1878	1879
Wood-coal	Indices	Undock	Induced	Wood-cage
Wide-cave	Wood-case	Wood-kayak	Weedicide	Weed-cap
1880	1881	1882	1883	1884
Wood-door	Wood-den	End-job	End-date	Wide-dome
Wide-door	Wide-jaw	Wide-jab	Wood-deity	Wood-dam
1885	1886	1887	1888	1889
Waddle	Wood-dais	Wood-decay	Wedded	Wood-edge
Noddle	End-days	Weed-juice	Nodded	Weed-dope
1890	1891	1892	1893	1894
Nudger	Indigene	Indigo-hue	Wood-gate	End-game
Nidgery	Widgeon	Wood-pub	Widget	Endogamy
1895	1896	1897	1898	1899
Woodpile	Wedges	Wood-pike	Wedged	Wood-peg
Wood-glue	Nude-pose	End-piece	Indigo-dye	Wide-gap

1900 Angrier Wagerer	1901 Nigerian Ingrain	1902 Angry-bee Yangzhou	1903 Ingrate Inaugurate	1904 Anagram Engram
1905 Engrave Inaugural	1906 Wipers Wagers	1907 Wee-price Woo-park	1908 Negroid Angered	1909 Engorge Wipe-rage
1910 Engineer Weaponry	1911 One-penny Nope-union	1912 Wage-nab Wig-web	1913 Ingenuity No-point	1914 Wigwam Nag-wife
1915 Inguinal Ungainly	1916 Weapons Ingenious	1917 No-panic Engine-key	1918 One-pound Unopened	1919 Wigwag Weeping
1920 Anaphora Young-hero	1921 Nephew Weigh-in	1922 Weepy-baby Wage-hub	1923 Night Weight	1924 Wage-boom Nip-home
1925 Enophile Unpayable	1926 Anaphase Wage-hoax	1927 Wage-book Wig-hook	1928 Nap-bed Wig-head	1929 Wig-bag Wage-hype
1930 Nugatory Wig-tree	1931 Neptune Negation	1932 Inept-yob Input-bay	1933 Negotiate Wage-equity	1934 Angiotomy Naptime
1935 Negative Wagtail	1936 Ingots Inputs	1937 Unpoetic Nepotic	1938 Neap-tide Unpitied	1939 Nag-tag Wipe-tape
1940 Young-fry Wage-free	1941 Wage-fine Young-man	1942 Nope-mob Wage-fib	1943 Nape-fat Nag-mate	1944 Nip-off Wipe-off
1945 Wage-file Young-foal	1946 Enigmas Away-games	1947 Weepy-face Young-mice	1948 Weepy-mood Wipe-mud	1949 Ion-pump Young-image
1950 Angler Unipolar	1951 Napoleon Angelina	1952 Englobe Ungava-bay	1953 Ungulate Unplait	1954 Engulf Napalm
1955 Nigella Anguilla	1956 Angels Angles	1957 Angelic Weepy-voice	1958 Unpaved Angled	1959 Negligee Angiology
1960 Wig-size Wage-soar	1961 Young-son Nap-soon	1962 Anguish Youngish	1963 Ingest Youngest	1964 Wage-sum Nap-sofa
1965 Young-soul Wig-sale	1966 Angiosis Wage-issue	1967 Nagasaki Weepy-sky	1968 Anapsid Young-side	1969 Young-sage Wig-usage
1970 Wig-care Nap-cure	1971 Napkin Nape-acne	1972 Young-cub Nape-ache	1973 Wage-cut Young-cat	1974 Nap-café Wig-cameo

1975	1976	1977	1978	1979
Wipe-clue	Wage-case	Unpack	Wage-code	Wage-cap
Young-koala	Wag-keys	Unpick	Young-kid	Nape-cape
1980	1981	1982	1983	1984
Wage-diary	Wiped-away	Wop-jibe	Wiped-out	Angioedema
Wipe-dry	Nap-den	Wog-jibe	Wage-data	Unpaid-fee
1985	1986	1987	1988	1989
Ungodly	Young-aides	Young-duke	Unguided	Wag-dog
Wage-deal	Wage-dues	Wig-decoy	Young-dad	Nip-edge
1990	1991	1992	1993	1994
Nigger	Nippon	Wipe-pooh	Nugget	Nip-gum
Nipper	Noggin	Nap-pub	Nagyagite	Wig-gem
1995	1996	1997	1998	1999
Nipple	Nappies	Anagogic	Engaged	Wage-gap
Wiggle	Young-guys	Wage-peak	Unpaged	Wipe-page

ALPHA BETA 2000 – 2999

2000 Barrier Horror	2001 Horizon Borrow	2002 Hurrah Buzzy-bee	2003 Burrito Berry-tea	2004 Horrify Bar-room
2005 Barrel Brazil	2006 Bearers Berries	2007 Burr-oak Brazuca	2008 Horrid Hazard	2009 Barrage Herzog
2010 Bronze Brewery	2011 Brown Brawny	2012 Bernabeu Horny-boy	2013 Hornet Baronet	2014 Barnum Hornify
2015 Brawl Baronial	2016 Burns Horns	2017 Brink Bronco	2018 Brand Brandy	2019 Boring Bring
2020 Barber Harbour	2021 Bourbon Harbin	2022 Brouhaha Hairy-baby	2023 Herb-tea Barbet	2024 Abraham Brahma
2025 Bearable Borehole	2026 Herbs Bribes	2027 Barbecue Bra-hook	2028 Bribed Bare-body	2029 Herbage Bear-hug
2030 Barter Hertz	2031 Britain Baritone	2032 Birth Breath	2033 Burette Bratty	2034 Hour-time Hire-team
2035 Brutal Hurtle	2036 Brutes Hearts	2037 Heretic Hieratic	2038 Aborted Berated	2039 Heritage Beer-tap
2040 Briefer Hormuz	2041 Harmony Hormone	2042 Brumby Bar-mob	2043 Hermit Barefoot	2044 Beer-foam Bar-off
2045 Briefly Bramley	2046 Briefs Brooms	2047 Bromic Bare-face	2048 Barmaid Bermuda	2049 Beer-mug Hero-image
2050 Bravery Broiler	2051 Berlin Barlow	2052 Brave-boy Hazel-hoe	2053 Brevity Harlot	2054 Harlem Heirloom
2055 Braille Brill	2056 Brevis Bravoes	2057 Hair-lice Bearlike	2058 Bravado Herald	2059 Harelip Horology
2060 Bursar Bursary	2061 Abrasion Bryson	2062 Brush Harsh	2063 Breast Burst	2064 Heroism Heurism
2065 Abrasive Hoarsely	2066 Brass Harass	2067 Brisk Brescia	2068 Bruised Braised	2069 Bar-soap Bruise-ego
2070 Barker Broker	2071 Broken Hearken	2072 Birch Broche	2073 Bract Haircut	2074 Abrocoma Hieracium

2075	2076	2077	2078	2079
Barclay	Braces	Brick	Barcode	Breakage
Biracial	Brakes	Brock	Brocade	Breakup
2080	2081	2082	2083	2084
Border	Burden	Hire-job	Heredity	Boredom
Hoarder	Broadway	Herd-boy	Hard-toy	Bear-jam
2085	2086	2087	2088	2089
Hurdle	Birds	Broad-oak	Bearded	Bridge
Bridle	Beards	Bardic	Boarded	Abridge
2090	2091	2092	2093	2094
Burger	Aborigine	Borough	Abrupt	Bregma
Harper	Bargain	Burgh	Abrogate	Hero-game
2095	2096	2097	2098	2099
Burgle	Herpes	Hairpiece	Brigade	Bragg
Hair-gel	Burps	Bra-piece	Brigid	Brigg
2100	2101	2102	2103	2104
Honorary	Benzene	Hyena-rib	Benzoate	Bow-room
Ebenezer	Benzoin	Howrah	Bone-rot	Bin-rim
2105	2106	2107	2108	2109
Benzyl	Honours	Benzoic	Hayward	Bioenergy
Binaural	Binaries	By-work	Byword	Hyena-rage
2110	2111	2112	2113	2114
Banner	Bony-inion	Hannah	Bonnet	Biennium
Bonanza	How-now	Bone-nib	Honey-nut	Bonny-M
2115	2116	2117	2118	2119
Biennial	Bananas	Hunnic	Banned	Boning
Biannual	Bunions	Ebony-ink	Binned	Bowing
2120	2121	2122	2123	2124
Banbury	Bonbon	Beanie-baby	Henbit	Bonhomie
Honey-bear	Henbane	Ebony-baby	Howbeit	Bony-beef
2125	2126	2127	2128	2129
Bean-hole	Henhouse	Bone-hook	Bonehead	Beanbag
Bowable	Bonobos	Hen-beak	Bowhead	Bin-bag
2130	2131	2132	2133	2134
Hunter	Huntaway	Beneath	Banquet	Bantam
Banter	Benton	Bony-youth	Hewitt	Hawaii-time
2135	2136	2137	2138	2139
Bentley	Hints	Bent-key	Haunted	Bone-type
Buoyantly	Bounties	Bony-tyke	Hunted	Hen-tag
2140	2141	2142	2143	2144
Bonfire	Honeymoon	Benumb	Benefit	Banff
Bone-free	Bin-man	Hyena-mob	Bone-fat	Hawaii-mafia
2145	2146	2147	2148	2149
Binomial	Bone-fuse	Bionomic	Bona-fide	Bone-image
Bone-meal	Boon-fees	Benefice	Bin-food	Bin-mop

2150 Howler However	2151 Bowline Bow-low	2152 Hawaii-aloha Bone-lab	2153 Banality Bawl-out	2154 Beewolf He-wolf
2155 Honolulu Howell	2156 Bowels Howls	2157 Bone-lace By-walk	2158 Bowled Bawled	2159 Bowleg Bon-voyage
2160 Hawser Bansuri	2161 Benson Hanson	2162 Banish Banshee	2163 Honest Boneset	2164 Hansom Yahwism
2165 Hansel Heinously	2166 Bonuses Obnoxious	2167 Honey-sauce Bean-sauce	2168 Bean-seed Bow-aside	2169 Bean-soup Bonus-pay
2170 Banker Bouncer	2171 Heineken Bin-can	2172 Bench Hunch	2173 Bounce-out Bank-quay	2174 Bunkum Bank-fee
2175 Biweekly Bouncily	2176 Banks Bionics	2177 Hawick Honey-cake	2178 Hawked Banked	2179 Hencoop Beanie-cap
2180 Boundary Hinder	2181 Abandon Bandana	2182 Handy-boy Howdah	2183 Bandit Hand-out	2184 Bone-deaf Ebony-dame
2185 Handle Bundle	2186 Hands Bonds	2187 Bone-decay Hand-key	2188 Banded Bonded	2189 Bandage Bondage
2190 Hanger Hunger	2191 Benign Bang-on	2192 Hang-hoe Bingo-bay	2193 Abnegate Honeypot	2194 Bung-fee Ban-opium
2195 Bangle Bungle	2196 Hinges Bangs	2197 Bow-piece Hang-key	2198 Hanged Hinged	2199 Hang-up Hen-egg
2200 Bayberry Hebraize	2201 Hebrew Bahrain	2202 Rhubarb Baby-rib	2203 Hobart Baby-art	2204 Baby-room Bioherm
2205 Bihourly Haberlea	2206 Hubris Babirusa	2207 Hauberk Hebraic	2208 Hybrid Beebread	2209 Baby-rage Hobo-rag
2210 Baboonery Abhenry	2211 Abbey-nun Hobo-inn	2212 Hobnob Hub-web	2213 Baby-unit Bee-hunt	2214 Baby-name Baby-waif
2215 Hobnail Baby-owl	2216 Baby-wise Baboons	2217 Bubonic Bee-hawk	2218 Behind Boy-band	2219 Ebbing Bhang
2220 Bibber Bobber	2221 Baby-bone Bobbin	2222 Hubbub Baby-bib	2223 Hobbit Hohhot	2224 Baby-boom Baby-bum

2225	2226	2227	2228	2229
Babble	Hobbies	Baby-book	Babyhood	Babbage
Bubble	Bobbies	Bib-hook	Bobbed	Baby-bop
2230	2231	2232	2233	2234
Abbey-tour	Bhutan	Boob-tube	Habituate	Baby-team
Bib-tear	Hibitane	Baby-tab	Habitat	Booby-time
2235	2236	2237	2238	2239
Habitual	Habits	Hebetic	Habitude	Baby-tag
Bob-tail	Habitus	Baby-tyke	Hebetude	Booby-tape
2240	2241	2242	2243	2244
Hob-fairy	Bahamian	Bee-bomb	Boob-fat	Ebb-off
Hob-fire	Bohemian	Baby-fib	Baby-foot	Hob-fume
2245	2246	2247	2248	2249
Abba-movie	Bahamas	Baby-face	Baby-food	Baby-mug
Baby-foal	Bay-homes	Abbey-mice	Abbey-mead	Hobo-image
2250	2251	2252	2253	2254
Behaviour	Babylon	Baby-vibe	Bibelot	Behalf
Hobelar	Bubaline	Boob-lobe	Hublot	Beebalm
2255	2256	2257	2258	2259
Bay-hill	Bibles	Biblike	Behold	Baby-lip
Bee-bully	Baubles	Baby-voice	Behaved	Hub-log
2260	2261	2262	2263	2264
Boob-size	Hobson	Yobbish	Behest	Bahaism
Baby-size	Baby-son	Babyish	Babysit	Babyism
2265	2266	2267	2268	2269
Bi-basal	Abbess	Bibasic	Abbasid	Baby-spy
Abhesive	Bee-houses	Baby-seek	Bob-aside	Boob-sag
2270	2271	2272	2273	2274
Baby-care	Hoboken	Baby-cub	Bobcat	Baby-coma
Baby-cry	Baby-cow	Hibachi	Baby-cot	Abbey-café
2275	2276	2277	2278	2279
Baby-koala	Abbacies	Buy-back	Abbey-code	Hubcap
Hub-coil	Bubkes	Hob-cook	Baby-cade	Baby-cap
2280	2281	2282	2283	2284
Beheader	Abbey-dean	Boob-job	Baby-diet	Booby-doom
Baby-dry	Baby-jaw	Bob-a-job	Abbe-duty	Behead-foe
2285	2286	2287	2288	2289
Abbeydale	Baby-dose	Baby-doc	Beheaded	Baby-dog
Bob-Dole	Hybodus	Hobo-joke	Bhajji	Hobo-dope
2290	2291	2292	2293	2294
Baby-gro	Bubo-pain	Baby-pooh	Abbey-gate	Baby-game
Baby-gear	Abbey-pew	Hobo-pub	Baby-goat	Hobo-goof
2295	2296	2297	2298	2299
Baby-pool	Baby-peas	Booby-gook	Boob-pad	Baby-pig
Baby-play	Hobo-guise	Baby-pace	Baby-guide	Baby-poop

2300 Arbitrary Betrayer	2301 Butyrin Hot-urine	2302 Heat-rub Bi-turbo	2303 Beetroot Hit-rate	2304 Beauty-room Boot-room
2305 Betrayal Bee-trail	2306 Heaters Biters	2307 Beatrice Boat-race	2308 Hatred Betrayed	2309 Hot-rage Bee-trap
2310 Hotwire Botanize	2311 Between Hot-wine	2312 Botany-bay Bet-web	2313 Heat-unit Bitnet	2314 Hate-name Hot-info
2315 Heat-wave Butanol	2316 Batons Hot-wax	2317 Botanic Beatnik	2318 Obtund Obtained	2319 Beating Biting
2320 Bother Hither	2321 Heathen Bethany	2322 Hot-hob Beauty-boob	2323 Bat-bite Hot-beauty	2324 Hit-home Hot-hoof
2325 Bath-oil Bethel	2326 Baths Boathouse	2327 Boat-hook Hot-bake	2328 Hot-bed Hot-head	2329 Beet-bug Hatha-yoga
2330 Butter Battery	2331 Button Batten	2332 Bequeath Hot-tub	2333 Hoity-toity Hittite	2334 Bottom About-time
2335 Battle Bottle	2336 Ubiquitous Boutiques	2337 Biotitic Haiti-quake	2338 Beatitude Batted	2339 Hot-tip Hot-tap
2340 Beautifier Hot-fire	2341 Batman Hitman	2342 Hate-mob Hot-fib	2343 Hotfoot Heat-mat	2344 Bite-off Hot-fume
2345 Beautiful Botfly	2346 Betimes Hot-fuse	2347 Beatific About-face	2348 Beautified Beatified	2349 Bitmap Heat-map
2350 Hitler Butler	2351 Hotline Hot-oven	2352 Hate-vibe Beauty-lab	2353 Hate-vote Bite-vet	2354 Hot-lime Beet-leaf
2355 Hot-lava Hate-love	2356 Beetles Beatles	2357 Bootlace By-talk	2358 Boatload Beetled	2359 Bootleg Bite-lip
2360 Boot-size Heat-soar	2361 Hot-sun Bee-toxin	2362 Hot-ash Boat-shoe	2363 Bequest Hot-seat	2364 Beauty-sofa Bet-safe
2365 Boot-sale Hot-seal	2366 Hot-issue Biotaxis	2367 Hot-sauce Biotoxic	2368 Hot-soda Bite-side	2369 Hot-soup Beauty-spa
2370 Hot-car Beauty-care	2371 Beautician Betoken	2372 Batch Bitch	2373 Hot-city Hate-act	2374 Bet-café Beta-coma

2375 Bat-cave Hot-coal	2376 Hot-case Boat-cox	2377 Hot-cake Hot-cocoa	2378 Bytecode Bat-kid	2379 Bat-cage Hot-cup
2380 Hut-door Heat-dry	2381 Hot-June Butadiene	2382 Hot-job Hate-jibe	2383 Hot-jet Beauty-diet	2384 Heat-doom Hot-dome
2385 Hot-deal Heatedly	2386 Hot-days Hot-ideas	2387 Beta-decay Beauty-juice	2388 Hot-diode Betided	2389 Hotdog Heated-up
2390 Bait-prey Hot-pyre	2391 Hatpin Hot-pan	2392 Bet-pub Hot-ghee	2393 Hotpot Hot-pit	2394 Butea-gum Beauty-gem
2395 Hot-glue Heat-gel	2396 Biotypes Hot-pies	2397 Hot-poke Heat-peak	2398 Beauty-god Heat-guide	2399 Hot-pipe Beat-egg
2400 Bio-freeze Euhemerize	2401 Home-run Boom-zone	2402 Beef-rib Bum-rub	2403 Hoof-rot Home-art	2404 Biform Homeroom
2405 Humoral Humeral	2406 Humerus Humorous	2407 Hayfork Homeric	2408 Humoured Byford	2409 Hay-forage Bum-rap
2410 Hymnary Homeware	2411 Hominin Home-win	2412 Home-web Hoof-nub	2413 Humanity Beaumont	2414 Hafnium Homonym
2415 Bimanual Humanely	2416 Humans Bimanous	2417 Hymnic Boom-week	2418 Humanoid Hymnody	2419 Beaming Booming
2420 Bomber Humber	2421 Bambino Hambone	2422 Home-hub Bomb-bee	2423 Bumboat Home-beauty	2424 Home-boom Beefy-bum
2425 Humble Bumble	2426 Bombs Home-base	2427 Home-bake Beam-hook	2428 Homebody Bombed	2429 Home-bug Bum-bag
2430 Beefeater Haematuria	2431 Himation Haematin	2432 Bee-moth By-mouth	2433 Haematite Home-equity	2434 Hematoma Home-team
2435 Bimetal Heftily	2436 Hamites Home-ties	2437 Haematic Homeotic	2438 Haematoid Hefted	2439 Homotype Hefty-pay
2440 Buffer Hammer	2441 Buffoon Boffin	2442 Home-fob Boom-fib	2443 Buffet Beef-meat	2444 Bum-fume Home-fame
2445 Baffle Buffalo	2446 Hummus Home-fax	2447 Home-mice Beefy-face	2448 Home-made Hummed	2449 Home-map Beam-image

2450 Hay-fever Bifilar	2451 Home-alone Hemline	2452 Home-lab Boom-vibe	2453 Hamlet Humility	2454 Biofilm Home-life
2455 Befall Home-leave	2456 Himalayas Humvees	2457 Homelike Boom-voice	2458 Befouled Home-video	2459 Homologue Home-leg
2460 Bum-size Home-soiree	2461 Hem-sew Beef-saw	2462 Hamish Beamish	2463 Home-site Homestay	2464 Home-safe Hem-seam
2465 Home-sale Home-soil	2466 Biomass Beam-axis	2467 Beef-sauce Biomusic	2468 Bemused Home-side	2469 Home-usage Beef-soup
2470 Haymaker Homecare	2471 Beef-cow Boomkin	2472 Hemi-cube Boom-echo	2473 Home-kit Home-city	2474 Beef-café Home-cameo
2475 Bifacial Bifocal	2476 Home-keys Beam-cues	2477 Beefcake Ham-cook	2478 Homicide Home-code	2479 Home-copy Home-keep
2480 Humidor Home-dry	2481 Hamden Homodyne	2482 Bum-jab Home-job	2483 Humidity Beef-diet	2484 Humidify Home-demo
2485 Bimodal Humidly	2486 Humidex Home-ideas	2487 Beef-juice Ham-decay	2488 Homey-dad Humid-day	2489 Beefed-up Hoof-dog
2490 Bumper Hamper	2491 Hempen Homogeny	2492 Bumph Humph	2493 Humpty Beef-pot	2494 Home-game Homogamy
2495 Hampole Bumpily	2496 Bumps Humps	2497 Bump-key Home-peace	2498 Bumped Bum-pad	2499 Home-page Bump-up
2500 Blazer Blurry	2501 Heavy-rain Blue-zone	2502 Blurb Holy-orb	2503 Bivariate Hilarity	2504 Holy-ram Heavy-arm
2505 Beverly Bay-laurel	2506 Hilarious Hoovers	2507 Holy-ark Holozoic	2508 Holyrood Hovered	2509 Beverage Halurgy
2510 Bilinear Blower	2511 Blown Hole-in-one	2512 Holy-web Bevin-boy	2513 Blunt Havant	2514 Holy-name Bee-venom
2515 Heavenly Blue-Nile	2516 Heavens Bylaws	2517 Balance Blank	2518 Bland Blonde	2519 Belong Oblong
2520 Belabour Bulbar	2521 Heel-bone Holy-bow	2522 Blabby Blue-baby	2523 Halibut Bilobate	2524 Balham Holy-home

2525	2526	2527	2528	2529
Bilabial	Bulbs	Holy-book	Holyhead	Hula-hoop
Heavy-haul	Blobs	Bluebook	Able-body	Heavy-bag
2530	2531	2532	2533	2534
Blitz	Hilton	Health	Obliquity	Heavy-atom
Belter	Bolton	Blithe	Bolt-out	Blue-team
2535	2536	2537	2538	2539
Obliquely	Bolts	Baltic	Ablated	Built-up
Heavy-tool	Belts	Biolytic	Belated	Belt-up
2540	2541	2542	2543	2544
Balefire	Halfway	Helium-buoy	Hayloft	Bailiff
Belfry	Blue-moon	Holy-fib	Helmet	Bluff
2545	2546	2547	2548	2549
Baleful	Halifax	Bulimic	Bloomed	Blimp
Blue-movie	Beliefs	Holm-oak	Half-day	Half-pay
2550	2551	2552	2553	2554
Believer	Hallow	Ball-boy	Ballet	Holy-life
Hillary	Hollow	Bellboy	Ballot	Hallam
2555	2556	2557	2558	2559
Bivalve	Balls	Holly-oak	Ballad	Blue-lip
Bellevue	Bells	Balalaika	Bullied	Heavy-leg
2560	2661	2662	2563	2564
Belsize	Holy-son	Abolish	Blast	Balsam
Hole-size	Heavy-sin	Blush	Holiest	Baalism
2565	2566	2567	2568	2569
Obviously	Bless	Blue-sky	Heaviside	Bile-soap
Holy-soul	Bliss	Obelisk	Blue-side	Blue-sage
2570	2571	2572	2573	2574
Bulker	Balcony	Bleach	Bluecoat	Bio-vacuum
Bilker	Halcyon	Belch	Holy-city	Ebola-coma
2575	2576	2577	2578	2579
Helical	Helices	Black	Bile-acid	Blue-cap
Bleakly	Blokes	Block	Blue-cod	Bulk-up
2580	2581	2582	2583	2584
Builder	Blue-jean	Heavy-job	Heavy-duty	Heal-deaf
Boulder	Build-on	Holiday-bay	Hold-out	Holy-dome
2585	2586	2587	2588	2589
Boldly	Holidays	Blue-joke	Blooded	Hold-up
Baldly	Blades	Bile-juice	Bloodied	Bay-ledge
2590	2591	2592	2593	2594
Helper	Halogen	Hayleigh	Obligate	Belgium
Bulgaria	Bologna	Haulage-bay	Boil-pot	Hologamy
2595	2596	2597	2598	2599
Blue-glue	Bleeps	Biologic	Heel-pad	Boil-egg
Heel-peel	Blogs	Heelpiece	Helipad	Hole-peg

2600	2601	2602	2603	2604
Be-sorry	Bus-zone	Absorb	Base-rate	Box-room
Bus-rear	Box-iron	House-robe	Bus-route	Houseroom
2605	2606	2607	2608	2609
Observe	Boxers	Busy-race	Absurd	House-rage
Hose-reel	Abusers	Box-ark	Bus-ride	Box-zip
2610	2611	2612	2613	2614
Houseware	Hosanna	Busy-web	Absent	Housewife
Boys-wear	House-wine	Box-nub	Base-unit	Boys-name
2615	2616	2617	2618	2619
Hexanol	Basins	Absence	Boxwood	Boxing
Boys-only	Beeswax	Obeisance	Bio-sand	Housing
2620	2621	2622	2623	2624
Basher	Bees-honey	Hushaby	Houseboat	Heysham
Busy-hour	Bash-in	Bush-boy	Bush-tea	House-beam
2625	2626	2627	2628	2629
Boxhaul	Bushes	House-book	Busybody	Bishop
Bushel	House-boys	Hash-key	Abashed	House-bug
2630	2631	2632	2633	2634
History	Bestow	Best-buy	Hesitate	Bus-time
Buster	Hasten	Hose-tube	Ohio-state	Busy-team
2635	2636	2637	2638	2639
Hostel	Hosts	Host-ace	Boosted	Hostage
Hostile	Busts	Hoist-key	Boasted	Housetop
2640	2641	2642	2643	2644
Besmear	Houseman	House-fob	Housemate	Busy-mum
Bus-fare	Baseman	Boys-mob	Biosafety	Hose-fume
2645	2646	2647	2648	2649
Housefly	House-mouse	House-mice	Housemaid	Bus-map
Buxomly	Hoax-fax	House-mace	Busy-mode	Hoax-image
2650	2651	2652	2653	2654
Basilar	Baseline	Busy-lab	Absolute	House-loom
Base-layer	Bus-lane	Bias-vibe	Obsolete	Busy-life
2655	2656	2657	2658	2659
Absolve	House-lease	Basilica	Busload	Basal-age
Abusively	Hoax-visa	Hose-leak	Boys-aloud	Busy-loop
2660	2661	2662	2663	2664
Box-size	Abyssinia	House-shoe	Box-seat	Hassium
Busy-user	Bee-season	Bossy-boy	Busiest	Box-safe
2665	2666	2667	2668	2669
Bisexual	Bosses	Abyss-key	Bossed	Hyssop
Hassle	Hisses	Boss-key	Hissed	Hussy-up
2670	2671	2672	2673	2674
Obscure	Obscene	Beseech	Basket	Basic-fee
Boxcar	Buskin	Bosch	Biscuit	Baskimo

2675	2676	2677	2678	2679
Biosocial	Basics	Basic-key	Basked	Bioscopy
Bascule	Husks	Obese-cook	Basic-idea	Housekeep
2680	2681	2682	2683	2684
House-door	Boxed-in	House-job	Hose-jet	House-dome
Busy-diary	Obsidian	Busy-job	Base-data	Bus-jam
2685	2686	2687	2688	2689
House-deal	Besides	Hasidic	Busy-dad	Housedog
Bus-delay	Busy-days	Hoax-joke	Biased-idea	Box-edge
2690	2691	2692	2693	2694
Besieger	Hexagon	Boys-gab	Ibex-goat	Busy-gym
Hesperia	Hoosegow	Busy-pub	House-pet	Boys-game
2695	2696	2697	2698	2699
Bus-pool	House-apex	Bespoke	Besieged	Hosepipe
House-gala	Base-gas	Hospice	Bus-guide	Busy-page
2700	2701	2702	2703	2704
Book-array	Bicorn	Hay-crib	Bike-route	Book-room
Boy-crazy	Beak-iron	Aboukir-bay	Hike-rate	Bike-room
2705	2706	2707	2708	2709
Bakerloo	Bakers	By-crook	Bike-ride	Hook-zip
Bike-rail	Bikers	Bike-race	Bacardi	Bike-rage
2710	2711	2712	2713	2714
Bakeware	Baconian	Beacon-buoy	Abacinate	Hay-knife
Baconer	Book-now	Bike-nub	Bike-nut	Book-info
2715	2716	2717	2718	2719
Beknave	Bacons	Book-week	Bookend	Baking
Bacon-oil	Beacons	Hook-nook	Boy-kind	Booking
2720	2721	2722	2723	2724
Book-hero	Beech-way	Beach-boy	Bookie-bet	Bochum
Abkhazia	Book-ban	Beech-hue	Bike-hut	Beecham
2725	2726	2727	2728	2729
Bookable	Beeches	By-choice	Book-ahead	Book-bag
Beech-oil	Beaches	Beach-ice	Hook-head	Biochip
2730	2731	2732	2733	2734
Bacteria	Ubication	Bike-tube	Boycott	Book-time
Hectare	Biocytin	Book-tab	Book-quote	Bike-team
2735	2736	2737	2738	2739
Bioactive	Be-cautious	Hectic	Book-today	Book-top
Book-tale	Book-taxi	Hike-tyke	Bike-tide	Book-tape
2740	2741	2742	2743	2744
Book-fair	Bookman	Bike-fob	Book-mate	Book-off
Bake-fire	Hake-fin	Hokmah	Bake-meat	Bake-off
2745	2746	2747	2748	2749
Book-meal	Becomes	Book-make	Bake-food	Bee-camp
Bake-meal	Hook-fix	Bake-fake	Book-mad	Book-image

2750 Bicolour Booklore	2751 Baculine Bike-lane	2752 Boy-club Bio-clean	2753 Booklet Bakelite	2754 Becalm Book-leaf
2755 Bacilli Baklava	2756 Booklouse Bike-lease	2757 Bucolic Booklice	2758 Becloud Hook-load	2759 Book-log Bioecology
2760 Book-size Bike-user	2761 Bay-casino Bye-cousin	2762 Bookish Bake-ash	2763 Book-set Bike-seat	2764 Book-exam Hook-safe
2765 Book-sale Bike-axle	2766 Abacuses Book-issue	2767 Bay-kiosk Hocus-key	2768 Bake-soda Hook-aside	2769 Bike-usage Book-expo
2770 Backer Hacker	2771 Beckon Hackney	2772 Backhoe Book-cab	2773 Bucket Back-out	2774 Back-fee Book-café
2775 Bicycle Heckle	2776 Bucks Hacks	2777 Back-key Haycock	2778 Backed Hacked	2779 Hiccup Back-pay
2780 Abecedary Book-diary	2781 Hooked-on Booked-in	2782 Hook-jab Book-job	2783 Book-date Baked-oat	2784 Bike-demo Bay-academy
2785 Biocidal Book-deal	2786 Biacids Book-ideas	2787 Bookie-joke Bike-decoy	2788 Bookie-odd Booked-day	2789 Book-edge Hooked-up
2790 Beekeeper Hook-prey	2791 Bake-pan Hook-gun	2792 Book-pub Hook-gob	2793 Bake-pot Haiku-poet	2794 Book-game Bike-gym
2795 Book-gala Hokey-guile	2796 Biceps Buy-copies	2797 Book-epic Beak-poke	2798 Book-guide Hook-pad	2799 Book-page Bike-peg
2800 Abjurer Hydrozoa	2801 Bedizen Hadrian	2802 Body-robe Bad-rib	2803 Hydrate Body-art	2804 Headroom Bedroom
2805 Bedrail Head-rule	2806 Hiders Hydras	2807 Headrace Hydric	2808 Hydride Abjured	2809 Bad-rage Bed-rag
2810 Headwear Bad-war	2811 Hoedown Head-inion	2812 Body-nob Bad-whey	2813 Headnote Obedient	2814 Bad-name Hide-info
2815 Bejewel Body-wave	2816 Head-noose Bedouins	2817 Hedonic Obedience	2818 Body-need Head-end	2819 Heading Hiding
2820 Body-hair Head-bare	2821 Hyoid-bone Head-bow	2822 Abu-Dhabi Head-bob	2823 Body-heat Bad-bout	2824 Head-home Bad-beef

2825	2826	2827	2828	2829
Hide-hole	Head-box	Hide-hook	Bedhead	Bedbug
Head-above	Bad-boys	Bad-book	Head-hood	Body-bag
2830	2831	2832	2833	2834
Bead-tree	Body-tone	Hadith	Bad-equity	Bedtime
Bed-tray	Bad-tune	Head-youth	Head-tout	Bad-team
2835	2836	2837	2838	2839
Hide-tool	Bidets	Bed-quake	Hydatid	Body-type
Bad-tale	Head-tax	Bad-teak	Bed-tidy	Head-top
2840	2841	2842	2843	2844
Bad-fairy	Abdomen	Hoodie-mob	Bed-mate	Head-off
Hide-more	Headman	Bad-fib	Body-fat	Bed-foam
2845	2846	2847	2848	2849
Headful	Bad-fox	Hide-face	Body-food	Body-image
Bad-flu	Head-fix	Head-mike	Bad-mood	Body-map
2850	2851	2852	2853	2854
Bad-liar	Headline	Body-vibe	Head-vote	Hoodlum
Head-over	Bad-view	Head-lobe	Bad-lot	Bedlam
2855	2856	2857	2858	2859
Bedevil	Head-louse	Head-lice	Bad-lead	Head-lag
Hide-love	Bud-vase	Bad-look	Bed-load	Bad-league
2860	2861	2862	2863	2864
Bedsore	Hudson	Bad-shoe	Bedsit	Bad-sum
Body-size	Body-sway	Hide-sob	Headset	Body-exam
2865	2866	2867	2868	2869
Hideously	Body-axis	Hide-seek	Bedside	Heads-up
Biodiesel	Bad-ass	Body-soak	Bad-seed	Body-expo
2870	2871	2872	2873	2874
Body-care	Bodkin	Headache	Abdicate	Body-cam
Head-core	Bad-coin	Hide-cub	Abduct	Bad-café
2875	2876	2877	2878	2879
Head-coil	Bodacious	Bedeck	Bed-code	Head-cap
Hide-cave	Bad-case	Hijack	Bad-kid	Bad-copy
2880	2881	2882	2883	2884
Bidder	Hidden	Buddha	Body-data	Head-dome
Body-odour	Abidjan	Body-jab	Bad-diet	Bad-dime
2885	2886	2887	2888	2889
Huddle	Buddies	Bad-joke	Bedded	Buddy-up
Buddle	Bad-days	Head-dyke	Budded	Bed-edge
2890	2891	2892	2893	2894
Badger	Bedpan	Bad-pub	Budget	Bad-game
Headgear	Headpin	Bed-pooh	Head-gate	Badge-fee
2895	2896	2897	2898	2899
Bed-pole	Badges	Headpiece	Hedged	Bad-egg
Body-gel	Hedges	Head-poke	Budged	Budge-up

2900	2901	2902	2903	2904
Huge-roar	Bog-iron	Hog-rib	Huge-rat	Hyperaemia
Big-zero	Heparin	Bee-grub	Big-rout	Hygroma
2905	2906	2907	2908	2909
Bygrave	Bigorexia	Biopiracy	Begird	Hyperopia
Boy-girl	Hope-rise	By-grace	Hope-road	Boy-George
2910	2911	2912	2913	2914
Bio-power	Big-win	Bug-web	Hognut	Hyponym
Bygone-era	Bignonia	Hygiene-bay	Huguenot	Big-name
2915	2916	2917	2918	2919
Big-nail	Bygones	Hygienic	Bogwood	Bigwig
Huge-wave	Hognose	Biogenic	Hogweed	Bagwig
2920	2921	2922	2923	2924
Higher	Hyphen	Biphobia	Height	Hyphema
Bugbear	Hipbone	Highboy	Haughty	High-aim
2925	2926	2927	2928	2929
Highly	Highs	Big-book	Bighead	Hip-hop
Huge-hole	Boughs	High-key	Hophead	High-up
2930	2931	2932	2933	2934
Bigotry	Hypotonia	Bypath	Baguette	Bigtime
Hug-tree	Beep-tone	Hog-taboo	Bugatti	Hepatoma
2935	2936	2937	2938	2939
Bi-petal	Bigots	Hepatic	Bigoted	Bug-tape
Bogey-tale	He-goats	Haptic	Heptad	Bag-tag
2940	2941	2942	2943	2944
Big-fry	Hegemony	Huge-mob	Bigfoot	Bug-off
Bogey-fairy	Hypomania	Bogey-fib	Hog-meat	Hype-fame
2945	2946	2947	2948	2949
Hopeful	Bigamous	Big-mac	Hope-mad	Hype-image
Bagful	Bug-fix	Huge-mice	Hope-fade	Bogey-imp
2950	2951	2952	2953	2954
Bipolar	Biplane	Bug-lab	Hoplite	Bug-life
Bugler	Hipline	Hope-vibe	Be-polite	Bay-golf
2955	2956	2957	2958	2959
Big-value	Bagels	Big-leak	Haploid	Big-leap
By-golly	Bugles	Huge-lake	Beguiled	Hagiology
2960	2961	2962	2963	2964
Big-size	Hip-sway	Big-shoe	By-post	Hypoxemia
Hip-X-ray	Boa-poison	Bogus-boy	By-past	Huge-sum
2965	2966	2967	2968	2969
Big-sale	Bypass	Hypoxic	Hop-aside	Bug-spy
Bogusly	Bagasse	Big-ask	Bogey-side	Hog-soup
2970	2971	2972	2973	2974
Hip-care	Big-cow	Hug-cub	Big-cat	Big-cameo
Beep-car	Huge-ocean	Bug-cab	Hepcat	Bug-café

2975	2976	2977	2978	2979
Big-clue	Biopics	Bipack	Hug-kid	Bogey-copy
Huge-cave	Big-case	Big-cake	Bogey-code	Big-cup
2980	2981	2982	2983	2984
Hope-door	Hog-jaw	Big-job	Hype-data	Huge-dam
Bug-jury	Bug-dean	Hag-jibe	Big-jet	Big-dome
2985	2986	2987	2988	2989
Bipedal	Big-ideas	Big-joke	Big-dude	Heaped-up
Big-deal	Buy-goods	Bog-decay	Hug-dad	Big-dog
2990	2991	2992	2993	2994
Beggar	Happen	Happy-boy	Biggity	Big-game
Buggery	Hypopnea	Bug-pub	Hogget	Happy-oaf
2995	2996	2997	2998	2999
Haggle	Huggies	Huge-piece	Bugged	Baggage
Hopple	Hippies	Hug-peace	Bagged	Bag-pipe

ALPHA BETA 3000 – 3999

3000 Terror Terrier	3001 Terrain Tarzan	3002 Otorrhea Tirzah	3003 Turret Taro-root	3004 Terrify Tyre-rim
3005 Quarrel Torril	3006 Quarries Equerries	3007 Terrace Tour-race	3008 Torrid Tarred	3009 Tear-rag Tour-rage
3010 Trainer Turner	3011 Tyranny Turn-away	3012 Tour-web Tree-neb	3013 Eternity Trinity	3014 True-name Quiz-enemy
3015 Eternal Trowel	3016 Turns Trains	3017 Trunk Trance	3018 Tornado Trend	3019 Turnip Trying
3020 True-hero Tree-bear	3021 Tribune Turbine	3022 Tar-baby Tyre-hub	3023 Tribute Terabyte	3024 Terbium Tour-boom
3025 Treble Trouble	3026 Tribes Treehouse	3027 Quiz-book Tour-bike	3028 Turbid Tree-bud	3029 Tree-hug True-hope
3030 Traitor Torture	3031 Triton Tartan	3032 Truth True-oath	3033 Quartet Tourette	3034 Tritium Teratoma
3035 Turtle Quartile	3036 Treats Tarts	3037 Autoerotic True-teak	3038 Treated Tree-toad	3039 Tree-top True-type
3040 Tremor Termer	3041 Termini Tramway	3042 Tour-mob Queer-fib	3043 Termite Turf-out	3044 Tariff Tear-off
3045 Trifle Tearful	3046 Terms Trams	3047 Tarmac True-face	3048 Termed Turfed	3049 Tramp Trump
3050 Trailer Trover	3051 Treeline Tram-way	3052 Tri-lobe Trail-by	3053 Treelet Trivet	3054 True-life Tree-leaf
3055 Travel Trolley	3056 Trails Trials	3057 Tyre-leak True-look	3858 Trailed Tour-video	3059 Trilogy Aquariology
3060 Treasure Trouser	3061 Torsion Tyrosine	3062 Trash Outrush	3063 Trust Tourist	3064 Tourism Truism
3065 Tarsal Tersely	3066 Tress Tarsus	3067 Tear-sac Too-risky	3068 Torsade Trioxide	3069 Tree-sap Troy-siege
3070 Tracer Trocar	3071 Tar-acne Turkana	3072 Torch Trachea	3073 Atrocity Tract	3074 Tour-café Trace-foe

3075 Treacle Utricle	3076 Atrocious Trikes	3077 Track Truck	3078 Traced Truce-day	3079 True-copy Trice-up
3080 Trader Outrider	3081 Trojan Trade-in	3082 Tired-boy Tyro-job	3083 Tour-duty Trijet	3084 Queerdom Triduum
3085 Tardive Treadle	3086 Trades Tirades	3087 Traduce Triadic	3088 Traded True-deed	3089 Trudge Queer-dog
3090 Trooper Torpor	3091 Atropine Trepan	3092 Trophy Trough	3093 Target Tar-pit	3094 True-gem Tour-game
3095 Triple Tripoli	3096 Trips Traps	3097 Tragic Tropic	3098 Torpedo Tragedy	3099 Trip-up Tyre-gauge
3100 Itinerary Tweezer	3101 Outworn Tanzania	3102 Tuna-rib Tiny-ruby	3103 Itinerate Toe-wart	3104 Tenerife Tonearm
3105 Twirl Tenurial	3106 Towers Toners	3107 Outwork Twerk	3108 Toward Outward	3109 Towrope Twerp
3110 Tanner Tenner	3111 Tannin Queen-Anne	3112 Town-yob Twin-boy	3113 Tenant Twenty	3114 Teen-wife Tune-info
3115 Tunnel Queen-envoy	3116 Tennis Twins	3117 Tenancy Twinkie	3118 Tanned Tinned	3119 Twinge Twang
3120 Tenebrae Tow-bar	3121 Tin-bin Tuna-bone	3122 Tiny-baby Ten-bob	3123 Towboat Two-bit	3124 Tyneham Tin-beef
3125 Tenable Atonable	3126 Queen-bees Teen-boys	3127 Tiny-book Tow-hook	3128 Towhead Tan-body	3129 Tone-beep Tiny-bug
3130 Tweeter Tantra	3131 Tin-tin Taunton	3132 Outwith Tenth	3133 Quantity Quintet	3134 Quantum Quantify
3135 Quaintly Quantile	3136 Tents Tenets	3137 Quantic Tonetic	3138 Tinted Tweeted	3139 Tintype Tin-top
3140 Queen-Mary Twofer	3141 Tin-man Tuna-fin	3142 Queen-Mab Teen-mob	3143 Equanimity Tin-meat	3144 Tune-off Queen-mum
3145 Tinfoil Tuneful	3146 Autonomous Equanimous	3147 Autonomic Two-face	3148 Queen-Maud Tin-food	3149 Taeniafuge Tiny-imp

3150 Tan-layer Tiny-liar	3151 Towline Tune-low	3152 Queen-Leah Tiny-lobe	3153 Tonality Twilit	3154 Tin-leaf Tiny-elf
3155 Atenolol Twill	3156 Towels Toe-nails	3157 Toe-walk Tiny-voice	3158 Tune-loud Tin-lid	3159 Quinology Tin-leg
3160 Tensor Tonsure	3161 Tension Queensway	3162 Outwash Queenish	3163 Twist Tiniest	3164 Twosome Quinism
3165 Tonsil Utensil	3166 Tenses Teniasis	3167 Tuna-sauce Queens-key	3168 Tensed Tyneside	3169 Tense-up Tuna-soup
3170 Tanker Tinker	3171 Tin-can Tuna-can	3172 Quench Tench	3173 Tenacity Tonicity	3174 Queen.com Teen-café
3175 Tinkle Tunicle	3176 Tanks Tenacious	3177 Teaneck Tonic-key	3178 Tanked Tweaked	3179 Tankage Tin-cup
3180 Tender Tinder	3181 Tendon Quinidine	3182 Teen-job Tine-jab	3183 Tin-deity Tuna-diet	3184 Tandem Tone-deaf
3185 Tweedle Tone-dial	3186 Tweeds Tiny-dose	3187 Tin-juice Toon-joke	3188 Twaddy Tended	3189 Toe-wedge Tuned-up
3190 Teenager Tanager	3191 Tea-wagon Tenpin	3192 Outweigh Teenage-boy	3193 Tin-pot Tongue-tie	3194 Tone-gym Queen-gem
3195 Tangle Tingle	3196 Tongs Twigs	3197 Tiny-piece Teen-geek	3198 Tin-god Tone-guide	3199 Twiggy Tiny-egg
3200 Taborer Teaberry	3201 Throne Thorn	3202 Throb Thereby	3203 Authority Throat	3204 Atheroma Theorem
3205 Ethereal Thrive	3206 Thorax Tubers	3207 Tea-break Outbreak	3208 Thread Thyroid	3209 Therapy Autoharp
3210 Thin-air Thenar	3211 Athenian Toe-bunion	3212 The-web Thawb	3213 Thanet Thwaite	3214 Ethanium Taboo-name
3215 Ethanol Thinly	3216 Athens Euthanasia	3217 Think Thank	3218 Outbound Thawed	3219 Thing Tubing
3220 Youth-bar The-hero	3221 Autobahn Tibia-bone	3222 The-abbey Youth-hub	3223 Tebibyte Youth-beauty	3224 The-boom Tube-beam

3225 Quibble The-Hale	3226 Thebes Tabbies	3227 Oath-book Youth-hike	3228 Tabbed The-bad	3229 The-Hague Youth-hope
3230 Theatre Toe-biter	3231 Tahitian Tibetan	3232 Thoth Tabitha	3233 Youth-quota Tube-tout	3234 Youth-team The-time
3235 Toy-beetle Tub-tile	3236 Autobots Thetis	3237 Earthquake Tabetic	3238 Athetoid The-tide	3239 The-top Tibet-yoga
3240 Theme-zoo Youth-fear	3241 Thiamine Thymine	3242 Thumb Toy-bomb	3243 Theft Tube-foot	3244 Thymoma Youth-fame
3245 Youthful Tubful	3246 Thames Thomas	3247 Euthymic Youth-face	3248 Ethmoid Tube-feed	3249 Thump Tube-map
3250 Tabular Tubular	3251 Ethylene Tubulin	3252 Qabalah Table-bay	3253 Athlete Tablet	3254 Thulium Thalami
3255 The-oval Tee-ball	3256 Tables Thieves	3257 Aquaholic Tube-leak	3258 Tabloid Toehold	3259 Theology Ethology
3260 Tube-size This-year	3261 The-sun This-way	3262 The-shoe This-boy	3263 Atheist Youth-site	3264 Atheism The-same
3265 The-soul Tube-seal	3266 Thesis Outhouses	3267 Tabasco Tub-soak	3268 Ethoxide Youth-side	3269 Thesp Tuba-expo
3270 Tea-beaker Tub-care	3271 Ethician Ethocaine	3272 The-cube Youth-echo	3273 The-act Tib-cat	3274 Thecoma Youth-café
3275 Ethical Thecla	3276 Ethics Tie-hooks	3277 Tobacco Thick	3278 Youth-code Thioacid	3279 Youth-cup The-cape
3280 Theodore The-jury	3281 The-den Youth-dean	3282 Youth-job The-job	3283 Youth-date Yeti-hideout	3284 Oath-doom The-Duma
3285 The-ideal Youth-jail	3286 Orthodox Tea-buds	3287 Theodicy The-duke	3288 Athodyd The-dead	3289 Toby-jug The-edge
3290 The-poor Tubipora	3291 Ethiopian The-open	3292 Thigh Though	3293 The-pit Tube-gate	3294 Youth-game The-gym
3295 Youth-play The-ugly	3296 Thugs Tea-bags	3297 Ethiopic The-peak	3298 The-good Orthopod	3299 The-gap Thuggee

3300 Utterer Quatorze	3301 Attorney Quatrain	3302 Atterby Utterby	3303 Titrate Attrite	3304 Yttrium Quiet-room
3305 Tutorial Equatorial	3306 Tutors Otters	3307 Ataturk Quit-race	3308 Tetrad Auto-trade	3309 Tutorage Taut-rope
3310 Auto-tuner Taut-wire	3311 Aquitanian Quiet-Inn	3312 Ottawa-bay Quit-web	3313 Quotient Attenuate	3314 Titanium Tuition-fee
3315 Tea-towel Equational	3316 Tetanus Titans	3317 Teutonic Titanic	3318 Attend Attained	3319 Touting Quoting
3320 Tether Tither	3321 Tithonia Too-thin	3322 Quiet-baby Tithby	3323 Titbit Yottabyte	3324 Quiet-hum Tatham
3325 Equitable Quotable	3326 Tithes Tethys	3327 Tooth-key Quote-book	3328 Toothed Tithed	3329 Tote-bag Quote-hype
3330 Quitter Tottery	3331 Quotation Equitation	3332 Tatty-bye Quiet-oath	3333 Etiquette Tete-a-tete	3334 Quit-time Quiet-time
3335 Tattle Teetotal	3336 Tattoos Tatties	3337 Quiet-quake Tattoo-ace	3338 Attitude Tattooed	3339 Quiet-tug Equity-tip
3340 Tautomer Titfer	3341 Ottoman Quitman	3342 Quiet-mob Toyota-fob	3343 Yeti-outfit Ottomite	3344 Quit-mafia Quote-mum
3345 Attomole Titmal	3346 Toffees Totems	3347 Titmice Totemic	3348 Quiet-mood Too-timid	3349 Quiet-image Tote-mop
3350 Titular Tutelary	3351 Quote-law Taut-line	3352 Quiet-vibe Equity-lib	3353 Totality Titivate	3354 Quiet-life Total-fee
3355 Totally Total-oil	3356 Titles Tootles	3357 Autotelic Outtalk	3358 Titled Tootled	3359 Tautology Tutelage
3360 Quite-sure Tot-size	3361 Autotoxin Ototoxin	3362 Quiet-sob Tot-shoe	3363 Attest Quietist	3364 Quietism Autotoxemia
3365 Quota-sale Quiet-soul	3366 Tutsis Quite-sexy	3367 Autotoxic Ototoxic	3368 Quiet-side Quit-side	3369 Quote-sage Quit-saga
3370 Toyota-car Tot-cry	3371 Quiet-ocean Tout-con	3372 Attach Titchy	3373 Tot-cot Quit-kit	3374 Quiet-café Quit-coma

3375 Quite-cool Quit-cave	3376 Aquatics Atticus	3377 Attack Titicaca	3378 Quiet-kid Quote-code	3379 Toyota-coupe Quiet-cop
3380 Quote-diary Quit-door	3381 Quotidian Tout-den	3382 Quit-job Quiet-dub	3383 Equity-audit Quote-data	3384 Quite-deaf Quiet-demo
3385 Quiet-dove Toyota-deal	3386 Quote-ideas Quiet-days	3387 Quote-joke Quite-dicey	3388 Quiet-dude Equity-deed	3389 Quiet-dog Quite-deep
3390 Quite-poor Quiet-pair	3391 Quetiapine Equity-gain	3392 Quiet-pub Tout-gab	3393 Tout-pout Tot-pot	3394 Quiet-game Tot-gym
3395 Quiet-plea Quit-play	3396 Toe-tips Tea-tips	3397 Autotypic Quiet-peace	3398 Quite-good Equity-guide	3399 Quote-page Quiet-peep
3400 Atomizer Itemizer	3401 Aquamarine Time-zone	3402 Time-orb Team-robe	3403 Temerity Time-rate	3404 Aquiform Team-room
3405 Tumoral Team-rule	3406 Aquifers Timers	3407 Team-race Tofurkey	3408 Team-radio Otford	3409 Team-rage Time-zap
3410 Timoneer Team-war	3411 Time-now Outfawn	3412 Time-web Tame-nob	3413 Time-unit Outmount	3414 Team-name Time-info
3415 Autumnal Toy-manual	3416 Time-wise Team-noise	3417 Team-week Time-once	3418 Time-end Team-need	3419 Timing Teeming
3420 Timber Tambour	3421 Tame-hyena Time-bin	3422 Team-hub Tame-hobo	3423 Timbit Team-bet	3424 Time-beam Team-home
3425 Tumble Automobile	3426 Tombs Tomboys	3427 Time-book Team-hike	3428 Time-ahead Team-head	3429 Team-hope Tame-hog
3430 Team-tour Tufter	3431 Automaton Tomatine	3432 Timothy Time-tube	3433 Team-quota Tomtit	3434 Tomtom Team-time
3435 Automotive Time-tool	3436 Tufts Tomatoes	3437 Automatic Tame-tyke	3438 Automated Tufted	3439 Item-tag Team-tape
3440 Quaffer Tammuz	3441 Autoimmune Tiffany	3442 Tame-mob Time-fib	3443 Teammate Tuffet	3444 Time-off Team-fame
3445 Tamiflu Tomfool	3446 Toffees Tiffs	3447 Team-face Toffee-ice	3448 Quaffed Team-feud	3449 Team-image Time-map

3450	3451	3452	3453	3454
Time-over	Outflow	Team-vibe	Tumult	Tame-life
Q-fever	Timeline	Atom-lab	Tumulate	Eat-flame
3455	3456	3457	3458	3459
Outfall	Tumulus	Tame-voice	Outfield	Etymology
Autofill	Tamils	Tea-milk	Team-lead	Time-lag
3460	3461	3462	3463	3464
Atomiser	Toe-fusion	Outfish	Atomist	Atomism
Outmeasure	Eta-meson	Team-sub	Utmost	Time-exam
3465	3466	3467	3468	3469
Timeously	Time-axis	Team-sky	Tameside	Team-spy
Time-save	Team-issue	Auto-music	Atomised	Time-saga
3470	3471	3472	3473	3474
Automaker	Team-icon	Too-much	Tomcat	Team-café
Time-cure	Tame-cow	Time-echo	Team-kit	Time-cameo
3475	3476	3477	3478	3479
Artificial	Autofocus	Tom-Cook	Time-code	Time-keep
Time-clue	Team-case	Team-cake	Tame-kid	Atomic-age
3480	3481	3482	3483	3484
Team-diary	Quay-meadow	Team-job	Timidity	Team-demo
Timid-aura	Team-don	Tame-jab	Timed-out	Tea-madam
3485	3486	3487	3488	3489
Timidly	Team-ideas	Time-decay	Outmoded	Tame-dog
Time-delay	Time-dose	Team-joke	Timid-idea	Time-edge
3490	3491	3492	3493	3494
Temper	Tampon	Tampa-bay	Tempt	Team-game
Tamper	Timpani	Tempeh	Tame-pet	Team-gym
3495	3496	3497	3498	3499
Temple	Tampax	Timepiece	Time-guide	Time-gap
Team-goal	Tea-mugs	Team-peak	Tamped	Team-page
3500	3501	3502	3503	3504
Equalizer	Tavern	Quail-rib	Tolerate	Tularaemia
Utilizer	Outlearn	Aquila-orb	Tile-art	Tile-roof
3505	3506	3507	3508	3509
Equal-role	Tailors	Tailrace	Equalized	At-large
TV-aerial	Quivers	Teleozoic	Utilized	Telergy
3510	3511	3512	3513	3514
Outliner	Talwin	Italian-boy	Talent	Talinum
Outlawry	Equilenin	Tail-nab	Atlanta	Teleonomy
3515	3516	3517	3518	3519
Tylenol	Talons	Tie-link	Outlined	Aqualung
Tale-weave	Outlaws	Tale-week	Toyland	Tiling
3520	3521	3522	3523	3524
Toolbar	Tailbone	Tea-lobby	Talbot	Tile-home
Equilibria	Taliban	Tool-hub	Tail-bite	Toy-album

3525	3526	3527	3528	3529
Tile-blue	Toolbox	Tale-book	Tail-bud	Tool-bag
Toil-hole	Equal-bias	Tool-hook	Equal-bid	Tile-heap
3530	3531	3532	3533	3534
Toiletry	Etiolation	Otolith	Toilette	Equal-time
Autolatry	Retaliation	Tilth	Quality-tea	Utility-fee
3535	3536	3537	3538	3539
Quail-tail	Toilets	Autolytic	Tilted	Teletype
Retaliative	Outlets	Toltec	Quilted	Tooltip
3540	3541	3542	3543	3544
Qualifier	Tail-fin	Outlimb	Out-lift	Tail-off
Telomere	Tail-fan	Tale-fib	Tele-footy	Toil-fame
3545	3546	3547	3548	3549
Tele-movie	Qualms	Tool-make	Talmud	Toe-lump
Toilful	Telefax	Toil-face	Qualified	Tile-mop
3550	3551	3552	3553	3554
Teller	Tallow	Ayatollah	Tallit	Equal-life
Tiller	Toll-way	Tall-boy	Tillite	Tellima
3555	3556	3557	3558	3559
Tell-lie	Tolls	Tall-oak	Quelled	Teleology
Equal-value	Televise	Tail-like	Outlived	Tillage
3560	3561	3562	3563	3564
Equaliser	Autolysin	Tie-leash	At-last	Atavism
Teleosaur	Toe-lesion	Toil-shoe	At-least	Toilsome
3565	3566	3567	3568	3569
Toil-soil	Autolysis	Tales-ace	Equalised	Tails-up
Telesale	Atlases	Tools-key	Utilised	Tool-usage
3570	3571	3572	3573	3574
Talker	Tool-icon	Toil-ache	Equivocate	Talcum
Tail-car	Talacen	Tail-cab	Toolkit	Telecom
3575	3576	3577	3578	3579
Equivocal	Talks	Tool-case	Talked	Talk-up
Tale-clue	Italics	Auto-lock	Tile-code	Tool-copy
3580	3581	3582	3583	3584
Autoloader	Toluidine	Tool-jab	Equal-duty	Tool-demo
Tile-door	Tale-doyen	Tile-job	Tail-jut	Tile-dome
3585	3586	3587	3588	3589
Toil-daily	Tea-ladies	Tea-vodka	Tool-aided	Equal-edge
Equal-deal	Equal-days	Tile-dyke	Equal-deed	Tool-dig
3590	3591	3592	3593	3594
Tale-guru	Auto-login	Outlaugh	Tail-gate	Tale-poem
Tail-prey	Telogen	Quail-pooh	Talipot	Tele-game
3595	3596	3597	3598	3599
Tool-pool	Tulips	Tailpiece	Tool-guide	Tailpipe
Teleplay	Autologous	Etiologic	Tail-pad	Quail-egg

3600	3601	3602	3603	3604
Taxi-array	Tsarina	Teasy-robe	Tax-rate	Taxi-zoom
Tsar-era	Taxi-run	Tax-rob	Taxi-route	Taser-aim
3605	3606	3607	3608	3609
Quasi-royal	Teasers	Outsource	Outsized	Tsar-ego
Tax-rule	Tasers	Taxi-race	Tax-raid	Taxi-rage
3610	3611	3612	3613	3614
Outswear	Taxi-union	Taxi-web	Tax-unit	Taxonomy
Tax-war	Tax-wine	Tax-nab	Tysonite	Tsunami
3615	3616	3617	3618	3619
Quasi-wool	Toxins	Toy-snake	Outsound	Taxing
Tax-waive	Texans	Tea-sink	Tax-need	Teasing
3620	3621	3622	3623	3624
Tax-bureau	Outshine	Toshiba	Tee-shot	Tax-boom
Tisbury	Auto-show	Taxi-hub	Outshoot	Taxi-home
3625	3626	3627	3628	3629
Taxable	Taxi-base	Tax-hike	Quashed	Teashop
Quasi-halo	Tie-shoes	Taxi-book	Taxi-ahead	Toyshop
3630	3631	3632	3633	3634
Toaster	Question	Toe-stub	Testate	Testify
Texture	Taxation	Tee-south	Outstate	Equisetum
3635	3636	3637	3638	3639
Textile	Tests	Autistic	Toasted	Outstep
Textual	Testis	Quixotic	Tested	Auto-stop
3640	3641	3642	3643	3644
Tax-free	Taxman	Taxi-mob	Too-soft	Taxi-fume
Taxi-fare	Tasmania	Tax-fib	Taxi-feat	Tax-fame
3645	3646	3647	3648	3649
Autosomal	Taxi-fees	Toxaemic	Quasimodo	Taxi-map
Tax-file	Tax-fax	Queasy-face	Tax-food	Teasy-image
3650	3651	3652	3653	3654
Taxi-over	Tax-law	Tee-slab	Taxi-lot	Itself
Tax-over	Taxi-lane	Aqueous-lube	Taslet	Tax-life
3655	3656	3657	3658	3659
Outsell	Auto-sales	Teasy-look	Taxi-load	Taxology
Tax-value	Taxi-lease	Queasy-voice	Tousled	Outslug
3660	3661	3662	3663	3664
Tessera	Toss-away	Tussah	Toss-out	Tax-safe
Tosser	Quassin	Teasy-sib	Taxi-seat	Taxi-sofa
3665	3666	3667	3668	3669
Tassel	Tissues	Toss-key	Tissued	Tossup
Tussle	Tax-sex	Aqueous-sauce	Tossed	Taxi-usage
3670	3671	3672	3673	3674
Outscore	Tuscany	Taxicab	Toxicity	Toxic-foe
Tusker	Taxi-icon	Toe-scab	Tax-cut	Ataxic-aim

3675 Toxic-oil Tax-clue	3676 Tusks Tasks	3677 Tea-sack Toe-sock	3678 Tax-code Tasked	3679 Autoscopy Otoscopy
3680 Outsider Taxi-door	3681 Toxodon Tax-den	3682 Taxi-job Teasy-jibe	3683 Tax-data Aqueous-jet	3684 Taxi-jam Tax-doom
3685 Tax-deal Teesdale	3686 Tuxedos Toxoids	3687 Teasy-joke Aqueous-juice	3688 Tuxedoed Tax-deed	3689 Tax-dope Tosa-dog
3690 Tax-payer Auto-spare	3691 Teaspoon Ataxia-gene	3692 Tax-pub Taxi-gab	3693 Taxi-gate Ataxia-gait	3694 Tax-game Teasy-poem
3695 Taxi-pool Auto-spool	3696 Taxi-gas Teasy-pose	3697 Outspeak Too-spicy	3698 Outspeed Tax-guide	3699 Tax-peg Taxi-page
3700 Outcrier Tocororo	3701 Autocrine Toy-crane	3702 Quaker-bay Toy-crib	3703 Autocrat Quaker-oat	3704 Auto-crime Tea-cream
3705 Outcurve Oat-cereal	3706 Quakers Takers	3707 Autocracy Teak-ark	3708 Take-ride Tokyo-radio	3709 Outcrop Take-rap
3710 Tokenize Teak-ware	3711 Tycoon-way Take-none	3712 Auto-knob Tycoon-bay	3713 Take-note Tie-knot	3714 Take-wife Token-fee
3715 Outknave Tukwila	3716 Tokens Tycoons	3717 Taconic Take-once	3718 Teakwood Take-weed	3719 Quaking Taking
3720 Teacher Autochory	3721 Teochew Teach-in	3722 Touch-bee Tyke-bib	3723 Teak-boat Touch-toe	3724 Take-home Autochef
3725 Touchily Teak-bole	3726 Teaches Touches	3727 Tyke-bike Tea-choice	3728 Take-heed Touched	3729 Touch-up Auto-chip
3730 Teak-tree Etcetera	3731 Tectona Taction	3732 Take-oath Tacit-boo	3733 Tektite Tea-kitty	3734 Tectum Take-time
3735 Tactile Tacitly	3736 Tacitus Take-taxi	3737 Tactic Tic-tac	3738 Eutectoid Tacit-joy	3739 Take-tip Tyke-tag
3740 Take-free Take-more	3741 Take-money Tyke-fun	3742 Tea-combo Teak-fob	3743 Atacamite Take-fate	3744 Take-off Tea-coffee
3745 Taco-meal Take-fuel	3746 Outcomes Toke-fix	3747 Tic-face Teak-mace	3748 Take-food Tyke-feed	3749 Quay-camp Tokyo-map

3750 Takeover Auto-colour	3751 Take-loan Quake-line	3752 Quake-vibe Tea-club	3753 Takovite Take-vote	3754 Auto-claim Take-life
3755 Autoclave Outcall	3756 Auto-close Toe-clues	3757 Quaky-voice Tie-cloak	3758 Take-lead Too-cold	3759 Tocology Autecology
3760 Take-Xray Quake-size	3761 Tucson Tocsin	3762 Teak-ash Tie-cash	3763 Outcast Take-seat	3764 Take-exam Quake-safe
3765 Teak-sale Take-soul	3766 Take-issue Toe-kiss	3767 Taco-sauce Tea-kiosk	3768 Take-side Teak-seed	3769 Teak-sap Tie-cusp
3770 Quicker Ticker	3771 Quicken Tick-away	3772 Tea-couch Tee-coach	3773 Ticket Toccata	3774 Quick-aim Taco-café
3775 Tackle Tickle	3776 Tacks Ticks	3777 Outkick Take-coke	3778 Ticked Tacked	3779 Quick-pay Take-copy
3780 Auto-coder Teak-door	3781 Take-iodine Tic-jaw	3782 Take-job Tyke-jab	3783 Take-data Takedaite	3784 Quake-doom Teak-dam
3785 Take-daily Autacoidal	3786 Autacoids Take-days	3787 Take-juice Teak-decay	3788 Tea-caddy Tyke-judo	3789 Teak-edge Toke-dope
3790 Tyke-gear Toy-keeper	3791 Tea-coupon Tic-agony	3792 Taco-pub Tokay-pooh	3793 Take-pity Teak-gate	3794 Toke-opium Tyke-game
3795 Outcouple Teak-pole	3796 Tea-cups Take-ages	3797 Take-apiece Teak-pike	3798 Tokyo-guide Tie-cupid	3799 Take-gauge Teak-peg
3800 Tudor-era Aqua-dryer	3801 Outdraw Toy-drone	3802 Toad-rib Tidy-robe	3803 Quadrate Qadarite	3804 Autodrome Tidy-room
3805 Tee-drive Outdrive	3806 Outdoors Tudors	3807 Quadric Too-dark	3808 Tidy-road Tide-ride	3809 Tied-rope Tea-dreg
3810 Tidy-wear Tied-wire	3811 Tie-down Tide-wane	3812 Tidy-web Tied-nob	3813 Toe-joint Tidy-unit	3814 Tidy-wife Auto-dynamo
3815 Tide-wave Quid-envy	3816 Tied-noose Tidy-anus	3817 Tea-junkie Toe-dance	3818 Tied-end Toad-wood	3819 Tiding Tidy-wage
3820 Tied-hour Tidy-hair	3821 Toad-bone Tidy-bin	3822 Tide-ebb Tied-bib	3623 Tied-bout Tod-bite	3824 Tidy-home Quid-boom

3825	3826	3827	3828	3829
Tied-above	Tidy-house	Quadbike	Toad-head	Toad-hop
Toad-hole	Toad-hoax	Tied-hook	Tidy-bed	Tied-bag
3830	3831	3832	3833	3834
Toad-eater	Toady-tone	Tied-tube	Today-quote	Tide-time
Tidy-tray	Toy-audition	Tidy-tub	Tidy-tot	Tied-item
3835	3836	3837	3838	3839
Toad-tale	Tied-toes	Toady-tyke	Outdated	Tidy-top
Quid-outlay	Aqua-detox	Tidy-teak	Today-tide	Tied-tip
3840	3841	3842	3843	3844
Toad-fear	Toady-man	Too-dumb	Tidy-mat	Teed-off
Tidy-maze	Today-menu	Tied-fob	Toad-foot	Tidy-foam
3845	3846	3847	3848	3849
Today-mail	Tod-fox	Toady-face	Toad-food	Outjump
Toad-meal	Tidy-mix	Tied-mace	Toady-mood	Toady-image
3850	3851	3852	3853	3854
Tidal-air	Quid-loan	Tidal-bay	Toadlet	Tidy-life
Tide-over	Tideline	Toady-vibe	Auto-delete	Toad-ileum
3855	3856	3857	3858	3859
Toad-lily	Tied-loose	Toy-device	Quid-load	Tidology
Tidally	Tie-deals	Tied-lace	Tide-video	Toad-leap
3860	3861	3862	3863	3864
Tidy-sore	Tide-sway	Toadyish	Outjest	Toadyism
Toad-sera	Toad-axon	Tidy-shoe	Tidy-site	Tidy-sum
3865	3866	3867	3868	3869
Tediously	Tied-axis	Tedesco	Tedious-day	Tidy-spy
Tide-sail	Today-issue	Toy-desk	Tidy-side	Tied-spy
3870	3871	3872	3873	3874
Quad-core	Etidocaine	Tod-cub	Aqueduct	Tea-decaf
Tidy-car	Toad-icon	Tide-echo	Auto-eject	Quod-cum
3875	3876	3877	3878	3879
Tied-coil	Tidy-case	Tidy-cook	Tidy-kid	Tidy-copy
Tidy-cave	Tajiks	Tide-kayak	Toady-code	Tied-cage
3880	3881	3882	3883	3884
Tedder	Toad-jaw	Teddy-boy	Quiddity	Tide-doom
Tidder	Tidy-den	Tidy-job	Tidy-data	Tide-dam
3885	3886	3887	3888	3889
Toddle	At-odds	Tadjik	Teddy-day	Tide-edge
Tiddly	Teddies	Toady-idiocy	Toady-dude	Outdodge
3890	3891	3892	3893	3894
Toad-prey	Toad-gene	Oat-dough	Toe-digit	Tied-game
Tadger	Quid-gain	Toad-pooh	Tied-goat	Tidy-gym
3895	3896	3897	3898	3899
Tadpole	Tied-goose	Tide-pace	Tide-guide	Toad-egg
Tide-pool	Tidy-apex	Tied-piece	Quid-paid	Tidy-pig

3900 Top-array Tiger-aura	3901 Outgrow Top-zone	3902 Tag-robe Toy-grab	3903 Taproot Tea-party	3904 Taproom Top-roof
3905 Top-role Tea-girl	3906 Tigers Tigris	3907 Top-race Tea-price	3908 Tapered Tea-grade	3909 Toe-grip Auto-garage
3910 Auto-power Tap-wire	3911 Tea-gown Top-wine	3912 Tip-nib Top-nob	3913 Outpoint Type-note	3914 Toponym Top-name
3915 Top-envoy Tape-wave	3916 Autogenous Tap-noise	3917 Autogenic Tap-once	3918 Top-end Top-need	3919 Typing Taping
3920 Tougher Tephra	3921 Typhoon Toughen	3922 Aquaphobia Tough-boy	3923 Autophyte Tight	3924 Atopobium Equip-home
3925 Top-heavy Tap-hole	3926 Typhus Toughs	3927 Tough-ace Type-book	3928 Typhoid Tough-day	3929 Autophagy Tough-guy
3930 Tiptree Top-tray	3931 Tipton Tape-tune	3932 Otopathy Tauopathy	3933 Top-quota Top-equity	3934 Top-team Tag-item
3935 Top-tool Tagtail	3936 Outputs Tiptoes	3937 Autoptic Autopoietic	3938 Togated Tiptoed	3939 Tip-top Topotype
3940 Quagmire Typifier	3941 Top-man Tip-money	3942 Tape-fib Tip-mob	3943 Tap-foot Top-feat	3944 Tip-off Tape-memo
3945 Tape-movie Tag-file	3946 Autogamous Top-mix	3947 Typeface Top-make	3948 Top-mood Typified	3949 Top-image Togo-map
3950 Tip-over Top-layer	3951 Tapeline Aquaplane	3952 Tape-vibe Equip-lab	3953 Autopilot Tea-plate	3954 Ita-palm Top-life
3955 Top-value Outpoll	3956 Togolese Tea-please	3957 Top-voice Outplace	3958 Tape-video Top-lady	3959 Topology Typology
3960 Type-size Top-seer	3961 Top-son Tag-sin	3962 Outgush Tip-ash	3963 Outpost Typist	3964 Tap-safe Top-sum
3965 Topsail Topsoil	3966 Outguess Type-essay	3967 Autopsic Top-sauce	3968 Topside Top-seed	3969 Tip-spy Type-usage
3970 Top-car Top-care	3971 Tip-coin Top-icon	3972 Tip-cab Tape-echo	3973 Topcoat Top-cat	3974 Top-café Tape-cameo

3975	3976	3977	3978	3979
Topical	Topics	Tea-pack	Top-kid	Tape-copy
Typical	Tape-case	Topic-key	Outpaced	Type-copy
3980	3981	3982	3983	3984
Tap-door	Top-dean	Top-job	Tepidity	Tape-demo
Tip-jar	Topi-jaw	Tape-dub	Auto-update	Tip-dime
3985	3986	3987	3988	3989
Tepidly	Top-ideas	Tap-juice	Type-deed	Top-dog
Top-deal	Toe-pads	Type-joke	Tape-judo	Top-edge
3990	3991	3992	3993	3994
Tipper	Tappan	Top-pub	Tippet	Top-game
Tapper	Top-gain	Tape-gibe	Tappet	Type-poem
3995	3996	3997	3998	3999
Topple	Top-ups	Top-piece	Equipped	Top-page
Toggle	Tipp-ex	Tape-epic	Tagged	Tap-pipe

ALPHA BETA 4000 – 4999

4000 Mirror Freezer	4001 Marrow Furrow	4002 Myrrh Forerib	4003 Ferret Mozart	4004 Firearm Forearm
4005 Fizzle Muzzle	4006 Ferries Morris	4007 Ferric Fire-arc	4008 Married Furred	4009 Marriage Ferriage
4010 Frenzy Mariner	4011 Frown Forenoon	4012 Free-whey Forwhy	4013 Front Marinate	4014 Forename Frenum
4015 Fire-wave Fur-weave	4016 Morons Marines	4017 Frank Furnace	4018 Friend Frond	4019 Fringe Amazing
4020 Forebear Afro-hair	4021 Marihuana Free-bone	4022 Fairy-baby Fribby	4023 Fireboat Free-bet	4024 Free-home Fareham
4025 Friable Marble	4026 Firehose Freebase	4027 Fairy-book Fire-hook	4028 Forbid Morbid	4029 Fire-hoop Firebug
4030 Martyr Mortar	4031 Fortune Martian	4032 Froth Mirth	4033 Fortuity Fruit-tea	4034 Fortify Mortify
4035 Fertile Mortal	4036 Fruits Emeritus	4037 Mortice Amaurotic	4038 Fruited Merited	4039 Fruitage Foretop
4040 Farmer Murmur	4041 Foreman Mormon	4042 Farm-boy Marimba	4043 Format Forfeit	4044 Far-off Fire-off
4045 Formula Formal	4046 Forms Firms	4047 Formica Formic	4048 Formed Mermaid	4049 Frump Frame-up
4050 Forever Moreover	4051 Merlin Freeview	4052 Fear-vibe Free-lab	4053 Morality Frailty	4054 Free-life More-life
4055 Frill Morally	4056 Morals Forlese	4057 Frolic Fairylike	4058 Emerald Freeload	4059 Foreleg Mariology
4060 Foreseer Free-size	4061 Emersion Foreseen	4062 Fresh Marsh	4063 Frost Forest	4064 Fearsome Foursome
4065 Morsel Furiously	4066 Amaurosis Morass	4067 Forsake Fresco	4068 Foreside Aforesaid	4069 Free-usage Marsupia
4070 Marker Mercury	4071 African American	4072 March Markab	4073 Market Ferocity	4074 Americium Fierce-foe

4075	4076	4077	4078	4079
Miracle	Fracas	Frock	Forced	Free-copy
Fiercely	Marks	Frack	Marked	Mark-up
4080	4081	4082	4083	4084
Murder	Marijuana	Fair-job	Free-data	Freedom
Marauder	Freudian	Free-jab	Maize-diet	Foredoom
4085	4086	4087	4088	4089
Fardel	Fridays	Ford-key	Freddy	Fridge
Fair-deal	Frauds	Mazda-key	Forded	Firedog
4090	4091	4092	4093	4094
Forgery	Margin	Morph	Forget	Fair-game
Merger	Foreign	Morphea	Frigate	Free-gym
4095	4096	4097	4098	4099
Forgive	Frogs	Forepeak	Frigid	Free-egg
Fragile	Mirages	Fur-piece	Forged	Frappe
4100	4101	4102	4103	4104
Funerary	Fanzine	Menorah	Minority	Mean-army
Fenrir	Fun-run	Fine-robe	Minaret	Fine-rim
4105	4106	4107	4108	4109
Mineral	Minors	Minor-key	Main-road	Manrope
Funeral	Miners	Money-race	Fun-ride	Mania-rage
4110	4111	4112	4113	4114
Manner	Minnow	Fine-nib	Eminent	Mononym
Fawner	Fine-wine	Funny-boy	Money-unit	Mean-enemy
4115	4116	4117	4118	4119
Funnel	Minions	Finance	Manned	Mining
Funnily	Moneywise	Eminence	Fanned	Moaning
4120	4121	4122	4123	4124
Minibar	Main-bone	Man-boob	Man-bite	Moonbeam
Man-hour	Mini-bin	Moon-ebb	Main-bout	Money-boom
4125	4126	4127	4128	4129
Amenable	Minibus	Minibike	Manhood	Moneybag
Manhole	Funhouse	Fine-book	Main-body	Main-hope
4130	4131	4132	4133	4134
Mentor	Fountain	Month	Mint-tea	Meantime
Monitor	Mountain	Manitoba	Money-quota	Omentum
4135	4136	4137	4138	4139
Mantle	Minutes	Fanatic	Finitude	Montage
Mental	Fantasy	Moonquake	Fainted	Mintage
4140	4141	4142	4143	4144
Minimize	Main-menu	Mean-mob	Fan-fete	Minimum
Funfair	Moneyman	Fine-fib	Moan-fate	Mean-mafia
4145	4146	4147	4148	4149
Minimal	Minims	Moon-face	Manmade	Fine-image
Manful	Fine-mix	Fine-make	Minified	Mean-imp

4150 Omnivore Monolayer	4151 Mainline Minivan	4152 Minilab Fun-vibe	4153 Finality Moonlet	4154 Fun-life Final-fee
4155 Finally Manually	4156 Finals Fowls	4157 Manlike Moonlike	4158 Money-load Final-day	4159 Monologue Money-league
4160 Monsieur Mean-size	4161 Mansion Monsoon	4162 Finish Menasha	4163 Amnesty Finest	4164 Monism Monosomy
4165 Ominously Mainsail	4166 Menses Finesse	4167 Minsk Amnesic	4168 Monoxide Moonseed	4169 Money-usage Fine-sage
4170 Manicure Fencer	4171 Manikin Monacan	4172 Munch Munich	4173 Monocyte Monocot	4174 Minicam Manic-foe
4175 Manacle Monocle	4176 Monkeys Maniacs	4177 Finicky Mooncake	4178 Fenced Minced	4179 Mince-pie Main-copy
4180 Minder Mender	4181 Mundane Mindanao	4182 Fine-job Mini-jab	4183 Mandate Fanjet	4184 Fandom Mini-dome
4185 Fondle Mandala	4186 Funds Minds	4187 Monadic Mandaic	4188 Amended Funded	4189 Mendip Fine-edge
4190 Finger Manager	4191 Monogyny Minigun	4192 Mingy-boy Mango-bay	4193 Money-pot Moon-gate	4194 Monogamy Fungemia
4195 Monopoly Mingle	4196 Fangs Fungus	4197 Main-piece Moon-peak	4198 Monopodia Fanged	4199 Main-page Mini-egg
4200 February Mayberry	4201 Fibrin Embryony	4202 Amber-hue Amberboa	4203 Imbrute Fibrate	4204 Fibroma Embryoma
4205 Febrile Embroil	4206 Fibrous Embers	4207 Embark Embrace	4208 Fibroid Maharaja	4209 Embargo Umbrage
4210 Embower Mob-war	4211 Fab-wine Mob-union	4212 Fob-nob Fib-web	4213 Ambient Umbonate	4214 Fab-name Mob-enemy
4215 Embowel Fib-weave	4216 Fab-nose Fib-noise	4217 Ambience Mohawk	4218 Embowed Aim-beyond	4219 Fab-wage Mob-nag
4220 Fibber Imbiber	4221 Zimbabwe Moho-hen	4222 Fab-baby Mob-hub	4223 Imbibe-tea Mob-hate	4224 Fab-home Fob-boom

4225	4226	4227	4228	4229
Mabble	Mob-house	Fob-hook	Imbibed	Ambu-bag
My-bible	Fib-hoax	Fib-book	Mobbed	Mab-bogey
4230	4231	4232	4233	4234
Yamaha-tyre	Ambition	Imbathe	Mob-tout	Mahatma
Fib-query	Mob-queen	Fab-youth	Fab-quota	Fab-team
4235	4236	4237	4238	4239
May-beetle	Ambitious	Fab-tyke	Yamaha-quad	Umbo-top
Fib-tale	Ambits	Fib-quake	Mob-tide	Fab-toga
4240	4241	4242	4243	4244
Fab-four	Fab-money	Fab-fob	Mahomet	Fob-off
Mob-fear	Moob-man	Mab-fib	Fab-fete	Fib-memo
4245	4246	4247	4248	4249
Fab-meal	Mayhems	Mayhemic	Mahmood	Omaha-map
Mob-movie	Fab-mix	Fab-face	Fab-fad	Fab-image
4250	4251	4252	4253	4254
Fibular	Mob-law	May-blob	Mobility	Embalm
Ambler	Aim-blow	Mobile-bay	Ambulate	Emblem
4255	4256	4257	4258	4259
May-ball	Fabulous	Embolic	Fabled	Amblyopia
Mabelle	Embolus	Mob-like	Ambled	Moblog
4260	4261	4262	4263	4264
Fab-size	Fab-sun	Ambush	Fohist	Embosom
Fob-user	Mob-sway	Maybush	Fab-site	Fohism
4265	4266	4267	4268	4269
Mob-soul	Embassy	Fab-sauce	Fab-side	Mob-spy
Yamaha-sale	Emboss	Fab-sky	Fee-based	Fob-usage
4270	4271	4272	4273	4274
Mob-cry	Mohican	Fib-echo	Omaha-city	Fab-café
Moob-care	Fob-coin	Maybach	Moby-kit	Mob-cameo
4275	4276	4277	4278	4279
Imbecile	Fob-keys	Fee-back	Amebicide	Mobcap
Fab-cave	Fabaceous	Fab-cook	Fab-kid	Fib-copy
4280	4281	4282	4283	4284
Embodier	Fab-dean	Moob-job	Fab-diet	Mob-doom
Fib-diary	Mob-den	Fab-jab	Mob-data	Fab-dame
4285	4286	4287	4288	4289
Omaha-daily	Fab-days	Moob-juice	Embodied	Mob-dope
Fab-deal	Fabids	Fab-joke	Fob-jade	Fab-dog
4290	4291	4292	4293	4294
Fab-opera	Mahogany	Aim-high	Ambiguity	Fab-game
Ambi-pur	Fob-pen	Fab-pub	Mob-gate	Fob-gem
4295	4296	4297	4298	4299
Fab-gala	Ambiguous	Fab-piece	Mob-guide	Fob-peg
Fib-plea	Fab-pose	Mob-peace	Fab-God	Mob-pope

4300 Motorize Fitzroy	4301 Matron Motorway	4302 Foot-rub Afterbay	4303 Maturity Meteorite	4304 Amity-room Fat-ram
4305 Material Motorola	4306 Features Matrix	4307 Metric Footrace	4308 Matured Featured	4309 Ametropia Footrope
4310 Footwear Mutineer	4311 Motown Matawan	4312 Foot-web Fatwah	4313 Footnote Mutant	4314 Metonym Meet-wife
4315 Emotional Motional	4316 Emotions Mutinous	4317 Myotonic Metonic	4318 Fatwood Motioned	4319 Footing Meeting
4320 Mother Father	4321 Methane Meat-bone	4322 Fat-baby Faith-buoy	4323 Fitbit Meat-bite	4324 Fathom Fit-home
4325 Mutable Imitable	4326 Maths Moths	4327 Meat-hook Mythic	4328 Method Fathead	4329 Mythopoeia Fat-bag
4330 Matter Fetter	4331 Mutation Mutton	4332 Fattah Fat-youth	4333 Moquette Maquette	4334 Fit-team Meatotomy
4335 Mettle Mottle	4336 Mottos Fatuitous	4337 Mitotic Myotatic	4338 Fitted Mutated	4339 Foot-tap Meta-tag
4340 Metamere Fat-free	4341 Footman Footy-fan	4342 Fatimah Footy-mob	4343 Foot-mat Fat-mate	4344 Foot-off Feat-fame
4345 Fateful Fitful	4346 Motifs Fat-mix	4347 Fat-face Myotomic	4348 Mate-mood Fat-maid	4349 Foot-map Fat-image
4350 Metal-ore Mutualize	4351 Mytilene Fit-line	4352 Fat-lob Emit-vibe	4353 Fatality Futility	4354 Meatloaf Futile-aim
4355 Fatally Mutually	4356 Motives Motels	4357 Mute-voice Fatlike	4358 Fat-lady Mutual-aid	4359 Footy-league Fetology
4360 Footsore Fit-size	4361 Myotoxin Fate-sway	4362 Fetish Footy-shoe	4363 Metasequoia Moot-site	4364 Mutism Fat-sum
4365 Fatuously Fat-soul	4366 Mitosis Mutases	4367 Myotoxic Meat-sauce	4368 Fit-side Matsudo	4369 Foot-spa Meat-soup
4370 Foot-care Emit-cry	4371 Emoticon Fat-cow	4372 Match Fetch	4373 Fat-cat Footy-kit	4374 Fit-coma Moot-café

4375 Metical Fate-clue	4376 Miotics Emetics	4377 Fat-cook Moat-kayak	4378 Feticide Fit-kid	4379 Fit-cap Footy-cup
4380 Matador Fit-door	4381 Foot-jaw Meat-den	4382 Foot-jab Foot-dab	4383 Fetidity Metadata	4384 Feat-demo Foot-edema
4385 Fetidly Mutedly	4386 Omit-days Emit-ideas	4387 Fatidic Meat-decay	4388 Fat-dude Meet-dad	4389 Foot-deep Fat-dog
4390 Footgear Footy-pro	4391 Mitogen Mutagen	4392 Footage-boy Moot-pub	4393 Mitigate Foot-gout	4394 Fit-game Footy-gem
4395 Fate-plea Footy-play	4396 Fatigues Footages	4397 Footpace Metopic	4398 Fatigued Footpad	4399 Fit-peg Fat-pig
4400 Yammerer Mamzer	4401 Foofaraw Fomorian	4402 Mafia-robe Yummy-rib	4403 Effort Fumeroot	4404 Affirm Fume-room
4405 Memorial Immoral	4406 Affairs Memories	4407 Afforce Efforce	4408 Afford Offered	4409 Immerge Mafia-rage
4410 Immunize Feminize	4411 Feminine Memnon	4412 Off-web Mafia-web	4413 Moment Immunity	4414 Ammonium Immunome
4415 Ammonal Emmanuel	4416 Immense Offense	4417 Offence Affiance	4418 Offend Affined	4419 Foaming Fuming
4420 Member Fimbria	4421 Yummy-honey Maim-bone	4422 Mamba-bay Foamy-boob	4423 Offbeat Miami-heat	4424 Ammobium Offham
4425 Mumble Fumble	4426 Mombasa Off-base	4427 Off-hook Memo-book	4428 Mamhead Off-head	4429 Mum-hug Fame-hope
4430 Immature Ammeter	4431 Off-tune Fife-tune	4432 Fifth Fume-tube	4433 Muftiate Mimetite	4434 Off-time Mafia-team
4435 Immotile Mu-metal	4436 Fomites Muftis	4437 Mimetic Offtake	4438 Mufti-day Momotidae	4439 Memo-tape Off-top
4440 Mammary Mummery	4441 Muffin Mammon	4442 Mafia-mob Mummy-boy	4443 Muffetee Off-feet	4444 Mummify Eff-off
4445 Mammal Muffle	4446 Mummies Muffs	4447 Fame-face Iffy-make	4448 Miffed Muffed	4449 Miami-map Fume-fog

4450 Familiar Foam-layer	4451 Offline Family-way	4452 Fame-vibe Offley-Hay	4453 Affiliate Immolate	4454 Fame-life Yummy-loaf
4455 Familial Mum-love	4456 Females Families	4457 Mameluke Memo-leak	4458 Offload Mayfield	4459 Effulge Family-guy
4460 Affixer Effexor	4461 Effusion Mu-meson	4462 Famish Offish	4463 Offset Offsite	4464 Momism Mafia-safe
4465 Effusive Famously	4466 Mimesis Affixes	4467 Fume-sky Yummy-sauce	4468 Offside Affixed	4469 Foamy-soap Mafia-spy
4470 Officer Mimicry	4471 Fame-icon Memo-coin	4472 Affiche Office-boy	4473 Affect Effect	4474 Miami-café Mime-cameo
4475 Official Iffy-clue	4476 Officious Office-use	4477 Efficacy Office-key	4478 Office-aide Effaced	4479 Memo-copy Miami-cop
4480 Off-dry Memo-diary	4481 Mafia-den Emma-Jane	4482 Mafia-job Maim-jab	4483 Immediate Off-duty	4484 Fiefdom Femidom
4485 Miami-daily Mafia-deal	4486 Off-days Iffy-ideas	4487 Immediacy Yummy-juice	4488 Miami-Dade Mum-dad	4489 Off-edge Fume-dope
4490 Mampara Mumper	4491 Memo-pen Maim-gun	4492 Mafia-pub Foam-pooh	4493 Fumigate Effigiate	4494 Mime-game Memo-poem
4495 Effigial Foam-glue	4496 Effigies Mumps	4497 Off-peak Off-pace	4498 Memo-pad Miami-guide	4499 Memo-page Fife-pipe
4500 Flurry Floorer	4501 Fluorine Fleuron	4502 Male-robe Mule-rib	4503 Flirt Favourite	4504 Mail-room Male-ram
4505 Floral Malarial	4506 Flyers Floors	4507 Fluoric Mile-race	4508 Florid Florida	4509 Floorage Flare-up
4510 Flower Malware	4511 Melanin Flown	4512 Meal-web Flea-nab	4513 Flint Fluent	4514 Melanoma Filename
4515 Felinely Male-only	4516 Melons Felons	4517 Flank Flunk	4518 Flawed Flowed	4519 Feeling Fling
4520 Malabar Male-hair	4521 Fava-bean Fleabane	4522 Flabby Male-baby	4523 Fleabite Flyboat	4524 Fulham Move-home

4525	4526	4527	4528	4529
Moveable	Mailbox	Malbec	Male-body	Mailbag
Flyable	Mulhouse	Fly-hook	Mylohyoid	Fleabag
4530	4531	4532	4533	4534
Filter	Emulation	Filthy	Militate	Mealtime
Military	Foliation	Multi-buy	Mulatto	Flat-fee
4535	4536	4537	4538	4539
Flatly	Flats	Faulty-key	Melted	File-type
Emulative	Flatus	Flat-key	Malted	Fly-tip
4540	4541	4542	4543	4544
Flamer	Mailman	Flambeau	Malamute	Fluff
Feel-free	Melamine	Malambo	Flameout	Fly-off
4545	4546	4547	4548	4549
Fulfil	Films	Malefic	Filmed	Flump
Milfoil	Flimsy	Male-face	Flamed	Flame-pea
4550	4551	4552	4553	4554
Flavour	Fellow	Fellah	Mallet	Mollify
Flyover	Million	Mullah	Millet	Flyleaf
4555	4556	4557	4558	4559
Malleoli	Falls	Fallacy	Filled	Fall-guy
Fluvial	Mills	Flulike	Felled	Fillip
4560	4561	4562	4563	4564
Flexor	Emulsion	Flesh	Molest	Emulsify
Flexure	Flexion	Foolish	Falsity	Falsify
4565	4566	4567	4568	4569
Falsely	Floss	Flask	Flexed	False-age
Flexile	Aimless	Felsic	Fools-day	Fuel-usage
4570	4571	4572	4573	4574
Foul-cry	Falcon	Mulch	Felicity	Felicify
Fulcra	Folkway	Filch	Falcate	Meal-café
4575	4576	4577	4578	4579
Molecule	Folks	Flock	Filicide	File-copy
Flakily	Malicious	Flick	Flaked	Milk-pea
4580	4581	4582	4583	4584
Folder	Mildew	Flu-jab	Fluidity	Movie-dome
Fielder	Floodway	Flood-bay	Foldout	Foiled-aim
4585	4586	4587	4588	4589
Mildly	Fields	Melodic	Fielded	Fledge
Fluidly	Folds	Fluidic	Flooded	Foldup
4590	4591	4592	4593	4594
Filigree	Filipino	Flag-boy	Fleapit	Amalgam
Moviegoer	Malign	Foul-pooh	Flip-out	Male-game
4595	4596	4597	4598	4599
Foul-play	Flags	Myalgic	Feel-good	Floppy
File-pile	Flaps	Male-peak	Movie-guide	Flappy

4600	4601	4602	4603	4604
Measurer	Mesozoan	Fox-rib	Misroute	Fusarium
Miserere	Masurian	Masorah	Maserati	Fix-arm
4605	4606	4607	4608	4609
Miserly	Misers	Mesozoic	Misread	Measure-up
Misrule	Miseries	Mix-rice	Measured	Fix-rope
4610	4611	4612	4613	4614
Masonry	Mix-wine	Mason-bee	Masonite	Misname
Fusioneer	Fix-new	Mix-whey	Fax-note	Fax-info
4615	4616	4617	4618	4619
Mouse-owl	Mesons	Masonic	Moosewood	Amusing
Fusional	Mix-noise	Fox-nook	Foxwood	Mixing
4620	4621	4622	4623	4624
Fisher	Fashion	Fox-baby	Mishit	Moose-hoof
Masher	Fox-bone	Fish-bay	Foxbat	Fix-home
4625	4626	4627	4628	4629
Feasible	Fishes	Fix-hook	Mashed	Mishap
Fixable	Fuse-box	Fax-book	Meshed	Mushy-pea
4630	4631	4632	4633	4634
Fixture	Fasten	Musth	Misquote	Mistime
Mixture	Fixation	Fix-tab	Mosquito	Mystify
4635	4636	4637	4638	4639
Festive	Masts	Mistake	Mastoid	Mistype
Fistula	Fists	Mystic	Fixated	Mixtape
4640	4641	4642	4643	4644
Misfire	Foxman	Fox-fib	Misfit	Maximum
Foxfire	Fix-fine	Fix-fob	Myxomata	Fax-memo
4645	4646	4647	4648	4649
Maximal	Museums	Miasmic	Fox-food	Fix-image
Misfile	Maximus	Faux-face	Fax-mode	Mix-mug
4650	4651	4652	4653	4654
Fusilier	Muslin	Mix-vibe	Mesolite	Myself
Fox-lair	Maslow	Fox-lib	Maxalt	Muslim
4655	4656	4657	4658	4659
Maxilla	Measles	Fox-lake	Misled	Fuselage
Misally	Fix-lease	Fix-leak	Mislaid	Misology
4660	4661	4662	4663	4664
Emissary	Mission	Messiah	Miss-out	Massif
Fissure	Fission	Moss-bay	Fassaite	Fixism
4665	4666	4667	4668	4669
Fissile	Masses	Moss-key	Mossad	Message
Missile	Misses	Mix-sauce	Missed	Massage
4670	4671	4672	4673	4674
Mascara	Moscow	Fox-cub	Mascot	Music-fee
Masker	Musician	Mix-echo	Musket	Fox-coma

4675	4676	4677	4678	4679
Muscle	Masks	Music-key	Miscode	Miscopy
Musical	Mosaics	Mix-cake	Masked	Muskeg
4680	4681	4682	4683	4684
Moose-deer	Fox-den	Fix-job	Misdate	Myxoedema
Mouse-deer	Moose-jaw	Fox-jab	Fax-data	Mousedom
4685	4686	4687	4688	4689
Misdeal	Fix-dose	Fox-decoy	Misdeed	Fixed-pay
Misdial	Mouse-douse	Mix-juice	Fix-odd	Mixed-up
4690	4691	4692	4693	4694
Fox-prey	Misogyny	Fox-pub	Mix-pot	Misogamy
Fix-gaze	Fox-paw	Mouse-pooh	Aim-spot	Fix-game
4695	4696	4697	4698	4699
Misplay	Faux-pas	Myspace	Misguide	Misgauge
Misgive	Mix-ups	Mesopic	Mousepad	Fax-page
4700	4701	4702	4703	4704
Macarize	Micron	Microbe	Macerate	Macrame
Microzoa	Macaroni	Face-rub	Micrite	Make-room
4705	4706	4707	4708	4709
Maceral	Makers	Micro-key	Myocardia	Micropia
Makarov	Macros	Mice-race	Make-ready	Fake-rug
4710	4711	4712	4713	4714
Make-weary	Make-wine	Make-web	Look-into	Meconium
Face-war	Meek-nun	Fake-nib	Make-note	Make-name
4715	4716	4717	4718	4719
Make-wave	Mucinous	Make-nice	Fecund	Facing
Fake-wool	Make-noise	Fake-nuke	Aficionado	Making
4720	4721	4722	4723	4724
Macabre	Machine	Make-baby	Machete	Make-home
Moocher	Face-bow	Fake-boob	Makebate	Mice-boom
4725	4726	4727	4728	4729
Amicable	Fuchsia	Facebook	Much-ado	Make-big
Michael	Machos	Macbook	Make-bed	Face-bug
4730	4731	4732	4733	4734
Factor	Faction	Fake-oath	Fake-quote	Face-time
Factory	Fiction	Mice-taboo	Makatite	Factum
4735	4736	4737	4738	4739
Factual	Facts	Mycotic	Emaciated	Fake-tape
Fictive	Facetious	Faucet-key	Factoid	Face-tag
4740	4741	4742	4743	4744
Make-more	Make-fun	Macamba	Fake-feat	Faceoff
Fake-fur	Meek-man	Macomb	Face-fate	Make-off
4745	4746	4747	4748	4749
Make-move	Fake-mix	Make-face	Make-mad	Make-image
Facemail	Meek-mouse	Fake-make	Fake-food	Face-mop

4750 Macular Makeover	4751 Mclean Myoclonia	4752 Mice-lab Fake-alibi	4753 Facility Faculty	4754 Mycelium F-clef
4755 Facially Focally	4756 Facials Focalise	4757 Mukluk Fake-voice	4758 Macleod Make-void	4759 Mucilage Mycology
4760 Make-sure Face-sore	4761 Make-sane Face-sun	4762 Moksha Make-shy	4763 Face-east Mucosity	4764 Make-safe Mecism
4765 Mucosal Meek-soul	4766 Mycosis Focuses	4767 Make-sauce Face-soak	4768 Focused Make-sad	4769 Make-soup Face-soap
4770 Mockery Fucker	4771 Fake-coin Meccano	4772 Maccabee Face-ache	4773 Make-kite Fake-kit	4774 Make-cameo Fake-coma
4775 Fickle Mackle	4776 Mocks Fucks	4777 Focaccia Make-cake	4778 Mocked Amicicide	4779 Face-cap Mock-up
4780 Make-dry Fake-diary	4781 Macedonia Fucidin	4782 Face-dab Fake-job	4783 Fake-data Make-date	4784 Macadam Macadamia
4785 Make-deal Facedly	4786 Macodes Fake-ideas	4787 Make-joke Fake-juice	4788 Make-odd Face-deed	4789 Make-deep Fake-edge
4790 Make-pure Face-gear	4791 Make-gain Mucigen	4792 Mice-pooh Fake-pub	4793 Fake-gait Meek-poet	4794 Face-gem Make-game
4795 Face-gel Mice-play	4796 Make-ups Mucopus	4797 Makepeace Make-pace	4798 Make-good Fake-god	4799 Fukuppy Fake-gauge
4800 Federer Federary	4801 Modern Midiron	4802 Midrib Feeder-bay	4803 Moderate Majority	4804 Mudroom Mid-arm
4805 Federal Majorly	4806 Majors Feeders	4807 Midrace Major-key	4808 Fjord Madrid	4809 Mad-rage Feed-rope
4810 Media-war Feed-wire	4811 Madonna Meadow-way	4812 Food-web Medinah	4813 Midianite Fodient	4814 Midwife Media-info
4815 Maidenly Media-wave	4816 Meadows Maidens	4817 Midweek Food-nook	4818 Feed-weed Food-need	4819 Fading Feeding
4820 Food-bar Mad-hero	4821 Mud-hen Mad-bean	4822 Feed-baby Media-hub	4823 Food-bite Mud-hut	4824 Mad-home Food-boom

4825	4826	4827	4828	4829
Mud-hole	Mad-house	Food-bake	Maidhood	Mudbug
Mid-bole	Food-box	Mud-hike	Mad-bid	Media-hype

4830	4831	4832	4833	4834
Mediator	Mediation	Mid-tibia	Meditate	Food-item
Feudatory	Food-tin	Mad-youth	Food-quota	Mad-team

4835	4836	4837	4838	4839
Made-equal	Fujitsu	Media-autocue	Mediated	Mad-type
Mad-tale	Food-tax	Food-take	Mud-tide	Media-tape

4840	4841	4842	4843	4844
Modifier	Madman	Feed-fib	Food-fat	Feed-off
Feed-fear	Food-menu	Mad-mob	Mid-foot	Media-memo

4845	4846	4847	4848	4849
Medfly	Madams	Mid-face	Modified	Media-image
Food-mile	Mediums	Food-make	Mad-mood	Mud-mop

4850	4851	4852	4853	4854
Modular	Midline	Mid-lobe	Fidelity	Midlife
Medlar	Madeline	Mad-lab	Modality	Mad-life

4855	4856	4857	4858	4859
Medieval	Models	Medevac	Mad-lad	Food-log
Medulla	Medals	Majolica	Food-lady	Mid-leg

4860	4861	4862	4863	4864
Mid-size	Madison	Modish	Majesty	Fideism
Made-sure	Medusan	Mud-shoe	Modest	Maidism

4865	4866	4867	4868	4869
Midsole	Amidases	Mid-sky	Medusoid	Mood-sag
Food-sale	Food-axis	Mud-soak	Mid-side	Media-spy

4870	4871	4872	4873	4874
Mediocre	Medicine	Feed-cub	Medicate	Modicum
Fiduciary	Mad-cow	Media-echo	Mudcat	Food-café

4875	4876	4877	4878	4879
Medical	Medics	Medick	Medicaid	Madcap
Fiducial	Food-case	Mud-cake	Mad-kid	Midcap

4880	4881	4882	4883	4884
Fodder	Madden	Mud-dab	Fad-diet	Feud-doom
Madder	Food-den	Media-job	Muddy-toe	Food-demo

4885	4886	4887	4888	4889
Middle	Middies	Mad-joke	Muddied	Mad-dog
Fiddle	Maddox	Food-decay	Mad-dude	Muddy-up

4890	4891	4892	4893	4894
Media-guru	Amidogen	Food-pub	Fidget	Midgame
Food-prey	Mid-open	Media-gibe	Midget	Mud-gym

4895	4896	4897	4898	4899
Food-pool	Midges	Mad-pace	Food-guide	Food-pipe
Mud-play	Fudges	Mid-piece	Fudged	Mid-page

4900 Emperor Figurer	4901 Magazine Migraine	4902 Empire-bay Umpire-boo	4903 Import Impurity	4904 Emporium Map-room
4905 Imperial Improve	4906 Figures Empires	4907 Empiric May-park	4908 Figured Impaired	4909 Amperage Umpirage
4910 Empower Imaginary	4911 Impawn Mignon	4912 Fogey-nob Mug-neb	4913 Magnet Magnate	4914 Magnify Magnum
4915 Imaginal Magnolia	4916 Magnesia Magnus	4917 Myogenic Mega-nuke	4918 Impend Impound	4919 Imaging Impinge
4920 Amphora Mop-hair	4921 Fogbow Afghan	4922 Amphibia Mega-boob	4923 Fight Might	4924 Mega-ohm Image-beam
4925 Moghul Omphale	4926 Mug-house Megabase	4927 Mug-hook Map-book	4928 Mop-head Megabid	4929 Omophagia Image-hype
4930 Imputer Emptier	4931 Umpteen Megaton	4932 Empathy Myopathy	4933 Amputate Empty-out	4934 Omega-time Image-team
4935 Fugitive Emptily	4936 Impetus Amputees	4937 Mega-quake Fogey-tyke	4938 Emptied Imputed	4939 Impetigo Mop-top
4940 Fog-free Fag-fire	4941 Megafauna Image-man	4942 Mug-mob Imp-fob	4943 Map-fate Mega-foot	4944 Oaf-gaffe Mog-off
4945 Mugful Fag-fuel	4946 Magmas Image-fix	4947 Empyemic Mop-face	4948 Map-mode Image-mad	4949 Mega-amp Imp-image
4950 Employer Implore	4951 Fog-line Emplane	4952 Moplah Omega-vibe	4953 Impolite Maplet	4954 Amplify Fig-leaf
4955 Ampulla Fugally	4956 Impulse Moguls	4957 Emplace Fog-like	4958 Implode Implied	4959 Image-logo Mug-lip
4960 Imposer Mega-size	4961 Empoison Mop-sin	4962 Impish Fogeyish	4963 Impost Imagist	4964 Imagism Fogeyism
4965 Mega-sale Impiously	4966 Impasse Mopsus	4967 Amagasaki Mop-soak	4968 Imposed Fig-seed	4969 Mop-soap Fig-sap
4970 Magic-air Megacurie	4971 Magician Omega-icon	4972 Impeach Mapuche	4973 Impact Megacity	4974 Myopic-aim Fag-café

4975	4976	4977	4978	4979
Magical	Fugacious	Magic-key	Magic-day	Magic-pea
Map-clue	Fagaceous	Magick	Image-code	Image-copy
4980	4981	4982	4983	4984
Mop-dry	Mogadon	Mop-dab	Map-data	Imp-doom
Impeder	Megadyne	Image-job	Image-date	Map-dam
4985	4986	4987	4988	4989
Megadeal	Mopeds	Fig-juice	Megiddo	Fogdog
Amygdala	Mega-dose	Fog-decoy	Impeded	Map-edge
4990	4991	4992	4993	4994
Mugger	Impugn	Mug-pub	Faggot	Image-game
Foppery	Map-gene	Foggy-bay	Maggot	Fogey-goof
4995	4996	4997	4998	4999
Fipple	Magpies	Map-peak	Mugged	Map-page
Muggle	Moggies	Image-epic	Mapped	Foggage

ALPHA BETA 5000 – 5999

5000 Very-rare Over-zero	5001 Overrun Alizarin	5002 Lorry-bay Averrhoa	5003 Overrate Lazaret	5004 Overarm Variorum
5005 Overrule Vizierial	5006 Lorries Lazarus	5007 Verruca Lorry-key	5008 Lizard Override	5009 Overripe Larrup
5010 Learner Vernier	5011 Overween Vernonia	5012 Lazy-web Ivory-nib	5013 Variant Learnt	5014 Every-name Lazy-wife
5015 Vernal Avernal	5016 Larynx Overwise	5017 Variance Veronica	5018 Veranda Overawed	5019 Lozenge Veering
5020 Overhear Overbear	5021 Verbena Everyhow	5022 Every-bob Leery-baby	5023 Overheat Overbite	5024 Verbify Averham
5025 Overhaul Variable	5026 Verbs Lazy-bees	5027 Overbook Overbake	5028 Overhead Everybody	5029 Verbiage Overhype
5030 Overture Averter	5031 Everton Overtone	5032 Ovary-tube Lazy-youth	5033 Everett Very-quiet	5034 Overtime Every-time
5035 Virtual Overtly	5036 Vertex Varieties	5037 Overtake Lazy-tyke	5038 Averted Everted	5039 Vertigo Overtop
5040 Evermore Verifier	5041 Vermin Everyman	5042 Lazy-mob Ivory-fob	5043 Overfit Lazy-foot	5044 Veer-off Very-iffy
5045 Overfly Every-move	5046 Alarms Overmix	5047 Viremic Overmake	5048 Overfeed Verified	5049 Lazy-fag Liar-image
5050 Overlayer Leery-liar	5051 Overview Very-low	5052 Lazy-vibe Virile-boy	5053 Varlet Virility	5054 Overleaf Lazy-life
5055 Larval Overall	5056 Laurels Virilise	5057 Overlook Laurel-oak	5058 Overload Overloud	5059 Overlap Virology
5060 Overseer Oversize	5061 Aversion Eversion	5062 Overshoe Very-shy	5063 Everest Varsity	5064 Versify Voyeurism
5065 Aversive Variously	5066 Overseas Viruses	5067 Versace Verse-key	5068 Versed Overused	5069 Over-usage Lazy-sage
5070 Larker Overcare	5071 Larceny Lazy-cow	5072 Larch Lurch	5073 Veracity Voracity	5074 Overcome Lazio.com

5075 Lyrical Overcool	5076 Lyrics Larks	5077 Overcook Layer-cake	5078 Viricide Lurked	5079 Overkeep Ivory-cup
5080 Larder Verdure	5081 Overdone Viridian	5082 Lazy-job Overdub	5083 Overjet Viridity	5084 Every-dime Ivory-dome
5085 Lordly Luridly	5086 Overdose Lords	5087 Very-juicy Leery-joke	5088 Overjoyed Larded	5089 Lazy-dog Very-edgy
5090 Larger Verger	5091 Virgin Virginia	5092 Average-boy Large-bee	5093 Variegate Virgate	5094 Every-game Large-fee
5095 Largely Overplay	5096 Averages Virgos	5097 Lazy-pace Voyeur-peek	5098 Overaged Overpaid	5099 Average-age Overegg
5100 Lunar-year Lion-roar	5101 Lunarian Vanern	5102 Lion-rib Lanzhou	5103 Linearity Venerate	5104 Eelworm Alien-arm
5105 Venereal Linearly	5106 Viewers Loners	5107 Alien-race Lanark	5108 Vineyard Leeward	5109 Oil-energy Even-ripe
5110 Lanner Ovenware	5111 Vine-wine Lennon	5112 Lunan-bay Vein-web	5113 Lenient Linnet	5114 Vain-name Law-wife
5115 Ovine-wool Alien-envoy	5116 Lawns Linens	5117 Leniency Low-ink	5118 Vinewood Line-end	5119 Evening Lining
5120 Low-hair Law-bar	5121 Low-bow Ulna-bone	5122 Low-ebb Oven-hob	5123 Oven-heat Lion-bite	5124 Low-beam Alien-home
5125 Viewable Loanable	5126 View-box Law-bias	5127 Oven-bake Law-book	5128 Lionhood Low-bed	5129 Lane-hog Low-beep
5130 Venture Venter	5131 Alienation Venation	5132 Law-oath Vain-youth	5133 Eventuate Lunette	5134 View-time Law-team
5135 Eventual Lintel	5136 Events Vanities	5137 Lunatic Lentic	5138 Vented Eventide	5139 Vintage Vantage
5140 Oven-fire Low-fare	5141 Lawman Laywoman	5142 Loony-mob Alien-fib	5143 Low-fat Lean-meat	5144 Even-off Oven-fume
5145 Lawful Avian-flu	5146 Venomous Low-fees	5147 Venefice Alien-face	5148 Low-mood Linefeed	5149 Lion-image Lyon-map

5150 Lunular Lean-over	5151 Lanolin Low-line	5152 Linea-alba Lion-vibe	5153 Venality Veniality	5154 Linoleum Lowlife
5155 Vanilla Lineally	5156 Vowels Alewives	5157 Lone-voice Low-vice	5158 Vanload Vain-lady	5159 Law-logo Alien-leg
5160 Lion-size Lone-user	5161 Venison Lawson	5162 Vanish Oven-ash	5163 Lowest Lawsuit	5164 Lonesome Alienism
5165 Law-seal Lone-soul	5166 Lioness Lenses	5167 Evanesce Low-sky	5168 Linseed Lineside	5169 Line-sag Bonus-pay
5170 Lancer Linker	5171 Link-way Loan-coin	5172 Lunch Lynch	5173 Lancet Low-cut	5174 Link-fee Venue-café
5175 Lankily Lion-cave	5176 Links Avionics	5177 Oven-cook Oil-wick	5178 Linked Lanced	5179 Linkage Linkup
5180 Vendor Lender	5181 London Lion-den	5182 Low-jab Law-job	5183 Loan-date View-data	5184 Vanadium Land-fee
5185 Vandal Avondale	5186 Lands Lindsay	5187 Vandyke Landkey	5188 Vended Landed	5189 Low-edge Lean-dog
5190 Avenger Vinegar	5191 Long-way Lion-paw	5192 Long-boy Avian-pooh	5193 Elongate Languet	5194 Long-yam Looney-game
5195 Evangel Lingual	5196 Lungs Lounges	5197 Low-peak Even-pace	5198 Languid Long-day	5199 Language Long-ago
5200 Library Labourer	5201 Liberian Libran	5202 Labia-rub Lobo-rib	5203 Liberty Vibrate	5204 Librium Labarum
5205 Liberal Labral	5206 Laborious Vibe-rise	5207 Lubric Liberec	5208 Laboured Oilbird	5209 Alborg Viborg
5210 Lab-war Leibniz	5211 Lebanon Albanian	5212 Libyan-boy Albany-bay	5213 Lab-unit Lube-nut	5214 Olibanum Lab-name
5215 Aloha-wave Libyan-oil	5216 Elbows Albinos	5217 Lee-Bank Lab-week	5218 Elbowed Lie-beyond	5219 Oil-hinge Labia-wipe
5220 Libber Lobber	5221 Lobo-bone Lab-bin	5222 Lab-hob Vibey-baby	5223 Lobo-bite Lab-hit	5224 Vibey-home Lobo-boom

5225	5226	5227	5228	5229
Lob-above	Lobbies	Lobby-key	Lobbied	Lab-bug
Vibe-halo	Lab-bias	Lab-book	Lob-ahead	Lib-hype
5230	5231	5232	5233	5234
Oil-heater	Libation	Oil-bath	Lib-quote	Lobotomy
Lab-quiz	Lobation	Lobito-bay	Lab-quota	Lab-team
5235	5236	5237	5238	5239
Oil-beetle	Lobotes	Albitic	Lobated	Lab-tap
Lobo-tail	Lab-tax	Libya-quake	Lab-toad	Lobo-tag
5240	5241	5242	5243	5244
Lie-before	Albumin	Lib-mob	Labmate	Lib-fame
Albufera	Lobefin	Lobamba	Lobefoot	Lab-fume
5245	5246	5247	5248	5249
Labia-mole	Albumose	Lab-mice	Lab-made	Libya-map
Lab-file	Lab-fees	Lobo-face	Lobo-food	Lobo-image
5250	5251	5252	5253	5254
Lobular	Viable-way	Lablab	Viability	Lay-blame
Oil-boiler	Lobeline	Lib-vibe	Liability	Vibey-life
5255	5256	5257	5258	5259
Labella	Labels	Vibey-voice	Viable-idea	Lab-logo
Lab-levy	Libels	Lobelike	Lab-video	Lobo-leg
5260	5261	5262	5263	5264
Lobe-size	Lobo-axon	Ivy-bush	Elohist	Lab-exam
Lab-user	Elbasan	Lob-shoe	Vibist	Lib-axiom
5265	5266	5267	5268	5269
Vibey-soul	Lab-assay	Libya-sky	Lie-beside	Lab-usage
Olbas-oil	Vibe-axis	Elbe-soak	Oil-based	Lib-saga
5270	5271	5272	5273	5274
Albacore	Lib-icon	Vibe-echo	Albacete	Lab-café
Lobo-cry	Lob-coin	Lobo-cub	Lab-coat	Lobo-coma
5275	5276	5277	5278	5279
Vehicle	Lab-case	Layback	Lab-code	Lobo-cage
Lab-clue	Eel-hooks	Lubeck	Albucid	Lab-copy
5280	5281	5282	5283	5284
Lab-door	Lobo-den	Lube-job	Lab-data	Lib-dame
Lube-jar	Lab-dean	Vibe-dub	Lobed-toe	Lob-jam
5285	5286	5287	5288	5289
Lab-deal	Libidos	Labia-juice	Vibey-dude	Lobo-dog
Lib-duel	Lab-dose	Lab-joke	Alibi-deed	Lob-dope
5290	5291	5292	5293	5294
Lobo-prey	Albuginea	Vibey-pub	Lab-gate	Lib-game
Lab-agar	Lobo-paw	Lobo-pooh	Lobo-gut	Lab-opium
5295	5296	5297	5298	5299
Lube-gel	Vibe-pause	Lab-geek	Lab-guide	Lube-pipe
Lib-gala	Lobipes	Vibe-epic	Lobiped	Lab-pig

5300 Literary Ulterior	5301 Latrine Veteran	5302 Alter-boy Latrobe	5303 Literate Laterite	5304 Vitrify Elite-army
5305 Lateral Literal	6306 Litres Voters	5307 Literacy Liquorice	5308 Altered Leotard	5309 Liturgy Alter-ego
5310 Latinize Luteinize	5311 Quit-now Late-noon	5312 Aviation-bay Elite-web	5313 Latent Eloquent	5314 Vietnam Luteinoma
5315 Elite-navy Aviation-oil	5316 Latinos Lotions	5317 Latency Eloquence	5318 Latino-day Elite-need	5319 Voting Looting
5320 Lather Leather	5321 Lithuania Lothian	5322 Late-ebb Elite-babe	5323 Late-bet Vet-bite	5324 Lithium Lithify
5325 Lethal Evitable	5326 Laths Late-bus	5327 Lithic Vote-book	5328 Loathed Late-bid	5329 Late-hope Vote-hype
5330 Letter Litter	5331 Liquation Vitiation	5332 Ovate-tube Elite-youth	5333 Elite-quote Vote-tout	5334 Late-time Lutetium
5335 Little Late-tale	5336 Aliquots Litotes	5337 Lattice Lettuce	5338 Altitude Latitude	5339 Vote-tag Late-tip
5340 Liquefier Let-free	5341 Vitamin Late-moon	5342 Loot-mob Laity-fib	5343 Ultimate Vote-feet	5344 Let-off Elite-fame
5345 Late-meal Vote-mail	5346 Litmus Lit-fuse	5347 Ovate-face Elite-make	5348 Liquefied Elate-mood	5349 Elite-image Layout-map
5350 Vital-area Let-over	5351 Latvian Vituline	5352 Ovate-lobe Elite-vibe	5353 Vitality Veto-vote	5354 Late-life Ovate-leaf
5355 Vitally Let-all	5356 Vitalise Let-loose	5357 Elite-look Laity-voice	5358 Elite-lady Vote-yield	5359 Vitiligo Elite-league
5360 Lotus-ray Vat-size	5361 Vote-sway Oil-toxin	5362 Latish Loutish	5363 Elitist Latest	5364 Elitism Late-exam
5365 Late-soul Loot-sale	5366 Lotuses Latexes	5367 Vote-seek Lit-sky	5368 Elite-side Lie-outside	5369 Elite-sage Vet-usage
5370 Late-cry Loot-car	5371 Vatican Oil-tycoon	5372 Latch Letch	5373 Loquacity Veto-act	5374 Viaticum Elite-café

5375 Loot-cave Luticole	5376 Loquacious Latices	5377 Lite-cake Elite-cook	5378 Vaticide Elite-kid	5379 Elite-cop Loot-copy
5380 Liquid-air Vet-jury	5381 Late-June Lutidine	5382 Elite-job Late-jab	5383 Liquidity Liquidate	5384 Vote-demo Late-jam
5385 Late-July Liquid-oil	5386 Liquids Late-dose	5387 Lite-juice Elite-joke	5388 Vote-dad Vet-deed	5389 Vote-dupe Late-dig
5390 Elite-pair Vote-guru	5391 Vote-gain Litogen	5392 Elite-pub Laity-gab	5393 Litigate Oil-output	5394 Late-game Elite-gym
5395 Late-goal Elite-gala	5396 Litigious Latigos	5397 Vote-peace Late-peak	5398 Let-God Veto-guide	5399 Ovate-egg Aliquippa
5400 Oil-ferry Leaf-array	5401 Vomerine Life-zone	5402 Life-orb Elf-rib	5403 Alumroot Life-art	5404 Alfa-Romeo Oviform
5405 Life-zeal Lame-rule	5406 Loafers Lemurs	5407 Life-race Leaf-rake	5408 Alfred Ilford	5409 Life-urge Elf-rage
5410 Laminar Luminary	5411 Limonene Life-union	5412 Life-web Alfa-nob	5413 Element Lament	5414 Aluminium Alfa-wife
5415 Luminal Liminal	5416 Alumnus Lemons	5417 Almanac Alomancy	5418 Lemonade Almond	5419 Looming Leafing
5420 Limber Lumbar	5421 Life-ban Lima-bean	5422 Life-ebb IVF-baby	5423 Lifeboat Loaf-about	5424 Life-boom Life-beam
5425 Lambley Lambale	5426 Limbs Lambs	5427 Limbic Lambic	5428 Lambda Limbed	5429 Lumbago Life-hope
5430 Lifter Limiter	5431 Lift-away Life-tone	5432 Lame-youth Life-oath	5433 Lift-out Left-toe	5434 Life-time Lofty-aim
5435 Loftily Limitive	5436 Lofts Limits	5437 Loft-key Lift-yoke	5438 Limited Lifted	5439 Lift-up Life-type
5440 Life-fire Limmer	5441 Alum-mine Lame-man	5442 Elf-fib Limo-fob	5443 Lame-foot Life-mate	5444 Life-memo Lama-fame
5445 Alfa-male Lame-move	5446 Lammas Lummox	5447 Elf-face Lame-mice	5448 Lammed Luffed	5449 Alfa-omega Life-image

5450 Alfilaria Lifelore	5451 Lifeline Leaf-vein	5452 Life-vibe Lame-lobo	5453 Leaflet Lie-flat	5454 Alfalfa Elm-leaf
5455 Lamella Life-value	5456 Limulus Life-lease	5457 Lifelike Elflike	5458 Oilfield Alfold	5459 Lame-leg Leaf-logo
5460 Lamasery Life-size	5461 Limousine Life-sun	5462 Elfish Eel-fish	5463 Almost Alamosite	5464 Lamaism Lifesome
5465 Life-soul Leafy-soil	5466 Oil-mass Oil-mess	5467 Loo-mask Life-seek	5468 Lime-soda Elm-seed	5469 Lemsip Life-saga
5470 Life-care Lame-cure	5471 Limacine Life-icon	5472 Lame-cub Life-echo	5473 Lame-cat Leafy-city	5474 Life-acme Lame-cameo
5475 Life-clue Loamy-clay	5476 Ulmaceous Limaceous	5477 Lime-cake Leafy-cocoa	5478 Life-code Limacide	5479 Life-copy Elf-cup
5480 Limo-door Life-diary	5481 Life-dean Lie-midway	5482 Life-job Leaf-dab	5483 Life-duty Leafy-diet	5484 Life-doom Elfdom
5485 Life-jail Lame-deal	5486 Life-joys Lame-ideas	5487 Lime-juice Leaf-decay	5488 Life-odd Life-deed	5489 Lame-dog Leaf-edge
5490 Vampire Lamprey	5491 Lampoon Olympian	5492 Lymph Lamp-bay	5493 Limpet Lie-empty	5494 Life-game Lump-fee
5595 Lamp-oil Life-goal	5496 Lamps Lumps	5497 Olympic Life-peace	5498 Olympiad Limpid	5499 Limpopo Vamp-up
5500 Allurer Viverra	5501 Valerian Lily-iron	5502 Lover-boy Love-orb	5503 Levirate Leveret	5504 Vivarium Love-room
5505 Evil-rule Vuvuzela	5506 Lovers Leavers	5507 Live-race Oval-ark	5508 All-ready Louvered	5509 Allergy Leverage
5510 Livener Evil-war	5511 Livonian All-new	5512 Love-web Yellow-hue	5513 Violent Valiant	5514 Allonym Evil-name
5515 Love-wave Evil-wile	5516 Illinois Violins	5517 Alliance Violence	5518 Olivewood Allowed	5519 Living Loving
5520 Live-hero Love-bore	5521 Love-bone Evil-hyena	5522 Live-baby Love-boob	5523 Love-bite Live-bet	5524 Love-beam Leave-home

5525	5526	5527	5528	5529
Available	Value-house	Love-book	Love-bed	Love-bug
Valuable	Love-box	Evil-hook	Evil-head	All-hype
5530	5531	5532	5533	5534
Vulture	Evolution	Lilith	Levitate	All-time
Elevator	Volition	Evil-taboo	Allottee	Evil-team
5535	5536	5537	5538	5539
Volatile	Vaults	Voltaic	Elevated	Voltage
Evaluative	Violets	Lavatic	Violated	Allotype
5540	5541	5542	5543	5544
Live-fire	Illumine	Evil-mob	Live-footy	Leave-off
Love-more	Velamen	Love-fib	Evil-fate	Love-fame
5545	5546	5547	5548	5549
Live-movie	Volumes	Vivific	Vilified	Oil-lamp
Love-mail	Llamas	Euvolemic	Vivified	Lie-limp
5550	5551	5552	5553	5554
Alveolar	Villain	Lullaby	Alleviate	Alluvium
Evolver	Alluvion	Love-vibe	Velvet	Vellum
5555	5556	5557	5558	5559
Alluvial	Valves	Allelic	Evolved	Village
Vulval	Volleys	Viva-voce	Volleyed	Level-up
5560	5561	5562	5563	5564
Illusory	Illusion	Lavish	Loyalist	Loyalism
Vavasour	Allusion	Lavash	Violist	All-safe
5565	5566	5567	5568	5569
Illusive	Live-sex	Love-sake	Olive-seed	Love-saga
Allusive	Evil-axis	Olive-sauce	Evil-side	Live-expo
5570	5571	5572	5573	5574
Velcro	Volcano	Live-cub	Allocate	Yell.com
Love-care	Vulcan	Love-echo	Illicit	Love-café
5575	5576	5577	5578	5579
Oval-cave	Vivacious	Yale-lock	Love-kid	Oval-cup
Live-koala	Violaceous	Love-cake	Evil-code	Evil-cop
5580	5581	5582	5583	5584
Evil-doer	Love-den	Love-job	Validity	Allodium
Olive-jar	Allodynia	Evil-jibe	Lividity	Oval-dome
5585	5586	5587	5588	5589
Vividly	Lloyds	Olive-juice	Livedoid	Levodopa
Lividly	All-days	Love-joke	Alluded	Love-dope
5590	5591	5592	5593	5594
Allegory	Vulpine	Love-pub	Vulgate	Allogamy
Vulgar	Love-gene	Vole-pooh	Lava-pit	Love-game
5595	5596	5597	5598	5599
Illegal	Ellipse	Illogic	Alleged	Oval-egg
Live-play	Valgus	Love-epic	Love-guide	All-agog

5600 Laser-ray Luxury-area	5601 Also-ran Leisure-way	5602 Loose-robe Leisure-bay	5603 Luxuriate Lease-rate	5604 Lysozyme Lease-room
5605 Leisurely Lax-rule	5606 Luxuries Elixirs	5607 Oil-source Luxury-key	5608 Leisure-day Lousy-ride	5609 Lax-rope Oil-surge
5610 Visionary Loose-wear	5611 Lausanne Loose-union	5612 Loose-web Lousy-nob	5613 Loose-nut Luxe-unit	5614 Lysinemia Lousy-name
5615 Lesional Loose-nail	5616 Visions Lesions	5617 Ivy-snake Oil-sink	5618 Oil-sand Loosened	5619 Leasing Losing
5620 Lasher Loose-hair	5621 Lesbian Lisbon	5622 Lax-boob Loose-babe	5623 Lash-out Lose-heat	5624 Evesham Lease-home
5625 Visible Leasable	5626 Lashes Lesbos	5627 Lease-bike Lexibook	5628 Lashed Leashed	5629 Lose-hope Lesbigay
5630 Visitor Lustre	5631 Alsatian Listen	5632 Lesotho Lesath	5633 Lost-out Vastity	5634 Ileostomy Elastoma
5635 Laxative Vestal	5636 Vests Visits	5637 Elastic Lost-key	5638 Listed Vested	5639 Vestige Last-go
5640 Lismore Visa-free	5641 Lousy-man Loose-money	5642 Lousy-mob Lax-moob	5643 Lose-fat Loose-fit	5644 Loose-off Lose-fame
5645 Vaseful Lousy-meal	5646 Visa-fees Vasomax	5647 Lose-face Lexemic	5648 Lax-mode Lose-mojo	5649 Oil-sump Visa-image
5650 Visual-aura Elsevier	5651 Vaseline Vesuvian	5652 Lease-lab Loo-slab	5653 Lixiviate Vis-vitae	5654 Lixivium Loose-leaf
5655 Visually Elusively	5656 Voxels Visualise	5657 Lousy-look Loose-lace	5658 Loose-lead Visual-aid	5659 Lie-asleep Loose-lip
5660 Lesser Lessor	5661 Lessen Lesson	5662 Loosish Loose-shoe	5663 Lose-seat Lease-site	5664 Lysosome Lissom
5665 Vassal Vessel	5666 Losses Lassos	5667 Liassic Lexus-key	5668 Lassoed Aloes-seed	5669 Lux-soap Visa-saga
5670 Viscera Lascar	5671 Lexicon Oilskin	5672 Lease-cab Alaska-bay	5673 Lasket Loose-coat	5674 Viscum Oil-scam

5675	5676	5677	5678	5679
Vesicle	Luscious	Loose-cake	Viscid	Lease-copy
Lexical	Viscous	Lie-sick	Lousicide	Lexicog
5680	5681	5682	5683	5684
Loose-door	Elsdon	Lose-job	Lose-data	Avisodomy
Lax-jury	Loose-jaw	Loose-jibe	Lease-jet	Loose-jam
5685	5686	5687	5688	5689
Lose-deal	Lousy-days	Aloes-juice	Lease-deed	Lose-edge
Visa-delay	Loose-ideas	Lousy-joke	Lax-dude	Lousy-dog
5690	5691	5692	5693	5694
Vesper	Lasagne	Lease-pub	Oil-spot	Lose-game
Lisper	Vespine	Loose-pooh	Lax-gate	Lease-gem
5695	5696	5697	5698	5699
Vespula	Loosey-goosey	Oil-spike	Lexipedia	Visa-page
Visa-plea	Lax-apex	Lose-pace	Vespid	Loose-peg
5700	5701	5702	5703	5704
Alcazar	Lake-Orion	Elk-rib	Alacrity	Leaky-roof
Look-rear	Leak-urine	Lacy-robe	Ulcerate	Oily-cream
5705	5706	5707	5708	5709
Vicarial	Lookers	Leaky-arc	Lucozade	Vicarage
Look-real	Ulcers	Loco-rookie	Oil-crude	Oil-cargo
5710	5711	5712	5713	5714
Lacunar	Look-new	Vice-web	Vacant	Leak-info
Vicenza	Lacanian	Loco-nob	Vicinity	Alcyonium
5715	5716	5717	5718	5719
Voice-wave	License	Vacancy	Locoweed	Leaking
Lace-weave	Likewise	Laconic	Lakewood	Looking
5720	5721	5722	5723	5724
Voucher	Lichen	Leech-bay	Leachate	Alchemy
Lechery	Iliac-bone	Voice-ebb	Look-about	Voice-boom
5725	5726	5727	5728	5729
Alcohol	Leeches	Look-book	Look-ahead	El-cheapo
Likeable	Vocabs	Lace-hook	Leached	Look-big
5730	5731	5732	5733	5734
Lecture	Location	Leucothoe	Lactate	Victim
Victory	Vacation	Loco-youth	Loctite	Leucotomy
5735	5736	5737	5738	5739
Elective	Lactose	Lactic	Elected	Lace-top
Evocative	Lacteous	Lactuca	Evicted	Voice tape
5740	5741	5742	5743	5744
Lucifer	Laceman	Vice-mob	Locomote	Look-off
Look-far	Viceman	Lacombe	Look-fat	Voice-memo
5745	5746	5747	5748	5749
Voice-mail	Vacuums	Leukemic	Voice-mode	Lake-fog
Leak-fuel	Locums	Lucific	Vacuumed	Loci-map

5750 Locavore Avicularia	5751 Alkaline Iliac-vein	5752 Local-boy Voice-vibe	5753 Locality Alkylate	5754 Alkalemia Lay-claim
5755 Locally Vocally	5756 Locals Vocals	5757 Lookalike Vicelike	5758 Alkaloid Look-old	5759 Look-vague Voice-log
5760 Look-sure Lake-size	5761 Leucoxene Voice-sway	5762 Look-shy Lace-shoe	5763 Locust Vacuist	5764 Lookism Laicism
5765 Viciously Vacuously	5766 Vice-axis Look-sexy	5767 Yolk-sac Ale-cask	5768 Lakeside Lookaside	5769 Leek-soup Elk-leg
5770 Locker Licker	5771 Vaccine Lock-in	5772 Voice-echo Lucky-boy	5773 Leucocyte Locket	5774 Lucky-aim Alky-coma
5775 Luckily Ileocecal	5776 Locks Vicks	5777 Lock-key Oil-cock	5778 Locked Lackaday	5779 Lock-up Lockage
5780 Vocoder Voice-diary	5781 Vice-den Elk-jaw	5782 Vac-job Voice-dub	5783 Elucidate Lucidity	5784 Voice-demo Lucid-aim
5785 Lucidly Voice-dial	5786 Avocados Lucid-eyes	5787 Voice-decoy Loco-joke	5788 Look-odd Lucid-idea	5789 Look-deep Lake-edge
5790 Look-pure Lace-gear	5791 Leukopenia Look-again	5792 Alky-pub Voice-gab	5793 Look-opaque Evoke-pity	5794 Lake-game Voice-gem
5795 Alcogel Look-ugly	5796 Leak-gas Lycopus	5797 Vice-epic Voice-peak	5798 Look-good Voice-guide	5799 Alcopop Leak-pipe
5800 Loud-roar Al-Jazeera	5801 Lead-zone Void-urine	5802 Old-rob Loud-rub	5803 Old-rate Avid-rat	5804 Oil-drum Video-room
5805 Elderly Lead-role	5806 Leaders Evaders	5807 Lead-race Load-rice	5808 Eldorado Loud-radio	5809 Oil-drip Loud-rap
5810 Lead-wire Lead-war	5811 Lie-down Old-wine	5812 Video-web Old-nob	5813 Evident Vedanta	5814 Laudanum Old-enemy
5815 Leadenly Lead-envoy	5816 Ladinos Loud-noise	5817 Avoidance Evidence	5818 Ladywood Lead-end	5819 Leading Loading
5820 Oldbury Ledbury	5821 Old-bone Old-bean	5822 Lead-abbe Avid-baby	5823 Old-hat Loud-hoot	5824 Oldham Loud-boom

5825	5826	5827	5828	5829
Avoidable	Old-boys	Video-book	Aldehyde	Ladybug
Laudable	Video-box	Old-bike	Ladyhood	Loud-beep
5830	5831	5832	5833	5834
Laudatory	Laudation	Video-tube	Vidette	Old-time
Video-tour	Loud-tone	Loud-youth	Ladette	Lead-team
5835	5836	5837	5838	5839
Old-tale	Avoid-tax	Loud-quake	Viduity-aid	Videotape
Laudative	Old-taxi	Load-teak	Yield-quid	Lady-top
5840	5841	5842	5843	5844
Lead-free	Old-man	Lad-moob	Old-mate	Laid-off
Avoid-fear	Vodafone	Lead-mob	Lead-foot	Lead-off
5845	5846	5847	5848	5849
Old-fool	Old-foes	Old-face	Old-maid	Video-image
Video-move	Video-mix	Avid-mice	Video-mode	Old-map
5850	5851	5852	5853	5854
Laid-over	Lead-line	Lead-lab	Avadavat	Old-leaf
Old-layer	Ludlow	Loud-vibe	Lady-vote	Void-life
5855	5856	5857	5858	5859
Old-love	Aldolase	Ladylike	Old-lady	Lid-lag
Loud-yell	Avid-louse	Loud-voice	Ladled	Ludology
5860	5861	5862	5863	5864
Load-size	Lady-sway	Oldish	Eldest	Vedism
Old-user	Old-sin	Loudish	Voodooist	Voodooism
5865	5866	5867	5868	5869
Old-soul	Old-issue	Old-ski	Ladies-day	Video-usage
Lid-seal	Lead-axis	Video-sky	Lead-side	Lead-spy
5870	5871	5872	5873	5874
Lead-car	Lidocaine	Loud-echo	Oviduct	Videocam
Loud-cry	Ladykin	Video-cube	Viaduct	Old-café
5875	5876	5877	5878	5879
Lodicule	Load-case	Ladock	Old-code	Old-cape
Lead-clue	Lead-cause	Old-cook	Loud-kid	Vidcap
5880	5881	5882	5883	5884
Ladder	Aladdin	Old-job	Luddite	Video-demo
Loud-jeer	Loddon	Video-dub	Load-data	Old-dam
5885	5886	5887	5888	5889
Lady-diva	Old-days	Loud-joke	Old-dad	Lead-edge
Video-daily	Lead-ideas	Video-juke	Lidded	Old-dog
5890	5891	5892	5893	5894
Ledger	Load-gun	Loud-gab	Aldgate	Video-game
Lodger	Avoid-pain	Old-pub	Oil-depot	Old-gym
5895	5896	5897	5898	5899
Old-pal	Lodges	Video-epic	Video-guide	Lead-pipe
Video-play	Ledges	Lead-pace	Lodged	Loud-pop

5900 Vaporize Eulogizer	5901 Algerian Leporine	5902 Oil-probe Vaporub	5903 Evaporate Oviparity	5904 Leg-room Oil-proof
5905 Algarve Vague-role	5906 Vipers Vapours	5907 Oil-price Luge-race	5908 Leopard Lip-read	5909 Leipzig Lip-zip
5910 Legionary Legwear	5911 League-win Lignin	5912 Lagoon-bay Log-web	5913 Elegant Lignite	5914 Lignify Lignum
5915 Vaginal Lagoonal	5916 Vegans Lagoons	5917 Elegance Ivy-pink	5918 Legend Ligand	5919 Leaping Looping
5920 Algebra Laugher	5921 Leg-bone Laugh-away	5922 Aviophobia League-hub	5923 Light Alight	5924 Leg-hoof Lego-home
5925 Eligible Legible	5926 Log-house Laughs	5927 Logbook Liphook	5928 Leap-ahead Laughed	5929 Lap-hug Lug-bag
5930 Ligature Lop-tree	5931 Ligation Legation	5932 Logo-tab Loopy-youth	5933 Vegetate Vague-quote	5934 Vagotomy Lap-time
5935 Vegetal Lop-tool	5936 Legates Lego-toys	5937 Log-teak Lip-tic	5938 Leap-toad Voyage-tide	5939 Laptop League-top
5940 Oligomer Log-fire	5941 Logomania Lego-fun	5942 Loopy-mob Voyage-fib	5943 Vegemite Leg-fat	5944 Log-off Lop-off
5945 Lapful Lego-movie	5946 Legumes Logo-fees	5947 Oligemic Vague-face	5948 Oil-pomade Lipoamide	5949 Oil-pump Vague-image
5950 Loop-over Leap-over	5951 Leg-vein Vague-view	5952 Vague-alibi Loopy-vibe	5953 Legality Oil-glut	5954 Legal-fee Oil-palm
5955 Legally Lapilli	5956 Legalise Legalese	5957 Liplike Vague-look	5958 Legal-aid Leopold	5959 Algology Legal-age
5960 Leg-sore Lip-size	5961 Vepsian Log-saw	5962 Voguish Log-ash	5963 Legist Elegist	5964 Liposome Eulogism
5965 Lugsail Logo-seal	5966 Iliopsoas Lapses	5967 Alps-ice Leg-soak	5968 League-side Elapsed	5969 Lip-sip Log-sap
5970 Lip-care Voyage-car	5971 Logician Logo-icon	5972 Leg-ache Lego-cube	5973 Lego-city Lipocyte	5974 Log-café Vogue-cameo

5975	5976	5977	5978	5979
Logical	Logics	Alopecic	Algicide	League-cup
Loop-coil	Legacies	Log-cake	Log-code	Log-cage
5980	5981	5982	5983	5984
Avogadro	Lipid-ion	Log-job	Vapidity	Lapidify
Lapidary	Loopy-don	Leg-dab	Algidity	Logjam
5985	5986	5987	5988	5989
Vapidly	Lipids	Vague-joke	Log-deed	Lapdog
Logo-dove	Elapids	Leap-dyke	Vague-dude	Leap-deep
5990	5991	5992	5993	5994
Lapper	Leg-pain	Loopy-gab	Lappet	League-game
Logger	Lipopenia	Lip-gooby	Lip-pout	Lego-game
5995	5996	5997	5998	5999
Lay-people	Veggies	Leg-pace	League-guide	Luggage
Log-pile	Lay-eggs	Logo-piece	Logged	Lippage

ALPHA BETA 6000 – 6999

6000	6001	6002	6003	6004
Size-zero	Sorrow	Sore-rib	Sorority	Xray-room
Easy-error	Sea-arrow	Sorry-yob	Serrate	Sore-arm
6005	6006	6007	6008	6009
Sizzle	Seizures	Suez-race	Senior-aide	User-rage
Surreal	Size-rise	Soar-arc	Serried	Seize-rope
6010	6011	6012	6013	6014
Sorner	Sour-wine	Sour-whey	Serenity	Surname
Syria-war	Suzanne	Serene-bay	Sour-note	User-name
6015	6016	6017	6018	6019
Serenely	Sirens	Esurience	Serenade	Syringe
Sore-nail	Syrinx	Saranac	Sourwood	Sarong
6020	6021	6022	6023	6024
Sour-beer	Serbian	Sore-boob	Sure-bet	User-home
Size-hero	Exurban	Sarubobo	Sorbet	Sour-beef
6025	6026	6027	6028	6029
Exorable	Serbs	Seize-book	Sore-head	Sore-hip
Sizeable	User-bias	Usury-hike	User-abode	User-bug
6030	6031	6032	6033	6034
Sorter	Exertion	Xray-tube	Sort-out	Seriatim
Osier-tree	Serotine	Sore-tibia	Surtout	Sort-of
6035	6036	6037	6038	6039
Exertive	Sorts	Xerotic	X-rated	Serotype
User-tool	Sorties	Sore-tyke	Sorted	Saratoga
6040	6041	6042	6043	6044
Surfer	Sermon	Surf-bay	Surfeit	Seize-fame
Sure-fire	Sure-men	Sour-fib	Sure-foot	Usury-mafia
6045	6046	6047	6048	6049
Sure-move	Surmise	Surface	Surfed	Serfage
Surfle	Serfs	Sour-face	Sour-food	Suez-map
6050	6051	6052	6053	6054
Server	Sirloin	Xray-lab	Israelite	Easier-life
Surveyor	Sea-raven	Sour-vibe	Seriality	Sour-leaf
6055	6056	6057	6058	6059
Survive	Serialise	Service	Served	Serology
Serially	Israelis	Serve-ace	Surveyed	Serve-up
6060	6061	6062	6063	6064
Xeroxer	Sarsen	Sourish	Sorest	Sizeism
Suez-size	Sour-sin	Size-shoe	Sarasota	Xray-exam
6065	6066	6067	6068	6069
Seriously	Seeress	Sea-rescue	Sore-side	Soursop
Uxoriously	Xerosis	Sour-sauce	Osier-seed	Size-usage
6070	6071	6072	6073	6074
Sorcery	Saracen	Search	Sericite	Sarcoma
User-care	User-icon	Exarch	Surcoat	User-cameo

6075 Sea-oracle Xray-clue	6076 Exercise Exorcise	6077 Sirocco Sea-rock	6078 Sarcoid User-code	6079 Xray-copy Sore-cop
6080 Sordor Sardar	6081 Sardine Sardinia	6082 Easier-job Sore-jab	6083 Xray-data Sour-diet	6084 Exordium Sore-edema
6085 Exordial Sure-deal	6086 Sordes Xray-dose	6087 Sour-juice Soiree-joke	6088 Sordid Usury-deed	6089 Seized-up Sore-edge
6090 Surgery Usurper	6091 Surgery Sargon	6092 Seraph Sorgho	6093 Surgut Sore-gout	6094 Seize-opium Exergame
6095 Seraglio User-goal	6096 Gripes Syrups	6097 Exoergic Sour-puke	6098 User-guide Usurped	6099 Sergipe User-page
6100 Snorer Snoozer	6101 Sworn Sun-zone	6102 Sowerby Sun-orb	6103 Seniority Snort	6104 Swarm Sunroof
6105 Snarl Swerve	6106 Sunrise Sonorous	6107 Snarky Sow-rice	6108 Sword Snared	6109 Synergy Sewerage
6110 Sinner Sunnier	6111 Snow-in Suwannee	6112 Sunnah Snow-bay	6113 Asininity Sunnite	6114 Synonym Xenonym
6115 Sine-wave Sunnily	6116 Swans Sunnis	6117 Swanky Sin-week	6118 Sunny-day Saw-wood	6119 Swing Sewing
6120 Sun-bear Sunbury	6121 Sunbow Sin-bin	6122 Snobby Sun-hub	6123 Sun-hat So-what	6124 Sunbeam Sin-home
6125 Swayable Swahili	6126 Swabs Snobs	6127 Sunbake Sin-hook	6128 Sunbed Sinbad	6129 Sin-bag Sway-hip
6130 Senator Sanitary	6131 Sweeten Suntan	6132 Swathe Synth	6133 Snotty Sweet-tea	6134 Santa-Fe Sun-time
6135 Saintly Sweetly	6136 Sweets Saints	6137 Oxyntic Sinitic	6138 Sainted Sweated	6139 Santiago Sweet-pea
6140 Sin-free Sun-fry	6141 Sea-anemone Sea-woman	6142 Sin-mate Sane-mob	6143 Swift Exanimate	6144 Sniff Snuff
6145 Sawfly Sinful	6146 Swims Exanimous	6147 Isonomic Sun-face	6148 Sway-mood Sane-mode	6149 Swamp Asian-map

6150 Sway-over Snailery	6151 Sun-view Asian-lion	6152 Sin-vibe Sun-lab	6153 Senility Sunlit	6154 Sun-life Synovium
6155 Swell Swivel	6156 Snails Sea-waves	6157 Sun-like Easy-walk	6158 Axe-wield Sin-video	6159 Sinology Auxanology
6160 Sensory Sun-size	6161 Sow-sin Sane-son	6162 Swash Swish	6163 Sunset Soonest	6164 Sun-safe Sew-seam
6165 Sensual Sinuously	6166 Senses Sinuses	6167 Sun-soak Senesce	6168 Sinusoid Sow-seed	6169 Sea-wasp Sin-expo
6170 Snooker Sincere	6171 Sunken Sneak-away	6172 Synechia Sin-echo	6173 Sin-city Sun-city	6174 Sun-café Sin-acme
6175 Sneakily Snake-oil	6176 Snakes Sinks	6177 Snack Snick	6178 Snaked Sneaked	6179 Syncope Sneak-up
6180 Sender Sounder	6181 Sweden Sundew	6182 Sandy-bay Sane-job	6183 Send-out Sound-out	6184 Sin-doom Sun-dome
6185 Sandal Sundial	6186 Sands Sounds	6187 Synodic Syndic	6188 Sanded Sounded	6189 San-Diego Sendup
6190 Singer Sniper	6191 Ox-wagon Xenogeny	6192 Isoneph Singh	6193 Sawpit Swept	6194 Asian-game Xenogamy
6195 Single Senegal	6196 Songs Snaps	6197 Sun-peak Sin-epic	6198 Sun-guide Swiped	6199 Snappy Synagogue
6200 Sherry Sharer	6201 Shrew Shrine	6202 Shrub Suburb	6203 Shirt Short	6204 Ashram Shoe-room
6205 Soberly Shrove	6206 Shares Shores	6207 Shark Shriek	6208 Shred Shroud	6209 Sharp Shrug
6210 Shower Shiner	6211 Shown Shinny	6212 Shinobi Show-boy	6213 Shanty Shunt	6214 Sub-name Shy-wife
6215 Shawl Showily	6216 Shows Subways	6217 Shank Sea-bank	6218 Shandy Seabound	6219 Show-up Shooing
6220 Ishihara Sub-hour	6221 Ashbin Sheehan	6222 Shabby Ex-hubby	6223 Exhibit Axe-habit	6224 Shy-bum Sib-home

6225	6226	6227	6228	6229
Shoe-hole	Shoe-box	Shoe-hook	Subhead	Shoe-bag
Shoe-heel	Sib-bias	Sib-bike	Sobbed	Ash-heap
6230	6231	6232	6233	6234
Ashtray	Ashton	Sheath	Shitty	Sub-time
Shooter	Shut-in	Subtab	Shoot-out	Sub-atom
6235	6236	6237	6238	6239
Subtle	Sheets	Shy-tyke	Shouted	Sabotage
Subequal	Shots	Shiitake	Sheeted	Subtype
6240	6241	6242	6243	6244
Exhumer	Submenu	Shoe-fob	Shaft	Shimmy
Shofar	Shaman	Soho-mob	Shift	Shoo-off
6245	6246	6247	6248	6249
Ishmael	Shams	Shoe-make	Ashamed	Shampoo
Shoo-fly	Shamus	Shy-face	Exhumed	Soho-map
6250	6251	6252	6253	6254
Shaver	Shaven	Shiloh	Sublet	Shelf
Shiver	Subline	Shoe-lob	Usability	Sublime
6255	6256	6257	6258	6259
Shell	Sublease	Shoe-lace	Shield	Exobiology
Shovel	Sabulous	Ash-like	Should	Shoe-leg
6260	6261	6262	6263	6264
Shoe-size	Sibson	Shisha	Exhaust	Subsume
Ex-boxer	Sea-basin	Shush	Subset	Shiism
6265	6266	6267	6268	6269
Shoe-sole	Ex-boss	Suboxic	Subside	Sub-usage
Subsoil	She-ass	Shoe-soak	Subsidy	Shoe-sag
6270	6271	6272	6273	6274
Shaker	Shaken	Sheikh	Subacute	Shaky-aim
Sib-care	Ash-can	Sea-beach	Shakeout	Soho-café
6275	6276	6277	6278	6279
Shakily	Sebaceous	Shock	Shy-kid	Shake-up
Shekel	Shakes	Shack	Sub-acid	Shoe-cap
6280	6281	6282	6283	6284
Shudra	Shadow	Shoe-dab	Subedit	Shy-dame
Subduer	Sub-dean	Shy-jibe	Sub-duty	Shoe-demo
6285	6286	6287	6288	6289
Shadily	Shades	Shy-joke	Shoddy	She-dog
Subdual	Sheds	Shoe-decay	Subdued	Shy-dig
6290	6291	6292	6293	6294
Subpar	Subpoena	Ship-boy	She-goat	Subgame
Shaper	Shipway	Sheep-boy	Ship-out	Shoe-gum
6295	6296	6297	6298	6299
Shapely	Shapes	Sub-peak	Shoe-pad	Shaggy
Shoogly	Ships	Shoe-poke	Shaped	Subpage

6300 Exterior Starry	6301 Straw Strain	6302 Strobe Star-buy	6303 Start Street	6304 Stream Storm
6305 Astral Sterile	6306 Stars Stairs	6307 Strike Stroke	6308 Stride Steroid	6309 Storage Stripe
6310 Stanza Stoner	6311 Estonian Stow-away	6312 Stony-bay Stun-bee	6313 Extent Stunt	6314 Stonify Site-name
6315 Stanley Stonily	6316 Stones Stains	6317 Stance Stink	6318 Stand Extend	6319 Sting Stingy
6320 Soother Isothere	6321 Asthenia South-way	6322 South-bay Stubby	6323 Extubate Stub-out	6324 Asthma Ex-thief
6325 Stable Suitable	6326 Stabs Stubs	6327 Sothiac Site-book	6328 Stay-ahead Soothed	6329 Ex-thug Exit-hope
6330 Stature Sitter	6331 Station Situation	6332 Stith Staith	6333 Statute Squatty	6334 Osteotomy Set-time
6335 Settle Stately	6336 States Status	6337 Static Eustatic	6338 Satiated State-aid	6339 Sit-atop State-pay
6340 Steamer Stumer	6341 Stamina Stamen	6342 Exit-mob Ox-tomb	6343 Estimate Stomata	6344 Staff Stiff
6345 Stifle Stimuli	6346 Squamous Stems	6347 Stye-face Site-foci	6348 Steamed Stymied	6349 Stamp Stump
6350 Squalor Stealer	6351 Setline Stolen	6352 Set-vibe Site-lab	6353 Stilt Stylet	6354 Stay-aloof Steal-fee
6355 Still Stall	6356 Styles Stylus	6357 Stalk Steel-key	6358 Stolid Squalid	6359 Osteology Sitology
6360 Stay-sure Suit-size	6361 Exotoxin Seat-sway	6362 Squash Stash	6363 Exquisite East-exit	6364 Satisfy Satsuma
6365 Staysail Exit-soul	6366 Stasis Osteosis	6367 Easy-task Suet-sauce	6368 Set-aside Eastside	6369 Site-usage Seat-sag
6370 Squeaker Stoker	6371 Oxytocin Ex-tycoon	6372 Stocah Isotach	6373 Osteocyte Eastcote	6374 Sitcom Site-café

6375	6376	6377	6378	6379
Stoical	Stakes	Stick	Estacode	Steak-pie
Squeakily	Suitcase	Stock	Staked	Site-copy
6380	6381	6382	6383	6384
Studier	Osteodynia	Studio-boy	Exit-date	Stadium
Exit-door	Exit-den	Steady-boo	Site-duty	Study-aim
6385	6386	6387	6388	6389
Steadily	Studies	Study-key	St-Jude	Squidgy
Sit-idle	Studs	Steady-oak	Squaddie	Stodge
6390	6391	6392	6393	6394
Stupor	Estrogen	Staph	Step-out	Stigma
Steeper	Osteopenia	Stop-by	East-gate	Stupefy
6395	6396	6397	6398	6399
Staple	Steps	Isotopic	Stupid	Step-up
Steeple	Stages	Set-piece	Staged	Steppe
6400	6401	6402	6403	6404
Sea-ferry	Oxymoron	Somerby	Smart	Swarm
Safari-zoo	Safe-zone	Sumo-robe	Safe-route	Isoform
6405	6406	6407	6408	6409
Smear-oil	Isomerase	Smirk	Oxford	Exam-rage
Safe-rule	Ease-fears	Seamark	Smeared	Safe-rope
6410	6411	6412	6413	6414
Examiner	Safe-union	Seam-web	Seamount	Seminoma
Seminar	Asmonean	Safe-web	Easement	Same-name
6415	6416	6417	6418	6419
Seminal	Simonise	Exam-week	Examined	Seaming
Seafowl	Safe-ways	Sea-monk	Safe-end	Seeming
6420	6421	6422	6423	6424
Sombre	Somehow	Safe-baby	Same-boat	Safe-home
Safe-hour	Sumbawa	Exam-hub	Safe-bet	Sofa-bum
6425	6426	6427	6428	6429
Symbol	Safe-house	Exam-book	Somebody	Safe-hope
Sambal	Sofa-base	Safe-hook	Sofa-bed	Exam-hoop
6430	6431	6432	6433	6434
Oximeter	Soften	Smith	Smutty	Sometime
Sifter	Semitone	Smooth	Soft-toy	Same-team
6435	6436	6437	6438	6439
Softly	Softies	Osmotic	Safety-aid	Exam-tip
Safe-tool	Smuts	Somatic	Sifted	Same-type
6440	6441	6442	6443	6444
Summer	Summon	Safe-mob	Summit	Sofa-foam
Summary	Safe-man	Exam-fib	Summate	Safe-fume
6445	6446	6447	6448	6449
Exam-file	Suffix	Suffice	Safe-mode	Safe-image
Safe-move	Suffuse	Ex-officio	Exam-mood	Sofa-mop

6450 Similar Sea-floor	6451 Semolina Same-view	6452 Exam-lab Safe-alibi	6453 Exfoliate Simulate	6454 Simulium Useful-aim
6455 Small Smell	6456 Smiles Similes	6457 Soymilk Exam-leak	6458 Safe-lead Sea-mould	6459 Semiology Same-league
6460 Same-size Safe-user	6461 Samson Samsun	6462 Smash Sea-fish	6463 Safest Safe-exit	6464 Sufism Safe-exam
6465 Safe-soul Eximiously	6466 Osmosis Sea-moss	6467 Safe-sky Safe-ski	6468 Same-side Safe-side	6469 Safe-usage Exam-expo
6470 Smoker Safe-car	6471 Safe-coin Sufi-icon	6472 Smooch So-much	6473 Smoke-out Safe-city	6474 Semi-coma Sumo-cameo
6475 Exam-clue Safe-cave	6476 Smokes Safe-keys	6477 Smack Smock	6478 Safe-kid Semacode	6479 Safe-keep Exam-copy
6480 Semidry Ex-major	6481 Safe-den Exam-dean	6482 Safe-job Samadhi	6483 Safe-data Exam-date	6484 Exam-demo Semi-deaf
6485 Ex-model Safe-dive	6486 Some-days Sea-foods	6487 Samoyedic Safe-joke	6488 Safe-dude Same-odd	6489 Smudge Smidge
6490 Simper Semipro	6491 Sampan Safe-gun	6492 Safe-pub Sumph	6493 Exempt Safe-gate	6494 Smegma Safe-game
6495 Simple Sample	6496 Symposia Sumps	6497 Safe-peace Exam-pace	6498 Exam-guide Sympodia	6499 Smoggy Semi-pupa
6500 Slurry Solar-year	6501 Severn Silurian	6502 Soul-orb Sailor-boy	6503 Severity Sievert	6504 Sale-room Solarium
6505 Several Severely	6506 Sailors Savers	6507 Sea-lark Solo-race	6508 Salaried Severed	6509 Slurp Savoury-pie
6510 Slower Souvenir	6511 Savanna Salinan	6512 Slow-boy Soul-web	6513 Silent Salient	6514 Selenium Save-info
6515 Slowly Xylenol	6516 Sea-lions Sea-laws	6517 Silence Slinky	6518 Island Solenoid	6519 Slang Sling
6520 Sole-heir Axle-bar	6521 Axial-bone Sieva-bean	6522 Slobby Axle-hub	6523 Sailboat Soul-beauty	6524 Sealyham Sail-home

6525 Soluble Saveable	6526 Slabs Slobs	6527 Sail-hook Slob-ice	6528 Soil-bed Soul-abode	6529 Soil-bug Sale-hype
6530 Solitary Isolator	6531 Solution Sultana	6532 Sloth Sleuth	6533 Slutty Saltate	6534 Save-time Sale-item
6535 Axolotl Xylitol	6536 Slots Salts	6537 Auxilytic Soil-quake	6538 Solitude Salted	6539 Isolated Sale-tag
6540 Sulfur Sail-free	6541 Salmon Solomon	6542 Slim-boy Slum-bay	6543 Soul-mate Islamite	6544 Seal-off Slummy
6545 Slimly Soulful	6546 Selfies Slums	6547 Islamic Save-face	6548 Soul-food Sulfide	6549 Slump Self-pay
6550 Silver Slavery	6551 Sallow Sullen	6552 Silly-boy Soul-vibe	6553 Salivate Sell-out	6554 Slalom Save-life
6555 Sale-value Seville	6556 Salvos Slaves	6557 Slavic Slovakia	6558 Sleeved Solved	6559 Salvage Sell-up
6560 Sole-size Soul-seer	6561 See-vision Salesian	6562 Slash Slush	6563 Soloist Soul-exit	6564 Salsify Sivaism
6565 Save-soul Sail-solo	6566 Useless Sialosis	6567 Soul-seek Soil-soak	6568 Soul-seed Seal-side	6569 Sale-expo Sly-spy
6570 Slicer Sulker	6571 Silicon Silicone	6572 Slouch Sea-loch	6573 Select Solicit	6574 Silicify Soul-coma
6575 Sleekly Sulkily	6576 Slices Salacious	6577 Slack Slock	6578 Silicide Sliced	6579 Slice-up Soil-cup
6580 Soldier Solder	6581 Slide-in Sale-doyen	6582 Save-job Slide-by	6583 Solidity Save-data	6584 Seldom Solidify
6585 Solidly Salad-oil	6586 Salads Solids	6587 Solid-oak Slide-key	6588 Salad-day Soledad	6589 Sledge Sludge
6590 Savagery Sleeper	6591 Slogan Slipway	6592 Slough Sleigh	6593 Slept Soul-gate	6594 Save-game Solo-game
6595 Sleepily Savagely	6596 Slugs Savages	6597 Soul-peace Sale-peak	6598 Sloped Soul-guide	6599 Sloppy Sialagogue

6600 Assurer So-sorry	6601 Assyrian Sea-saurian	6602 Sexy-robe Ass-rib	6603 Assert Assort	6604 Sea-surf Sexy-room
6605 Sex-role Issue-rule	6606 Assizes Sixers	6607 Easy-source Sex-rookie	6608 Assured Ass-ride	6609 Sea-surge Sex-urge
6610 Seasoner Sex-war	6611 Susanne Sea-snow	6612 Ass-whey Sexy-nob	6613 Assent Essonite	6614 Sexy-wife Sea-swim
6615 Seasonal Sea-snail	6616 Seasons Saxons	6617 Essence Sea-snake	6618 Seasoned Sea-sand	6619 Assaying Issuing
6620 Sea-shore Ass-hair	6621 Ass-bone Issue-ban	6622 Sexy-boob Sioux-baby	6623 Sex-bite Ox-shit	6624 Sexy-bum Sashimi
6625 Asshole Issuable	6626 Sex-abuse Sashes	6627 Essay-book Axis-hook	6628 Sexy-body Asshead	6629 Sex-bug Sea-ship
6630 Sister Sea-star	6631 Sustain Sexton	6632 Sixth Sea-squab	6633 Sextet Ossett	6634 System Sex-item
6635 Systole Sextile	6636 Assets Sex-toys	6637 Asset-key Ossetic	6638 Existed Sexted	6639 Sex-tape Easy-step
6640 Assumer Issue-free	6641 Sex-fun Issue-money	6642 Sexy-moob Sex-fib	6643 Six-feet Ass-meat	6644 Issue-memo Sex-mime
6645 Sesame-oil Sex-file	6646 Assumes Exosomes	6647 Seismic Ass-face	6648 Assumed Ossified	6649 Oasis-map Sexy-image
6650 Assailer Sea-sailor	6651 Sex-line Oasis-view	6652 Assay-lab Sexy-vibe	6653 Sexuality Assault	6654 Sex-life Ass-life
6655 Sexually Ex-slave	6656 Sexualise Sea-seals	6657 Sexy-look Sea-silk	6658 Sex-video Sea-slide	6659 Sea-slug Sexology
6660 Oasis-size Asses-ear	6661 Session Ass-axon	6662 Essex-boy Sex-shy	6663 Assist Sexist	6664 Sexism Sissify
6665 Sessile Assuasive	6666 Assess Sussex	6667 Oasis-soak Aussie-sky	6668 Sex-seed Oasis-side	6669 Sex-saga Axis-sag
6670 Sex-cry Sexy-car	6671 Sex-icon Siskin	6672 As-such Sea-scuba	6673 Ex-scout Associate	6674 Oasis-cameo Sex-acme

6675 Ossicle Seascale	6676 Issue-keys Easy-excuse	6677 Sea-sick Sex-kooky	6678 Issue-code Aussie-kid	6679 Seascape Issue-copy
6680 Sea-sider Sex-diary	6681 Seaside-way Sex-den	6682 Issue-job Sex-jibe	6683 Assiduity Issue-date	6684 Axis-jam Issue-dime
6685 Sex-idol Issue-daily	6686 Assiduous Soya-seeds	6687 Sexy-joke Sex-decoy	6688 Sexy-dude Issue-deed	6689 Sexed-up Oasis-edge
6690 Assuager Exospore	6691 Assign Yes-sign	6692 Isis-pub Ass-pooh	6693 Sexpot Ass-gut	6694 Sex-game Oasis-gym
6695 Sex-pili Oasis-pool	6696 Sausages Ex-spouse	6697 Sea-space Sexy-epic	6698 Sea-speed Sex-guide	6699 Sexy-gig Ass-poop
6700 Scurry Scorer	6701 Screen Screw	6702 Scribe Scrub	6703 Secret Skirt	6704 Scream Scarf
6705 Scurvy Securely	6706 Scores Scars	6707 Scarce Secrecy	6708 Sacred Scared	6709 Scourge Scrap
6710 Scenario Skewer	6711 Skinny Oscinine	6712 Ask-why Escanaba	6713 Scanty Scent	6714 Seek-wife Ask-info
6715 Scowl Sea-convoy	6716 Scans Scones	6717 Science Skunk	6718 Second Ascend	6719 Asking Seeking
6720 Eschar Easy-chair	6721 Eschew Ask-how	6722 Scabby Sea-chub	6723 Sachet Escheat	6724 Scheme Ischemia
6725 School Sociable	6726 Scabies Sikhs	6727 Skyhook Easy-choice	6728 Scooby-doo Sky-abode	6729 Seek-hope Axe-chop
6730 Scooter Sector	6731 Section Suction	6732 Scathe Scythe	6733 Scatty Scott	6734 Scotoma Scutum
6735 Exactly Executive	6736 Scouts Skates	6737 Ascetic Sciatica	6738 Excited Executed	6739 Sky-top Exact-pay
6740 Sycamore Seek-more	6741 Ski-fan Saucy-man	6742 Sky-fob Saucy-mob	6743 Seek-mate Sky-footy	6744 Scuff Scoff
6745 Sky-movie Sky-mail	6746 Eskimos Scams	6747 Eskimo-ice Saucy-face	6748 Sky-media Seek-food	6749 Scamp Skimpy

6750 Secular Skiver	6751 Skyline Scalene	6752 Skylab Social-bee	6753 Escalate Excavate	6754 Exclaim Sea-clam
6755 Skill Skull	6756 Scales Scolex	6757 Skulk Saclike	6758 Scold Scald	6759 Scalp Sociology
6760 Excuser Ski-size	6761 Excision Soak-sun	6762 Ski-shoe Easy-cash	6763 Sea-coast Ski-site	6764 Excuse-me Ski-exam
6765 Skysail Excusal	6766 Excess Excuses	6767 Sky-ski Soak-sauce	6768 Excused Excised	6769 Sky-spy Soak-soup
6770 Soccer Sucker	6771 Sicken Suck-in	6772 Sick-bay Ex-coach	6773 Socket Sacket	6774 Skookum Sikkim
6775 Sickle Suckle	6776 Socks Sacks	6777 Sea-cock Suck-ice	6778 Succeed Saccade	6779 Skycap Sick-pay
6780 Exceeder Skijor	6781 Skidway Ascidian	6782 Skidby Seek-job	6783 Sky-jet Excaudate	6784 Sky-dome Ski-demo
6785 Suicidal Sky-dive	6786 Scads Scuds	6787 Soak-juice Skoda-key	6788 Exceeded Seceded	6789 Ski-dog Soak-deep
6790 Scooper Escaper	6791 Saucepan Skip-away	6792 Scypha Skegby	6793 Except Saucepot	6794 Sky-game Skip-fee
6795 Scapula Ski-pole	6796 Scoops Skips	6797 Scoop-ice Seek-peace	6798 Escapade Sky-god	6799 Skippy Scoop-up
6800 Oxidizer Side-array	6801 Sojourn Seed-rain	6802 Saudi-Arabia Suede-robe	6803 Siderite Seed-root	6804 Exoderm Side-room
6805 Sidereal Side-rail	6806 Side-rise Seed-rose	6807 Sea-drake Seed-rice	6808 Oxidized Side-road	6809 Side-zip Seed-ripe
6810 Side-wire Ex-donor	6811 Oxide-anion Ease-down	6812 Side-web Saudi-nob	6813 Oxidant Exodontia	6814 Sad-info Saudi-name
6815 Seed-wool Side-wave	6816 Sideways Sudanese	6817 Side-nook Sad-week	6818 Sad-end Side-need	6819 Seeding Exuding
6820 Sidebar Sudbury	6821 Seed-bean Side-bone	6822 Side-boob Sad-baby	6823 Sad-bit Side-hit	6824 Seed-boom Sad-home

6825	6826	6827	6828	6829
See-double	Seed-box	Side-hook	Seedbed	Seed-bug
Side-hole	Axe-jobs	Used-book	Seed-bud	Side-hop
6830	6831	6832	6833	6834
Seedeater	Sedation	Side-tube	Sad-quote	Seedtime
Side-tear	Sedition	Sad-youth	Seed-quota	Seed-team
6835	6836	6837	6838	6839
Sedative	Seditious	Sad-tyke	Sedated	Seed-top
Exudative	Used-toys	Side-tic	Sad-tide	Side-tip
6840	6841	6842	6843	6844
Seed-maize	Sideman	Sad-mob	Sodomite	Sod-off
Sad-fury	Sodium-ion	Side-moob	Side-foot	Sad-memo
6845	6846	6847	6848	6849
Sad-fool	Sodomise	Sad-face	Sad-mood	Sad-image
Side-move	Seed-mix	Side-facia	Seed-feed	Sea-dump
6850	6851	6852	6853	6854
Sea-diver	Side-line	Seed-lobe	Sedulity	Soda-lime
Sad-liar	Side-view	Side-lab	Sodality	Sad-life
6855	6856	6857	6858	6859
Sea-devil	Sedulous	Side-look	Sidled	Seed-logo
Sea-jelly	Side-eaves	Sad-voice	Side-load	Side-leap
6860	6861	6862	6863	6864
Side-sore	Side-sway	Soda-ash	Sadist	Sadism
Oxidiser	Sad-sin	Sad-sob	Side-exit	Side-seam
6865	6866	6867	6868	6869
Sad-soul	Sad-ass	Sad-sky	Oxidised	Side-sag
Sod-soil	Side-issue	Seed-soak	Used-side	Sad-saga
6870	6871	6872	6873	6874
Seducer	Soda-can	Seed-cob	Seed-coat	Side-café
Sidecar	Seed-cone	Side-cab	Sad-act	Sad-cameo
6875	6876	6877	6878	6879
Side-cave	Seedcase	Seedcake	Seduced	Seed-cup
Sad-clue	Side-cause	Sea-duck	Sad-kid	Sidcup
6880	6881	6882	6883	6884
Sadder	Sudden	Sad-job	Side-jet	Sad-doom
Side-door	Sodden	Side-jab	Sad-duty	Side-demo
6885	6886	6887	6888	6889
Saddle	Sad-days	Sadducee	Sea-daddy	Ex-judge
Side-deal	Sad-ideas	Sad-joke	Sad-deed	Side-dig
6890	6891	6892	6893	6894
Side-gaze	Side-pain	Soda-pub	Side-gate	Sad-poem
Sad-prey	Sad-gene	Sad-gab	Ex-deputy	Side-game
6895	6896	6897	6898	6899
Side-pool	Sea-dogs	Sidepiece	Seedpod	Side-gap
Sad-goal	Sedges	Sad-epic	Side-pad	Sad-page

6900 Superior Sprayer	6901 Sprain Aspirin	6902 Superb Saprobe	6903 Spirit Sport	6904 Sperm Supreme
6905 Spiral Seagrave	6906 Sugars Spears	6907 Spark Spork	6908 Spread Expired	6909 Superego Sprig
6910 Spyware Signer	6911 Spawn Spinney	6912 Spy-web Spin-boy	6913 Spent Signet	6914 Signify Saponify
6915 Signal Spinal	6916 Spans Spins	6917 Spank Spunk	6918 Expand Expend	6919 Sponge Expunge
6920 Sphere Sigher	6921 Syphon Sage-hen	6922 Sea-phobia Spy-hub	6923 Sight Sought	6924 Spy-home Usage-boom
6925 Spyhole Expiable	6926 Asphyxia Sighs	6927 Spy-hook Soap-book	6928 Saphead Xiphoid	6929 Soap-hype Spy-bag
6930 Spitz Expiatory	6931 Expiation Spot-on	6932 Spathe Ox-pith	6933 Spotty Expatiate	6934 Septum Sputum
6935 Spatial Spatula	6936 Spots Spouts	6937 Septic Exegetic	6938 Expiated Spouted	6939 Spit-up Spy-tape
6940 Spy-fear Spoofer	6941 Spumoni Soupfin	6942 Spy-fib Siege-mob	6943 Isogamete Soap-mat	6944 Spiff Soap-foam
6945 Spy-movie Soup-meal	6946 Spoofs Exogamous	6947 Exogamic Sage-face	6948 Sigmoid Spoofed	6949 Spy-image Soap-mop
6950 Explore Spoiler	6951 Spleen Explain	6952 Soap-lab Spy-vibe	6953 Exploit Split	6954 Sage-leaf Spy-life
6955 Spell Seagull	6956 Spoils Expulse	6957 Splice Ex-police	6958 Explode Spoiled	6959 Spoilage Splooge
6960 Exposure Espouser	6961 Sepsin Sipson	6962 Sea-gush Axe-gash	6963 Exposit See-past	6964 Spasm Spy-safe
6965 Spousal Exposal	6966 Sepsis Spouses	6967 Sip-sauce Spa-soak	6968 Exposed Espoused	6969 Sip-soup Spy-siege
6970 Speaker Spacer	6971 Spoken Soupcon	6972 Speech Sea-peach	6973 Expect Sagacity	6974 Specify Spycam

6975	6976	6977	6978	6979
Special	Spacious	Speck	Spaced	Space-age
Spicule	Spices	Spick	Spiced	Speak-up
6980	6981	6982	6983	6984
Spider	Speedway	Spy-job	Expedite	Axiopodium
Speeder	Sogdian	Say-goodbye	Sapidity	Siege-dam
6985	6986	6987	6988	6989
Speedily	Spades	Sip-juice	Spaded	Speed-up
Spy-jail	Spuds	Spy-decoy	Speeded	Spy-dog
6990	6991	6992	6993	6994
Supper	Sea-pigeon	Spy-pub	Spigot	Siege-game
Sipper	Soup-pan	Soupy-gooby	Soup-pot	Spy-gym
6995	6996	6997	6998	6999
Supple	Suppose	Spy-epic	Sapped	Sea-poppy
Supply	Sea-pigs	Isagogic	Sipped	Spuggy

ALPHA BETA 7000 – 7999

7000	7001	7002	7003	7004
Carrier	Carrion	Crazy-boy	Carrot	Career-aim
Currier	Czarina	Car-rob	Car-route	Car-roof
7005	7006	7007	7008	7009
Carrel	Carers	Car-race	Corrode	Carriage
Crazily	Couriers	Career-key	Carried	Car-rage
7010	7011	7012	7013	7014
Corner	Crown	Carnauba	Cornet	Acronym
Coroner	Cranny	Carnaby	Coronate	Cranium
7015	7016	7017	7018	7019
Crawl	Cranes	Cranky	Crowd	Carnage
Cranial	Crows	Cornice	Coronado	Caring
7020	7021	7022	7023	7024
Car-hire	Carbon	Crabby	Acrobat	Care-home
Care-bear	Carbine	Cry-baby	Acerbity	Car-boom
7025	7026	7027	7028	7029
Curable	Crabs	Acerbic	Carbide	Car-beep
Karbala	Cribs	Core-book	Carabid	Cure-hope
7030	7031	7032	7033	7034
Creator	Carton	Certhia	Curette	Certify
Crater	Cartoon	Curitiba	Critique	Care-team
7035	7036	7037	7038	7039
Creative	Cortex	Critic	Carotid	Cartage
Curtail	Crates	Eukaryotic	Created	Cortege
7040	7041	7042	7043	7044
Carefree	Acrimony	Crumb	Craft	Crummy
Carfare	Ceremony	Corymb	Cremate	Car-fume
7045	7046	7047	7048	7049
Careful	Crimes	Ceramic	Creamed	Cramp
Caramel	Kermis	Karmic	Ceramide	Crimp
7050	7051	7052	7053	7054
Carver	Caravan	Coral-bay	Cruelty	Ceruleum
Craver	Caroline	Cruel-boy	Cravat	Cure-lame
7055	7056	7057	7058	7059
Krill	Cervix	Crevice	Carload	Acarology
Corolla	Curves	Acrylic	Curved	Karyology
7060	7061	7062	7063	7064
Cruiser	Kerosene	Crash	Crust	Acrosome
Cursor	Coarsen	Crush	Crest	Karyosome
7065	7066	7067	7068	7069
Carousel	Across	Corsica	Crusade	Crisp
Curiously	Crisis	Kursk	Cursed	Corsage
7070	7071	7072	7073	7074
Croaker	Kraken	Crouch	Circuit	Crucify
Crookery	Coercion	Creche	Cruciate	Acrocomia

7075	7076	7077	7078	7079
Circle	Circus	Crack	Crooked	Cork-up
Crucial	Creeks	Crock	Corked	Corkage
7080	7081	7082	7083	7084
Carder	Cordon	Core-job	Credit	Car-jam
Corduroy	Croydon	Cordoba	Crudity	Card-fee
7085	7086	7087	7088	7089
Cordial	Cards	Cardiac	Carded	Cordage
Cradle	Cords	Card-key	Corded	Key-ridge
7090	7091	7092	7093	7094
Creeper	Cryogen	Cargo-bay	Carpet	Kerygma
Croupier	Kerogen	Coryphée	Crypt	Karyogamy
7095	7096	7097	7098	7099
Carpal	Corpse	Carapace	Croupade	Crappy
Carpel	Creeps	Crags	Car-guide	Craggy
7100	7101	7102	7103	7104
Knorr	Kanazawa	Cow-rib	Kunzite	Coenzyme
Cinerary	Canarian	Acne-rub	Co-write	Knee-room
7105	7106	7107	7108	7109
Knurl	Cowries	Cenozoic	Canard	Cow-rage
Econazole	Canorous	Knork	Coward	Keen-urge
7110	7111	7112	7113	7114
Cannery	Cannon	Cow-whey	Cannot	Coin-name
Canonry	Known	Knee-nub	Connote	Con-info
7115	7116	7117	7118	7119
Cannula	Canonise	Cyan-ink	Canned	Caning
Kennel	Conenose	Canonic	Conned	Coining
7120	7121	7122	7123	7124
Can-beer	Cowbane	Knobby	Cenobite	Cenobium
Con-brio	Knee-bone	Cow-baby	Ocean-heat	Cow-hoof
7125	7126	7127	7128	7129
Kneehole	Cowboys	Con-book	Cowhide	Cow-bug
Coinable	Knobs	Kiwi-beak	Ocean-bed	Coin-bag
7130	7131	7132	7133	7134
Centre	Canteen	Cynthia	Knotty	Aconitum
Counter	Contain	Canthi	Cantata	Kiwi-team
7135	7136	7137	7138	7139
Centile	Cents	Kinetic	Counted	Knee-top
Cantle	Knots	Cyanotic	Ocean-tide	Cone-tip
7140	7141	7142	7143	7144
Confer	Confine	Confab	Cow-foot	Con-mafia
Conifer	Conman	Coin-fob	Confute	Icon-fame
7145	7146	7147	7148	7149
Cow-meal	Confuse	Economic	Confide	Can-mop
Keen-move	Cinemas	Acne-face	Knifed	Ocean-map

7150 Conveyor Knavery	7151 Convene Ocean-line	7152 Con-alibi Knee-lobe	7153 Knelt Oak-wilt	7154 Ocean-life Coywolf
7155 Knoll Knell	7156 Convex Knives	7157 Convoke Conelike	7158 Conveyed Can-lid	7159 Iconology Oceanology
7160 Censor Censure	7161 Kansan Kinesin	7162 Cowish Kenosha	7163 Canoeist Key-West	7164 Consume Iconism
7165 Console Counsel	7166 Census Kinesis	7167 Kawasaki Ocean-soak	7168 Cyanosed Oceanside	7169 Knees-up Can-soup
7170 Cancer Conker	7171 Canakin Konkani	7172 Cinch Concha	7173 Conceit Iconicity	7174 Cow-coma Icon-cameo
7175 Cancel Council	7176 Concise Conics	7177 Knock Knack	7178 Coincide Concede	7179 Knee-cap Cone-cup
7180 Cinder Candour	7181 Canadian Condone	7182 Kind-boy Acne-jab	7183 Conduit Candiot	7184 Condom Candify
7185 Candle Kindle	7186 Cyanides Canids	7187 Conduce Can-juice	7188 Candid Candida	7189 Knee-deep Ocean edge
7190 Kangaroo Conger	7191 Cyanogen Knee-pain	7192 Cow-pooh Canopy-bay	7193 Cow-gate Coin-pot	7194 Cenogamy Kung-Fu
7195 Congeal Kingly	7196 Cowpox Kings	7197 Cowpoke Coin-piece	7198 Kneepad Canopied	7199 Knaggy Kiwi-egg
7200 Cherry Charry	7201 Churn Chorion	7202 Cherub Choirboy	7203 Chart Charity	7204 Charm Chrome
7205 Charley Choral	7206 Chorus Cheers	7207 Cherokee Choric	7208 Charade Keyboard	7209 Charge Iceberg
7210 Chewer Kohinoor	7211 Cheyenne Chinny	7212 Cobweb Cabin-boy	7213 Cabinet Chant	7214 Echo-name Archenemy
7215 Choanal Chain-oil	7216 Chains Chinese	7217 Chance Chunk	7218 Chained Chewed	7219 Change Aching
7220 Cobber Cab-hire	7221 Achy-bone Cube-bin	7222 Chubby Chihuahua	7223 Cohabit Cohobate	7224 Cobham Echo-boom

7225 Cobble Kibble	7226 Kebabs Cabbies	7227 Chibouk Echo-book	7228 Chabad Cash-aid	7229 Cabbage Chub-up
7230 Cheater Chequer	7231 Chitin Chutney	7232 Cheetah Ice-bath	7233 Chatty Chitty	7234 Each-time Cheque-fee
7235 Cubital Chital	7236 Cheats Cubits	7237 Chaotic Cubatic	7238 Cheated Chytide	7239 Archetype Chat-up
7240 Chimer Chimera	7241 Chimney Cabman	7242 Cabomba Chimb	7243 Achy-feet Cub-mate	7244 Chaff Chummy
7245 Chiefly Chamal	7246 Chimes Chums	7247 Cube-face Cab-make	7248 Chimed Chafed	7249 Champ Chump
7250 Achiever Cholera	7251 Echelon Chilean	7252 Kiblah Cable-buoy	7253 Chalet Cobalt	7254 Khalifa Cob-loaf
7255 Chill Chilli	7256 Chelsea Keyholes	7257 Chalk Chalice	7258 Child Achieved	7259 Chelp Chaology
7260 Chaser Chooser	7261 Chosen Cohesion	7262 Kibosh Cohosh	7263 Chaste Chest	7264 Chasm Chiasma
7265 Chisel Cohesive	7266 Chess Chasse	7267 Chase-cue Choice-key	7268 Chased Each-side	7269 Chase-up Cube-soap
7270 Choker Chakra	7271 Chicane Chicano	7272 Chichi Cheeky-boy	7273 Kobe-city Cub-cot	7274 Cub-coma Kobe-café
7275 Cubicle Cheekily	7276 Cheeks Choices	7277 Check Chick	7278 Cheeked Choked	7279 Chicago Choke-up
7280 Chider Chador	7281 Chadian Echidna	7282 Cub-jab Achy-job	7283 Cub-diet Cab-duty	7284 Cab-jam Echo-dome
7285 Cuboidal Caboodle	7286 Echo-ideas Achy-days	7287 Archduke Chadic	7288 Kabaddi Key-buddy	7289 Cube-edge Ache-dope
7290 Cub-prey Cab-gear	7291 Cheapen Chip-away	7292 Chough Cheap-buy	7293 Chagatai Chapati	7294 Chagoma Cheap-aim
7295 Chapel Cheaply	7296 Chaps Chips	7297 Each-piece Echo-peak	7298 Cheeped Cheap-day	7299 Chippy Choppy

7300 Caterer Cauterize	7301 Citizen Citroen	7302 Cat-rib Cute-robe	7303 Citrate Cut-rate	7304 Coat-room Key-term
7305 Actuarial Auctorial	7306 Actors Citrus	7307 Citric Icteric	7308 Acquired Catered	7309 Kite-rope Cat-rage
7310 Cautionary Auctioneer	7311 Act-now Eco-town	7312 City-web Action-boy	7313 Acquaint Octant	7314 Actinium Ketonemia
7315 Ice-towel Cut-nail	7316 Actions Auctions	7317 Actinic Cationic	7318 Cautioned Actioned	7319 Catnap Acting
7320 October Cythera	7321 Cat-bone Ice-thin	7322 Cute-baby City-hub	7323 Catboat Acute-bout	7324 Cotham Ecthyma
7325 Actable Citable	7326 Akathisia Cathouse	7327 Coat-hook Kite-beak	7328 Cathead Cathode	7329 Cat-bug Cut-hoop
7330 Cutter Cattery	7331 Cotton Kitten	7332 Cut-tube Cat-tab	7333 Coquette City-tout	7334 Cut-time City-team
7335 Cattle Kettle	7336 Acetates Cut-ties	7337 Ketotic Cute-tyke	7338 Actuated Acetated	7339 Cottage Cut-tape
7340 Act-fair City-mayor	7341 Catamenia Ketamine	7342 City-mob Coat-fob	7343 Catamite Cat-foot	7344 Cut-off City-mafia
7345 Cat-flu City-mail	7346 Cut-fees City-fox	7347 Cute-face Act-meek	7348 Citified Cut-food	7349 City-map Cute-image
7350 Cutlery Cutover	7351 Acetylene Catalonia	7352 Cat-lab Active-boy	7353 Activity Actuality	7354 City-life Act-aloof
7355 Actively Actually	7356 Octaves Actualise	7357 Catlike Acetylic	7358 Cut-lead Cute-lady	7359 Catalogue Cytology
7360 Coat-size Acute-sore	7361 Cytosine Act-soon	7362 Katyusha Act-shy	7363 Cat-suit Key-test	7364 Coat-seam Act-safe
7365 Cautiously Cytosol	7366 Ketosis Cytosis	7367 Acquiesce Ecotoxic	7368 Cot-side Cut-aside	7369 Catsup City-siege
7370 Acute-care Cat-cry	7371 Catkin Cetacean	7372 Catch Ketch	7373 Kit-Kat Cut-coat	7374 City-café Cat-coma

7375￼Cuticle￼Act-cool	7376￼Cetaceous￼Cut-keys	7377￼Cut-cake￼Oak-tick	7378￼Keto-acid￼City-kid	7379￼Kit-copy￼Kite-cage
7380￼Cut-dry￼Cat-diary	7381￼Cat-jaw￼Coyote-den	7382￼City-job￼Cat-jab	7383￼Cat-diet￼Cite-data	7384￼Acute-edema￼Act-deaf
7385￼Citadel￼Cut-deal	7386￼City-aides￼Act-ideas	7387￼Cute-joke￼City-duke	7388￼Act-odd￼Cute-dude	7389￼Cut-edge￼Act-dopey
7390￼Category￼Kite-prey	7391￼Octagon￼Acute-pain	7392￼City-pub￼Cat-pooh	7393￼Catgut￼City-gate	7394￼City-game￼Cat-gym
7395￼Act-play￼City-gala	7396￼Octopus￼Key-tags	7397￼Ectopic￼Cut-piece	7398￼City-guide￼Act-god	7399￼Kite-egg￼Cut-gap
7400￼Camorra￼Ice-freeze	7401￼Cameroon￼Cameron	7402￼Cameo-robe￼Camera-boy	7403￼Key-fruit￼Camerate	7404￼Aciform￼Key-frame
7405￼Cameral￼Cameo-role	7406￼Cameras￼Comoros	7407￼Ecofreak￼Key-force	7408￼Comrade￼Come-ready	7409￼Camargue￼Café-rage
7410￼Café-noir￼Come-near	7411￼Caymanian￼Come-now	7412￼Cayman-bay￼Café-web	7413￼Cement￼Acuminate	7414￼Cameo-name￼Café-info
7415￼Kimnel￼Cameo-wave	7416￼Acuminous￼Café-noise	7417￼Ecumenic￼Come-once	7418￼Camwood￼Key-find	7419￼Coming￼Coaming
7420￼Cambria￼Cumbria	7421￼Combine￼Ukambin	7422￼Café-hub￼Cameo-babe	7423￼Combat￼Comb-out	7424￼Cambium￼Come-home
7425￼Cymbal￼Cembalo	7426￼Key-fobs￼Camboose	7427￼Cameo-book￼Café-bookie	7428￼Combed￼Cambodia	7429￼Café-bug￼Cameo-hype
7430￼Cafeteria￼Cemetery	7431￼Kaftan￼Cameo-tune	7432￼Cometh￼Comet-ahoy	7433￼Kumquat￼Cafetite	7434￼Cymatium￼Cameo-time
7435￼Comitial￼Cafe-tale	7436￼Comatose￼Comets	7437￼Cymatic￼Acmatic	7438￼Come-today￼Café-tide	7439￼Come-top￼Cameo-tape
7440￼Coffer￼Coiffure	7441￼Common￼Caffeine	7442￼Café-mob￼Coma-fib	7443￼Commit￼Comfit	7444￼Come-off￼Cameo-fame
7445￼Coffle￼Camomile	7446￼Commas￼Cuffs	7447￼Key-office￼Cameo-face	7448￼Commode￼Cuffed	7449￼Acme-image￼Café-mug

7450 Cameleer Come-over	7451 Eco-flow Come-low	7452 Comely-boy Acme-vibe	7453 Camelot Cumulate	7454 Coma-life Eco-flame
7455 Icefall Come-alive	7456 Camels Cumulus	7457 Ice-milk Ice-flake	7458 Oakfield Camelid	7459 Café-logo Coif-vogue
7460 Ice-mixer Key-measure	7461 Come-soon Co-fusion	7462 Ice-fish Cameo-shy	7463 Acmeist Café-seat	7464 Acmeism Come-safe
7465 Camisole Coma-soul	7466 Camass Ice-mass	7467 Key-mask Oak-mosaic	7468 Come-aside Camisade	7469 Coma-saga Café-siege
7470 Kamikaze Comicry	7471 Cameo-coin Coom-can	7472 Comic-boy Café-echo	7473 Key-fact Cameo-act	7474 Acme-café Kaymakam
7475 Comical Coma-clue	7476 Comics Cimices	7477 Café-cake Cameo-kooky	7478 Comic-joy Acme-kid	7479 Coif-cap Café-cup
7480 Café-door Cameo-diary	7481 Comedian Camden	7482 Café-job Comedy-boy	7483 Cameo-date Café-duty	7484 Coma-doom Cameo-demo
7485 Key-module Kamadeva	7486 Comedies Acme-days	7487 Comedic Coom-decay	7488 Comedy-day Acme-judo	7489 Coma-dope Café-jug
7490 Camper Compare	7491 Company Campion	7492 Camp-boy Café-pub	7493 Compete Compute	7494 Coma-opium Café-game
7495 Compel Compile	7496 Campus Compose	7497 Coma-peace Cameo-epic	7498 Camped Come-good	7499 Cameo-page Café-egg
7500 Clearer Coverer	7501 Cavern Clarion	7502 Colour-hue Cover-boy	7503 Covert Clarity	7504 Clarify Cave-roof
7505 Clearly Colza-oil	7506 Coolers Colours	7507 Clerk Cleric	7508 Cleared Coloured	7509 Clergy Coverage
7510 Cleaner Culinary	7511 Clown Oak-Lawn	7512 Clean-boy Cool-whey	7513 Client Coolant	7514 Cool-name Cave-waif
7515 Colonel Colonial	7516 Claws Cleanse	7517 Clinic Clunky	7518 Clawed Cleaned	7519 Ceiling Clingy
7520 Calibre Kalahari	7521 Koala-bone Coalbin	7522 Clubby Cool-hob	7523 Celibate Kilobyte	7524 Coloboma Oklahoma

7525	7526	7527	7528	7529
Coalhole	Clubs	Celibacy	Cool-head	Clay-bog
Keelhaul	Celebs	Clue-book	Coal-bed	Coal-heap
7530	7531	7532	7533	7534
Culture	Coalition	Cloth	Clotty	Cool-time
Coulter	Cavatina	Calathea	Clatty	Colotomy
7535	7536	7537	7538	7539
Koala-tail	Cavities	Celtic	Coveted	Clay-top
Clay-tool	Clots	Cultic	Kilted	Clue-tip
7540	7541	7542	7543	7544
Calmer	Column	Climb	Calamity	Cliff
Clamour	Caveman	Colombia	Climate	Clammy
7545	7546	7547	7548	7549
Calmly	Climax	Clayface	Calmed	Clamp
Coal-fuel	Clumsy	Coalface	Claimed	Clump
7550	7551	7552	7553	7554
Caller	Civilian	Call-boy	Collate	Cave-life
Killer	Callow	Cool-vibe	Civility	Ice-volume
7555	7556	7557	7558	7559
Civilly	Calls	Claylike	Collide	College
Coevolve	Cells	Cool-look	Collude	Collage
7560	7561	7562	7563	7564
Closure	Claxon	Clash	Closet	Coliseum
Closer	Keelson	Calash	Oculist	Civism
7565	7566	7567	7568	7569
Closely	Class	Coalesce	Closed	Clasp
Clausal	Keyless	Cool-sky	Close-aide	Close-up
7570	7571	7572	7573	7574
Caulker	Calcine	Cliché	Calcite	Calcify
Calcar	Acalycine	Cloche	Co-locate	Calcium
7575	7576	7577	7578	7579
Calculi	Civics	Clock	Cloaked	Koala-cage
Acalculia	Calyces	Click	Caulked	Cool-cap
7580	7581	7582	7583	7584
Colder	Caledonia	Ceilidh	Cold-tea	Caladium
Co-leader	Euclidian	Cold-bay	Club-tie	Coal-dome
7585	7586	7587	7588	7589
Coldly	Clouds	Cold-ice	Clouded	Kludge
Cloudily	Colds	Cave-joke	Cloddy	Coiled-up
7590	7591	7592	7593	7594
Calgary	Cologne	Caliph	Coalpit	Cave-game
Kilgore	Clip-on	Clough	Colgate	Cool-gym
7595	7596	7597	7598	7599
Cool-pool	Clips	Ecologic	Clue-guide	Cloggy
Clypeal	Eclipse	Cool-pace	Kola-pod	Claggy

7600 Caesar-era Case-array	7601 Caesarean Casern	7602 Yaks-rib Cosy-robe	7603 Cosurety Coexert	7604 Cosy-room Ice-surf
7605 Case-rule Caesural	7606 Kaisers Key-series	7607 Key-source Cox-race	7608 Cosy-ride Case-ready	7609 Cause-rage Ice-surge
7610 Cousinry Cause-war	7611 Case-win Casino-way	7612 Coy-snob Casino-bay	7613 Case-note Caseinate	7614 Case-name Icy-swim
7615 Casanova Cousinly	7616 Cousins Casinos	7617 Ice-snake Cosy-nook	7618 Case-need Oaks-wood	7619 Casing Coaxing
7620 Cashier Kosher	7621 Cashew Cushion	7622 Kasbah Cash-boy	7623 Cash-out Cushite	7624 Cash-fee Cosy-home
7625 Causable Cushily	7626 Cosy-house Case-bias	7627 Casebook Akashic	7628 Cashed Cox-head	7629 Key-shop Cash-pay
7630 Castor Coaster	7631 Causation Castaway	7632 Coast-bay Case-tube	7633 Cast-out Key-state	7634 Costume Custom
7635 Castle Costly	7636 Costs Coasts	7637 Acoustic Caustic	7638 Custody Costed	7639 Key-stage Cost-up
7640 Ceasefire Cause-fear	7641 Cisman Casio-fan	7642 Coax-mob Casio-fob	7643 Casemate Kismet	7644 Case-memo Coax-mum
7645 Case-file Caseful	7646 Cosmos Case-mix	7647 Cosmic Casio-make	7648 Cosmid Coax-media	7649 Cosy-image Coax-imp
7650 Coax-lure Case-over	7651 Case-law Cox-lane	7652 Case-alibi Ice-slab	7653 Casualty Key-slot	7654 Oak-xylem Cosy-limo
7655 Casually Causally	7656 Casuals Key-sales	7657 Caselike Cosy-look	7658 Case-load Coax-lead	7659 Causalgia Icy-slope
7660 Kisser Case-size	7661 Cession Caisson	7662 Cosy-shoe Kissy-boy	7663 Coexist Cosset	7664 Case-seam Case-exam
7665 Cassava Cassia-oil	7666 Kisses Cassius	7667 Cossic Kiss-ace	7668 Kissed Cessed	7669 Cassiopeia Kiss-up
7670 Cascara Ice-scour	7671 Casio-icon Case-cone	7672 Casco-bay Cosy-cab	7673 Casket Ice-skate	7674 Key scam Ice-skim

7675	7676	7677	7678	7679
Cask-ale	Casks	Kiosk-key	Cascade	Icescape
Key-scale	Kiosks	Eco-sack	Ice-skid	Ice-scoop
7680	7681	7682	7683	7684
Case-diary	Yaks-jaw	Cosy-job	Case-date	Aces-demo
Case-jury	Case-dean	Case-dub	Cosy-duty	Case-doom
7685	7686	7687	7688	7689
Coax-daily	Oak-seeds	Coax-decoy	Coax-dad	Case-dig
Case-delay	Key-sides	Case-decay	Cosy-dude	Coax-dope
7690	7691	7692	7693	7694
Casper	Caspian	Coy-sigh	Cuspate	Aces-game
Ice-spray	Co-sign	Ecosophy	Cosy-pet	Yaks-gum
7695	7696	7697	7698	7699
Cosplay	Cusps	Ice-spike	Cusped	Case-page
Cuspal	Co-expose	Key-space	Ice-spade	Ice-seepage
7700	7701	7702	7703	7704
Accruer	Cicerone	Cookery-bay	Accurate	Ice-cream
Coke-zero	Eccrine	Oak-crib	Accrete	Cook-ram
7705	7706	7707	7708	7709
Accrual	Cookers	Accuracy	Accord	Cecropia
Cook-role	Kayakers	Cook-rice	Keycard	Ice-crag
7710	7711	7712	7713	7714
Cookware	Ciconine	Key-knob	Account	Oak-knife
Cocoonery	Cake-wine	Ace-cowboy	Cocoanut	Key-economy
7715	7716	7717	7718	7719
Ice-canal	Cocainise	Cook-once	Acacia-wood	Cooking
Ace-convoy	Yack-noise	Cake-week	Kakinada	Kayaking
7720	7721	7722	7723	7724
Co-chair	Keychain	Okeechobee	Cachet	Cook-beef
Coacher	Cocoa-bean	Coach-bay	Cake-bite	Cookie-boom
7725	7726	7727	7728	7729
Cochlea	Coaches	Cookbook	Coached	Cookie-bag
Cakehole	Cachexia	Cake-bake	Cokehead	Coach-up
7730	7731	7732	7733	7734
Accoutre	Coaction	Cook-taboo	Cocotte	Cook-time
Cocoa-tree	Cake-tin	Kooky-youth	Cake-quota	Kayak-team
7735	7736	7737	7738	7739
Coactive	Cactus	Cactaceae	Ice-coated	Cooktop
CCTV	Key-cities	Coca-toke	Kooky-tad	Coke-tap
7740	7741	7742	7743	7744
Cucumaria	Kakemono	Yacky-mob	Cook-meat	Ice-coffee
Cake-fair	Kooky-fan	Kooky-fib	Cake-fete	Cook-off
7745	7746	7747	7748	7749
Cake-meal	Cake-mix	Cake-make	Cook-food	Key-camp
Cacomelia	Coca-fix	Cookie-face	Cookmaid	Kooky-image

7750 Acicular Ice-cooler	7751 Cyclone Cycleway	7752 Key-club Kooky-vibe	7753 Occult Aciculate	7754 Acclaim Coca-leaf
7755 Kay-cello Kooky-love	7756 Icicles Ecclesia	7757 Cyclic Cakelike	7758 Accolade Occlude	7759 Cacology Cyclopia
7760 Accuser Cake-size	7761 Occasion Caucasian	7762 Cicisbeo Kookish	7763 Accost Cook-set	7764 Cacosmia Cook-safe
7765 Accusal Cake-sale	7766 Access Caucasus	7767 Oak-kiosk Cook-sauce	7768 Accused Caucasoid	7769 Cook-soup Kooky-spy
7770 Cocker Kicker	7771 Cockney Coke-can	7772 Cuckoo-bee Kick-boy	7773 Cockatoo Kick-out	7774 Cake-café Kick-foe
7775 Cackle Cockle	7776 Kicks Cocks	7777 Key-kick Kooky-cook	7778 Cockade Kicked	7779 Cock-up Kick-up
7780 Cookie-jar Ice-cider	7781 Akkadian Cycadean	7782 Kooky-jab Yucky-job	7783 Cake-diet Cook-duty	7784 Cocoa-dome Cook-demo
7785 Cook-daily Kooky-jail	7786 Cycads Cicadas	7787 Cocoa-juice Kooky-duke	7788 Acceded Cooked-idea	7789 Coca-dope Kooky-edge
7790 Occupier Key-copier	7791 Cake-pan Kakogawa	7792 Cocopah Cookie-pub	7793 Accept Occiput	7794 Acacia-gum Kooky-opium
7795 Cook-gala Key-couple	7796 Cacogeusia Cecopexy	7797 Cake-piece Kooky-epic	7798 Occupied Cocoa-pod	7799 Cocoa-pop Cook-egg
7800 Co-juror Code-zero	7801 Acid-rain Ecuadorian	7802 Ice-drib Cadiz-bay	7803 Kid-rate Acid-rot	7804 Kid-room Acid-rum
7805 Eco-drive Kid-zeal	7806 Ciders Cedars	7807 Aciduric Cedric	7808 Code-red Cody-road	7809 Ice-drop Kid-rage
7810 Kid-wear Code-wire	7811 Acid-wine Codeinone	7812 Kid-nab Acid-whey	7813 Cadent Code-unit	7814 Codename Kid-wife
7815 Kid-yowl Key-denial	7816 Kidneys Codons	7817 Cadence Ice-dance	7818 Cudweed Kid-need	7819 Kidnap Coding
7820 Cadbury Cudbear	7821 Kid-ban Kudu-bone	7822 Cade-baby Kid-bib	7823 Kid-bite Cod-bait	7824 Kudu-hoof Kid-home

7825	7826	7827	7828	7829
Codable	Codebase	Code-book	Codhead	Kid-hug
Acid-bile	Key-jobs	Kid-bike	Kidhood	Code-bug
7830	7831	7832	7833	7834
Co-editor	Code-tone	Cadet-boy	Codetta	Code-time
Kid-quiz	Key-audition	Kid-taboo	Kid-quota	Kid-tame
7835	7836	7837	7838	7839
Key-detail	Cadets	Acidotic	Cadet day	Code-tag
Kid-tale	Kid-toys	Kid-tyke	Caudated	Acid-tap
7840	7841	7842	7843	7844
Acidifier	Codomain	Code-fob	Code-feat	Cadmium
Codifier	Kidman	Kid-moob	Kid-foot	Acid-fume
7845	7846	7847	7848	7849
Kid-movie	Academies	Academic	Codified	Code-map
Code-file	Cadmus	Kid-face	Acidified	Ace-jump
7850	7851	7852	7853	7854
Cadaver	Cod-loin	Acid-lab	Kidult	Kid-life
Cajolery	Cod-line	Kid-alibi	Acidulate	Code-leaf
7855	7856	7857	7858	7859
Caudally	Acidulous	Key-advice	Cajoled	Kidology
Ice-jelly	Kid-visa	Acid-leak	Kid-video	Code-log
7860	7861	7862	7863	7864
Kid-size	Kid-son	Kid-shoe	Oak-joist	Kid-safe
Code-user	Acid-sin	Acid-ash	Codist	Code-safe
7865	7866	7867	7868	7869
Acid-soil	Acidosis	Oak-desk	Acid-seed	Cod-soup
Cod-sale	Ecdysis	Cod-sauce	Cod-side	Code-usage
7870	7871	7872	7873	7874
Kid-care	Caducean	Kid-echo	Co-educate	Acid-coma
Caducary	Acid-can	Ice-douche	Caducity	Kid-cameo
7875	7876	7877	7878	7879
Codicil	Caduceus	Iced-coke	Keyed-kid	Code-copy
Code-clue	Caudices	Iced-cake	Cued-code	Acid-cup
7880	7881	7882	7883	7884
Codder	Caddoan	Code-job	Code-data	Code-jam
Kadder	Caddow	Kid-jab	Kid-duty	Acid-doom
7885	7886	7887	7888	7889
Cuddle	Caddies	Acid-juice	Kidded	Acid-dip
Coddle	Caddis	Caddice	Caddied	Ace-judge
7890	7891	7892	7893	7894
Codger	Code-gene	Acid-PH	Cajeput	Code-game
Cadger	Kid-gun	Kid-gooby	Kid-goat	Acid-gum
7895	7896	7897	7898	7899
Cudgel	Coydogs	Codpiece	Code-guide	Codepage
Kid-play	Ice-jugs	Kid-pace	Kedged	Kid-gag

7900 Caperer Coprozoa	7901 Caprine Cyprian	7902 Ice-probe Cop-rob	7903 Cooperate Keyport	7904 Coprime Copy-room
7905 Capriole Key-groove	7906 Keepers Cigars	7907 Caprice Cup-race	7908 Capered Keep-ready	7909 Cooperage Key-grip
7910 Cage-wire Keep-near	7911 Cup-win Keep-new	7912 Cop-web Cop-nab	7913 Cogent Key-point	7914 Copy-name Keep-wife
7915 Cap-nail Cape-wool	7916 Coupons Cognise	7917 Cogency Keep-awake	7918 Kop-end Keep-need	7919 Keeping Coping
7920 Cypher Cougher	7921 Copy-ban Cage-hen	7922 Ecophobia Cop-baby	7923 Caught Cough-out	7924 Keep-home Okapi-hoof
7925 Capable Keepable	7926 Coughs Cepheus	7927 Copybook Cup-beak	7928 Coughed Keep-ahead	7929 Cough-up Keep-hope
7930 Capture Copter	7931 Captain Caption	7932 Keep-oath Keep-tab	7933 Capitate Cogitate	7934 Keep-time Cup-team
7935 Capital Captive	7936 Captious Cup-ties	7937 Coptic Ecopoetic	7938 Co-opted Cup-tied	7939 Cop-tip Cup-top
7940 Keep-far Cop-fear	7941 Keep-fine Cope-man	7942 Coup-mob Cup-fob	7943 Keepmoat Keep-mute	7944 Keep-off Cap-off
7945 Capful Cupful	7946 Key-games Keep-aims	7947 Keep-face Cage-mice	7948 Copy-mode Keep-food	7949 Keep-image Cape-map
7950 Copular Coupler	7951 Capelin Cipolin	7952 Coup-vibe Copy-lab	7953 Caplet Copulate	7954 Coagulum Keep-aloof
7955 Capella Keep-alive	7956 Coagulase Cupolas	7957 Acapulco Cuplike	7958 Coupled Cup-lid	7959 Couple-up Cup-lip
7960 Capsize Cap-size	7961 Keep-sane Cop-sin	7962 Cop-shoe Cup-sub	7963 Key-post Copyist	7964 Keep-safe Copy-exam
7965 Capsule Copiously	7966 Key-pass Copy-essay	7967 Keepsake Caps-key	7968 Capsid Keep-aside	7969 Cop-spy Cup-soup
7970 Cop-car Coupe-car	7971 Keep-keen Cop-icon	7972 Capuche Copy-echo	7973 Capacity Copycat	7974 Cop-café Cup-acme

7975 Keep-cool Copy-clue	7976 Capacious Cop-case	7977 Cup-cake Ice-pack	7978 Copy-code Cop-kid	7979 Keep-copy Cop-cap
7980 Keep-dry Cop-diary	7981 Ocypodian Cop-den	7982 Keep-job Cupid-boy	7983 Cupidity Keep-date	7984 Cup-dome Copy-jam
7985 Copy-daily Keep-idle	7986 Keypads Copy-ideas	7987 Cup-juice Cop-decoy	7988 Keep-odd Copy-dad	7989 Keep-dog Cape-edge
7990 Copper Cupper	7991 Keep-open Cap-gun	7992 Cop-pub Kippah	7993 Cuppa-tea Kippot	7994 Cup-game Cop-gym
7995 Coppola Coapply	7996 Cuppas Kippax	7997 Coppice Keep-peace	7998 Capped Cupped	7999 Keepy-uppy Copy-page

ALPHA BETA 8000 – 8999

8000 Day-error Jazz-era	8001 Dry-run Dry-iron	8002 Diarrhea Jarrah	8003 Dry-rot Door-art	8004 Jury-room Dry-rum
8005 Dazzle Dizzily	8006 Dryers Derris	8007 Jararaca Dry-rice	8008 Jazzed Jarred	8009 Jazz-up Door-rap
8010 Drainer Drawer	8011 Drawn Drown	8012 Dr-Who Drone-bee	8013 Odorant Draw-out	8014 Dear-wife Dare-enemy
8015 Adrenal Journal	8016 Draws Drains	8017 Drink Durance	8018 Adorned Drained	8019 Drainage Derange
8020 Durbar Dry-hair	8021 Durban Dry-bone	8022 Drabby Dry-hob	8023 Dry-heat Dry-beat	8024 Durham Dry-beef
8025 Adorable Durable	8026 Dribs Derbies	8027 Darbuka Door-hook	8028 Jarhead Derby-day	8029 Derby-pie Dry-bag
8030 Juratory Darter	8031 Adoration Duration	8032 Dearth Dorothy	8033 Dirty-tie Drott	8034 Jury-team Dry-time
8035 Adroitly Dirtily	8036 Darts Doritos	8037 Adriatic Diuretic	8038 Darted Dirtied	8039 Door-top Jury-tip
8040 Dreamer Dormer	8041 Doorman Dairyman	8042 Jeremiah Drambuie	8043 Draft Drift	8044 Draffy Doze-off
8045 Dermal Dreamily	8046 Dreams Drums	8047 Dermic Dormice	8048 Dairymaid Dermoid	8049 Dream-up Drum-up
8050 Driver Drover	8051 Driven Driveway	8052 Drive-by Dry-lube	8053 Derivate Deerlet	8054 Dry-leaf Dear-life
8055 Drill Drivel	8056 Drives Day-release	8057 Dry-look Deerlike	8058 Derived Derailed	8059 Drive-up Dry-lip
8060 Derisory Dear-sir	8061 Derision Dear-son	8062 Dry-sob Dryish	8063 Dearest Jurist	8064 Dorsum Dereism
8065 Derisive Dorsal	8066 Dress Dross	8067 Dry-sky Drosky	8068 Dry-seed Door-side	8069 Dry-soap Door-siege
8070 Darker Jerker	8071 Darken Dry-cow	8072 Diarchy Jericho	8073 Direct Dark-tea	8074 Dairy-café Jury-cameo

8075 Dracula Darkly	8076 Jerks Drakes	8077 Dreck Dark-ice	8078 Jerked Dark-day	8079 Dark-age Dry-cup
8080 Derider Joy-rider	8081 Jordan Dry-den	8082 Jury-job Dried-hay	8083 Dried-out Diary-date	8084 Dry-dam Dread-foe
8085 Dazedly Dry-July	8086 Dreads Druids	8087 Druidic Dardic	8088 Dreaded Derided	8089 Dredge Drudge
8090 Drapery Drooper	8091 Dragon Dragoon	8092 Drop-by Jury-pub	8093 Derogate Drop-out	8094 Diazepam Dry-opium
8095 Door-pole Drip-oil	8096 Drugs Drops	8097 Drop-key Jury-epic	8098 Draped Drooped	8099 Druggy Drippy
8100 De-ionizer Junior-year	8101 Denizen Denarian	8102 Junior-boy Dino-rib	8103 Juniority Dewret	8104 Dwarf Deworm
8105 Danazol Dowral	8106 Juniors Donors	8107 Aid-work Day-work	8108 Edward Deionized	8109 Donor-pay Junior-pay
8110 Dinner Downer	8111 Down-on Dawn-on	8112 Join-web Jaw-neb	8113 Jennet Downeyite	8114 Deny-info Join-enemy
8115 Downley Join-navy	8116 Downs Dennis	8117 Denounce Ordinance	8118 Downed Dawned	8119 Dining Joining
8120 Dunbar Danbury	8121 Jaw-bone Danubian	8122 June-baby Join-hub	8123 Jaw-bit Eden-beauty	8124 Denham Dunham
8125 Deniable Joinable	8126 Jaw-box Eden-house	8127 Jaw-hook Daw-beak	8128 Daw-head June-abode	8129 Dune-heap Deny-hope
8130 Denture Janitor	8131 Donation Dentine	8132 Do-with Dino-tibia	8133 Identity Dentate	8134 Identify Odontoma
8135 Dental Jointly	8136 Dents Donuts	8137 Dianoetic Deontic	8138 Dented Jointed	8139 Jaw-tape Joint-age
8140 Join-free Done-more	8141 Adwoman Day-woman	8142 June-mob Dino-fob	8143 Dynamite Jawfoot	8144 Adenomyoma June-memo
8145 June-move Done-meal	8146 Denims Dynamise	8147 Dynamic Jean-make	8148 Done-mode Join-media	8149 Doyen-image Jaw-mop

8150 Denver Jowler	8151 Jawline Donovan	8152 Din-vibe Jaw-lube	8153 Dwelt June-vote	8154 Jean-loom Dunelm
8155 Dwell Daniella	8156 Jewels Denials	8157 Jaywalk Jaw-like	8158 Donald Doweled	8159 Dunlop Dewlap
8160 Dinosaur Dowser	8161 Adenosine Dawson	8162 Danish Jewish	8163 Density Dynasty	8164 Jainism Densify
8165 Adnexal Densely	8166 Jinxes Jewess	8167 Dionysiac Janus-key	8168 Jinxed Dewaxed	8169 Jaw-sag Eden-saga
8170 Dancer Junker	8171 Duncan Jenkin	8172 Dench Jaw-ache	8173 Junket Dowcet	8174 Duncify Dinkum
8175 Dankly Junkily	8176 Donkeys Junkies	8177 Jaywick Dan-cake	8178 Danced Dinked	8179 Daw-cage Donkey-pee
8180 Dander Joinder	8181 Donjon Dunedin	8182 Jaw-jab Dandy-boy	8183 Denudate June-date	8184 Dandify Jaw-edema
8185 Dandle Dawdle	8186 Adenoids Dandies	8187 Jaundice Jaw-joke	8188 Denuded Done-deed	8189 Joined-up Dandy-guy
8190 Danger Juniper	8191 Dungeon Jungian	8192 Dinghy Eden-pub	8193 Audio-input Dying-out	8194 Join-game Jaw-gum
8195 Jungle Jangle	8196 Doings Dingoes	8197 Jaw-poke Join-piece	8198 Dunged Danged	8199 Daw-egg Join-gap
8200 Adherer Deburr	8201 Dehorn Debrine	8202 Debarb Deborah	8203 Dehort Jabarite	8204 Debrief Dharma
8205 Job-role Jab-rule	8206 Debris Day-hours	8207 Daybreak Debark	8208 Debride Diehard	8209 Aid-barge Jab-rage
8210 Debonair Duobinary	8211 Johnny Johanna	8212 Job-web Jab-nib	8213 Day-hunt Job-unit	8214 Job-info Dub-name
8215 Dubai-envoy Job-envy	8216 Johns Diabinese	8217 Debunk Jayhawk	8218 Debond Deboned	8219 Daubing Jibing
8220 Jobbery Dibber	8221 Dobbin Dubbin	8222 Jubbah Job-hub	8223 Adhibit Adobe-hut	8224 Daube-beef Job-boom

8225 Dabble Dibble	8226 Adobe-house Job-base	8227 Job-book Jab-hook	8228 Dubbed Dabbed	8229 Job-hop Jab-bug
8230 Debtor Doubter	8231 Jobation Debt-woe	8232 Job-oath Dub-youth	8233 Dubitate Job-quote	8234 Debit-fee Job-time
8235 Dib-tool Job-tale	8236 Diabetes Doubts	8237 Diabetic Adiabatic	8238 Debated Debited	8239 Debitage Dub-tape
8240 Day-before Jab-fear	8241 Job-money Juba-fan	8242 Audio-bomb Job-mob	8243 Job-mate Jab-foot	8244 Debuff Dhimmi
8245 Job-file Job-move	8246 Joy-homes Job-mix	8247 Jab-face Dab-face	8248 Job-mood Jibe-mode	8249 Dubai-map Dab-mop
8250 Doubler Diabolize	8251 Dublin Job-line	8252 Jehovah Jubilee-bay	8253 Debility Edibility	8254 Diabolify Jhelum
8255 Dehull Edible-oil	8256 Doubles Edibles	8257 Diabolic Debulk	8258 Doubled Job-lead	8259 Double-up Job-log
8260 Debaser Jab-sore	8261 Adhesion Dobson	8262 Job-sub Dab-ash	8263 Dubiosity Job-site	8264 Job-safe Job-exam
8265 Adhesive Dubiously	8266 Deboss Job-issue	8267 Dehisce Dehusk	8268 Debased Dib-seed	8269 Job-saga Dab-soap
8270 Ad-hocery Job-care	8271 Dibucaine Job-icon	8272 Debauch Debouch	8273 Job-cut Job-kit	8274 Jab-coma Job-acme
8275 Debacle Job-clue	8276 Daybooks Audiobooks	8277 Dieback Doohickey	8278 Job-code Jab-kid	8279 Dub-copy Jab-cop
8280 Job-diary Dab-dry	8281 Job-done Jab-jaw	8282 Jab-dab Jab-job	8283 Job-data Jab-date	8284 Job-demo Job-doom
8285 Job-delay Job-deal	8286 Aid-bodies Jab-dose	8287 Jihadic Jab-doc	8288 Aid-buddy Jab-dad	8289 Dab-edge Day-badge
8290 Job-guru Job-peer	8291 Job-gain Jab-pain	8292 Dubai-pub Dhegiha	8293 Daube-pot Dib-pit	8294 Dub-poem Jab-game
8295 Job-pool Job-plea	8296 Job-apex Jab-apes	8297 Juba-epic Jab-pace	8298 Job-guide Dab-pad	8299 Die-happy Job-page

8300 Auditory-area Jet-roar	8301 Detrain Dietarian	8302 Diatribe Audi-turbo	8303 Detroit Jequirity	8304 Auditorium Deuterium
8305 Editorial Auditorial	8306 Auditors Editors	8307 Day-truce Audio-trace	8308 Dotard Detrude	8309 Deterge Day-trip
8310 Detainer Auditioner	8311 Diet-inn Date-wine	8312 Data-web Date-nob	8313 Detent Détente	8314 Edit-info Dote-wife
8315 Ideational Jet-wave	8316 Editions Detainees	8317 Diatonic Audit-week	8318 Detained Detuned	8319 Dating Dieting
8320 Dithery Jethro	8321 Dethaw Data-bin	8322 Dote-baby Data-hub	8323 Death-queue Jetboat	8324 Jet-home Aid-thief
8325 Editable Auditable	8326 Database Idiot-box	8327 Datebook Diet-book	8328 Jet-ahead Jetbead	8329 Jute-bag Data-bug
8330 Jotter Jittery	8331 Dietician Dotation	8332 Edit-tab Jet-tub	8333 Duty-quota Dye-tattoo	8334 Audit-team Duty-time
8335 Adequately Dettol	8336 Jetties Ditties	8337 Dietetic Data-autocue	8338 Dotted Jetted	8339 Diet-tip Data-tape
8340 Duty-free Jet-fire	8341 Diet-menu Audit-money	8342 Idiot-mob Jet-fob	8343 Diatomite Jet-feet	8344 Jet-off Jet-fume
8345 Dutiful Jet-fuel	8346 Diatoms Day-times	8347 Diatomic Data-fake	8348 Data-feed Date-mood	8349 Data-map Edit-image
8450 Detailer Data-layer	8351 Dateline Duty-line	8352 Data-lab Date-vibe	8353 Audio-quality Idiot-veto	8354 Edit-life Jet-life
8355 Datively Date-love	8356 Details Joy-tales	8357 Data-leak Jutelike	8358 Detailed Data-load	8359 Jetlag Data-log
8360 Detoxer Data-size	8361 Datsun Edit-sin	8362 Dotish Idiotish	8363 Detest Data-set	8364 Detoxify Jetsam
8365 Duteously Data-sale	8366 Date-issue Edit-essay	8367 Jet-ski Detusk	8368 Detoxed Diet-soda	8369 Data-usage Diet soup
8370 Jet-car Data-care	8371 Dietician Idioticon	8372 Detach Ditch	8373 Detect Data-kit	8374 Datacom Dot-com

8375 Diet-cola Data-clue	8376 Adequacies Jet-keys	8377 Diet-coke Detick	8378 Data-code Dote-kid	8379 Data-copy Jute-cap
8380 Data-diary Diet-dairy	8381 Jet-din Date-den	8382 Idiot-job Data-dub	8383 Edit-data Dote-date	8384 Data-jam Diet-demo
8385 Edit-daily Date-delay	8386 Duty-days Diet-dose	8387 Diet-juice Idiot-joke	8388 Date-deed Dote-dad	8389 Jut-edge Idiot-adage
8390 Jet-gear Data-guru	8391 Dote-upon Jet-gun	8392 Diet-pub Idiot-gab	8393 Diet-pot Duty-gate	8394 Idiot-goof Data-game
8395 Data-pool Duty-goal	8396 Idiot-pose Data-pause	8397 Jet-pace Duty-peak	8398 Jet-pad Idiot-guide	8399 Data-page Jet-pipe
8400 Admirer Defrayer	8401 Deaf-run Doom-zone	8402 Adam-rib Demo-robe	8403 Demerit Udmurt	8404 Deform Deiform
8405 Admiral Defrayal	8406 Deaf-ears Dimerous	8407 Dimeric Demark	8408 Admired Defraud	8409 Defrag Demerge
8410 Domineer Demeanour	8411 Dominion Demonian	8412 Jam-web Dome-neb	8413 Adamant Dementia	8414 Damnum Dominium
8415 Demonial Domanial	8416 Demons Domains	8417 Defence Defiance	8418 Demand Diamond	8419 Defang Edifying
8420 Jamboree Dumber	8421 Dumb-way Jambon	8422 Deaf-baby Dumb-boy	8423 Jam-bite Dam-boat	8424 Jim-Beam Dumb-oaf
8425 Jumble Dumbly	8426 Jambox Demobs	8427 Domebook Dim-bookie	8428 Dome-head Damehood	8429 Dim-hope Doom-bogey
8430 Diameter Odometer	8431 Demotion Ideomotion	8432 Deaf-youth Defy-taboo	8433 Domett Duftite	8434 Domatium Demo-team
8435 Daftly Deftly	8436 Edematous Adamites	8437 Idiomatic Demotic	8438 Defeated Daft-idea	8439 Dome-top Demo-tape
8440 Differ Dimmer	8441 Deaf-man Demiman	8442 Doom-fib Demo-mob	8443 Deaf-mute Defy-fate	8444 Demo-memo Dammam
8445 Doomful Dim-fool	8446 Diffuse Dummies	8447 Deaf-mice Dim-face	8448 Jammed Dammed	8449 Dummy-up Dim-imp

8450	8451	8452	8453	8454
Daimler	Demilune	Demo-lab	Default	Deaf-elf
Defiler	Dim-view	Doom-vibe	Deflate	Doom-life
8455	8456	8457	8458	8459
Joyfully	Defiles	Domelike	Defiled	Edema-leg
Dime-value	Deflux	Dam-leak	Defilade	Doom-voyage
8460	8461	8462	8463	8464
Admeasure	Damson	Dim-sub	Demist	Doom-safe
Doomsayer	Jameson	Demo-shoe	Day-feast	Dim-exam
8465	8466	8467	8468	8469
Damsel	Admass	Damask	Doomsday	Dam-siege
Adams-ale	Dim-ass	Dome-sky	Demised	Dim-spy
8470	8471	8472	8473	8474
Defacer	Jamaican	Do-much	Defect	Demo-cameo
Diemaker	Dime-coin	Dome-echo	Deficit	Dome-café
8475	8476	8477	8478	8479
Domicile	Defocus	De-muck	Defaced	Demo-copy
Edificial	Dim-case	Deaf-cook	Democide	Deaf-cop
8480	8481	8482	8483	8484
Jam-jar	Jamdani	Edema-jab	Dimidiate	Dumdum
Jam-door	Diamidine	Dim-job	Doom-date	Demideify
8485	8486	8487	8488	8489
Audio-module	Doom-days	Dim-joke	Dim-deed	Dam-edge
Doom-delay	Diomedes	Jam-juice	Demo-judo	Doom-dope
8490	8491	8492	8493	8494
Jumper	Dampen	Damp-hay	Jump-out	Demo-game
Damager	Jump-in	Jumpy-bee	Dumpty	Doom-poem
8495	8496	8497	8498	8499
Dimple	Damages	Dime-piece	Damaged	Demagogue
Damply	Dumps	Dome-peak	Dumped	Jump-up
8500	8501	8502	8503	8504
Devourer	Daily-rain	Adverb	Advert	Delirium
Dialyzer	Idle-run	Dove-rib	Divert	Ideal-room
8505	8506	8507	8508	8509
Dual-role	Dealers	Divorce	Idealized	Diverge
Ideal-rule	Divers	Daily-race	Idolized	Deaverage
8510	8511	8512	8513	8514
Diviner	Devonian	Java-web	Divinity	Ideal-wife
Delaware	Julianna	Dovenby	Deviant	Daily-info
8515	8516	8517	8518	8519
Divinely	Divans	Advance	Divined	Dealing
Juvenile	Javanese	Deviance	Daily-need	Diving
8520	8521	8522	8523	8524
Daily-hour	Java-bean	July-baby	Jailbait	Ideal-home
Jail-bar	Dove-bone	Daily-ebb	Daily-beat	Dial-home

8525 Delible Delayable	8526 Jailhouse Daily-base	8527 Daily-book Dual-hook	8528 Ideal-body Idle-head	8529 Daily-hope Daily-hug
8530 Adultery Idolatry	8531 Devotion Deviation	8532 Duluth Jail-tab	8533 Daily-quota Adult-toy	8534 Ideal-team Idle-time
8535 Dovetail Devoutly	8536 Adults Duvets	8537 Deltaic Dialytic	8538 Deltoid Devoted	8539 Daily-tip Ideal-type
8540 Daily-fear Duel-fury	8541 Dolmen Dolman	8542 Delimb Idle-fib	8543 Delimit Dolomite	8544 Dilemma Deal-off
8545 Doleful Daily-mail	8546 Daily-fees Ideal-mix	8547 Dual-face Ideal-make	8548 Idle-mode Daily-food	8549 Ideal-image Java-map
8550 Delivery Dollar	8551 Javelin Jillion	8552 Delilah Dolly-boy	8553 Devaluate Jollity	8554 Jollify Daily-life
8555 Devolve Jovially	8556 Dolls Devils	8557 Dovelike Idyllic	8558 Devalued Jelled	8559 Develop Divulge
8560 Adviser Delusory	8561 Delusion Division	8562 Dovish Delish	8563 Delist Idealist	8564 Dualism Idealism
8565 Divisive Jealously	8566 Dialysis Joyless	8567 Adolesce Jalisco	8568 Advised Devised	8569 Daily-usage Jail-spy
8570 Dual-core Daily-care	8571 Divicine Java-icon	8572 Daily-echo Daily-ache	8573 Advocate Delicate	8574 Dulcify July-cameo
8575 Duolocal Dual-coil	8576 Delicious Devices	8577 Advocacy Delicacy	8578 Dial-code Ideal-kid	8579 Dual-copy Jail-cage
8580 Divider Deluder	8581 Davidian Duel-den	8582 Daily-job Duel-jab	8583 Ideal-date Daily-duty	8584 Divadom Daily-memo
8585 Dual-deal Daily-deal	8586 Daily-dose Idle-days	8587 Davidic Idle-joke	8588 Divided Deluded	8589 Divide-up Dual-edge
8590 Daily-prey Idle-pry	8591 Duel-gun Daily-gain	8592 Delphi Adelphia	8593 Delegate Divagate	8594 Daily-game Duel-gym
8595 Daily-play Dive-pool	8596 Dialogues Joy-leaps	8597 Delegacy Dialogic	8598 Daily-guide Deluged	8599 Dove-egg Ideal-gap

8600 Disarray Desirer	8601 Audio-siren Days-rain	8602 Adsorb Disrobe	8603 Desert Disroot	8604 Disarm Disroof
8605 Deserve Disraeli	8606 Desires Audi-series	8607 Dysuric Aid-source	8608 Desired Daisy-road	8609 Douse-urge Idea-surge
8610 Disinure Disney-zoo	8611 Disown Disunion	8612 Ideas-web Disney-bay	8613 Disunity Aids-unit	8614 Dysnomia Joyous-wife
8615 Douse-envy Days-only	8616 Dioxins Aid-sense	8617 Aids-week Ideas-nook	8618 Audio-sound Daisy-weed	8619 Dousing Dosing
8620 Dasher Disbar	8621 Dasheen Audio-show	8622 Ideas-hub Deus-abbey	8623 Dish-out Ajax-boot	8624 Adisham Daisy-boom
8625 Disable Daisy-blue	8626 Disabuse Dishes	8627 Dashiki Ajax-book	8628 Dished Dashed	8629 Dish-up Aids-bug
8630 Destroy Jester	8631 Destiny Dystonia	8632 Dusty-bay Deus-oath	8633 Disquiet Days-quota	8634 Justify Diastema
8635 Distal Jostle	8636 Deists Diastase	8637 Justice Dystocia	8638 Dusted Joisted	8639 Dustup Dystopia
8640 Douse-fire Days-of-yore	8641 Jasmine Desman	8642 Disembay Joyous-mob	8643 Day-safety Ajax-footy	8644 Days-off Ajax-fame
8645 Dismal Dysmelia	8646 Days-fees Odious-fox	8647 Disomic Joyous-face	8648 Dismayed Desmid	8649 Daisy-image Adios-amigo
8650 Daysailer Dieselize	8651 Disavow Daisy-lane	8652 Dyes-lab Joyous-vibe	8653 Desalt Desolate	8654 Daisy-leaf Day-asylum
8655 Disloyal Disvalue	8656 Dyslexia Dieselise	8657 Dislike Daisylike	8658 Ajax-video Dixie-lid	8659 Doxology Dyslogia
8660 Dossier Dosser	8661 Jesusian Odyssean	8662 Ajax-shoe Joyous-sob	8663 Desist Disseat	8664 Dysosmia Diseasome
8665 Dossal Jussive	8666 Diseases Jesses	8667 Jessica Dysoxic	8668 Diseased Dissuade	8669 Disusage Daisy-sap
8670 Descry Dioscuri	8671 Doeskin Ajax-icon	8672 Dusky-hue Disco-boy	8673 De-excite Daisy-cut	8674 Adios-coma Ajax.com

8675	8676	8677	8678	8679
Descale	Discs	Daysack	Discoid	Diascopy
Discal	Desks	Desk-key	Dusky-day	Day-escape
8680	8681	8682	8683	8684
Jus-dare	Disdain	Days-job	Days-date	Disdeify
Deoxidize	Disjoin	Aids-jab	Dose-diary	Disedify
8685	8686	8687	8688	8689
Disodile	Deoxidise	Daisy-juice	De-seeded	Disedge
Days-delay	Joyous-ideas	Odious-joke	Joyous-dad	Odious-dope
8690	8691	8692	8693	8694
Despair	Design	Joseph	Despot	Ajax-game
Disagree	Dyspnea	Dysaphia	Dispute	Joyous-poem
8695	8696	8697	8698	8699
Dispel	Disguise	Adspeak	Dose-guide	Ideas-page
Display	Dispose	Eduspeak	Jaspoid	Aides-gag
8700	8701	8702	8703	8704
Jacuzzi	Dacron	Joker-boy	Decorate	Decorum
Decrier	Decurion	Juicy-rib	Jakarta	Day-crime
8705	8706	8707	8708	8709
Decrial	Decrease	Idiocracy	Decreed	Juicy-ripe
Duke-rule	Decrees	Audio-creak	Decried	Juke-rap
8710	8711	8712	8713	8714
Deaconry	Decennia	Dyke-neb	Decent	Day-cinema
Dicey-war	Juicy-wine	Joke-web	Decant	Dicey enemy
8715	8716	8717	8718	8719
Decanal	Decoy-noise	Decency	Jocund	Joking
Diaconal	Joke-nose	Joke-nook	Juicy-end	Decaying
8720	8721	8722	8723	8724
Decohere	Jacobean	Juicy-boob	Jacobite	Joachim
Joke-hour	Deciban	Joke-hub	Juicy-bit	Aid-chief
8725	8726	8727	8728	8729
Decibel	Jacobs	Joke-book	Juicehead	Joke-bag
Educable	Duchies	Audio-choice	Dykehead	Decay-bug
8730	8731	8732	8733	8734
Doctor	Education	Juice-tube	Dictate	Dictum
Educator	Ejection	Joke-taboo	Diktat	Joke-time
8735	8736	8737	8738	8739
Ductile	Dakotas	Deictic	Educated	Juice-tap
Ductal	Ductus	Docetic	Ejected	Joke-tape
8740	8741	8742	8743	8744
Jacamar	Decoyman	Juicy-moob	Decimate	Duke-fame
Decumaria	Joke-man	Dye-comb	Decaf-tea	Decay-fume
8745	8746	8747	8748	8749
Decimal	Decoy-fox	Docimacy	Joke-mood	Decamp
Juicy-meal	Juicy-mix	Duke-mace	Juicy-food	Day-camp

8750	8751	8752	8753	8754
Declare	Decline	Juke-vibe	Docility	Declaim
Jocular	Declaw	Docile-boy	Ejaculate	Juicy-leaf
8755	8756	8757	8758	8759
Jekyll	Dicelous	Decloak	Deceived	Decalogue
Ducally	Jaculus	Jokelike	Joke-aloud	Audio-clip
8760	8761	8762	8763	8764
Decisory	Decision	Duke-shoe	Jocosity	Dioecism
Dice-size	Diocesan	Aid-cash	Docusate	Jokesome
8765	8766	8767	8768	8769
Decisive	Dioceses	Juicy-sauce	Deceased	Docusoap
Audaciously	Day-cases	Dicey-ski	Dice-side	Juicy-sap
8770	8771	8772	8773	8774
Dicker	Deccan	Day-coach	Jacket	Juice-café
Docker	Juice-can	Dice-cube	Docket	Juke-cameo
8775	8776	8777	8778	8779
Jackal	Ducks	Jack-oak	Decked	Dockage
Deckle	Jockeys	Juicy-cake	Docked	Jack-up
8780	8781	8782	8783	8784
Decider	Joke-dean	Juicy-job	Deciduity	Dukedom
Decoder	Juke-den	Dicey-jab	Juicy-diet	Deacidify
8785	8786	8787	8788	8789
Decadal	Decades	Decadic	Decided	Juiced-up
Decidual	Deciduous	Juicy-joke	Decoded	Dyke-edge
8790	8791	8792	8793	8794
Day-keeper	Decagon	Duke-pub	Dyke-gate	Deuce-game
Audio-copier	Idiocy-gene	Day-cough	Juice-pot	Juicy-pome
8795	8796	8797	8798	8799
Decouple	Juicy-goose	Joke-poke	Decapod	Decoupage
Decuple	Audio-copies	Decay-pace	Dice-pad	Joke-page
8800	8801	8802	8803	8804
Adjurer	Adjourn	Djerba	Dead-rite	Daydream
Deodorize	Dead-run	Dyed-robe	Dead-rat	Dead-room
8805	8806	8807	8808	8809
Adderley	Udders	Odd-race	Adjured	Aid-drop
Judo-rule	Deodorise	Audio-jerk	Dyed-red	Judo-rage
8810	8811	8812	8813	8814
Deadener	Die-down	Dead-wahoo	Jejunity	Duodenum
Duodenary	Djinny	Judean-boy	Dead-ant	Jejunum
8815	8816	8817	8818	8819
Duodenal	Dedans	Dejunk	Addenda	Adding
Jejunal	Add-ons	Dead-week	Deadwood	Eddying
8820	8821	8822	8823	8824
Odd-hour	Dead-bone	Odd-baby	Deadbeat	Dedham
Dyed-hair	Dead-hen	Judo-hub	Odd-bit	Odd-bum

8825 Addable Dead-hole	8826 Deadhouse Deedbox	8827 Odd-book Judo-hook	8828 Deadhead Dead-ahead	8829 Dead-hope Odd-bug
8830 Additory Adjutory	8831 Addition Dedition	8832 Judith Deed-oath	8833 Dead-quiet Add-quota	8834 Odd-time Dead-time
8835 Additive Dado-tile	8836 Jujitsu Oddities	8837 Odd-take Judo-tyke	8838 Dead-toad Odd-tad	8839 Adjutage Deed-tape
8840 Add-more Dead-fire	8841 Dead-man Odd-man	8842 Odd-fib Djembe	8843 Dead-meat Judo-feat	8844 Didymium Dad-mum
8845 Add-fuel Dead-mail	8846 Odd-mix Didymous	8847 Odd-face Dead-mice	8848 Odd-mood Dead-media	8849 Do-damage Odd-fag
8850 Doodler Dead-layer	8851 Deadline Dead-even	8852 Deadly-boa Odd-lab	8853 Dud-vote Odd-lot	8854 Odd-life Dead-leaf
8855 Add-value Add-all	8856 Doodles Dedalus	8857 Odd-look Add-voice	8858 Addled Doodled	8859 Dead-leg Judo-logo
8860 Dead-sure Odd-size	8861 Addison Odds-on	8862 Yiddish Jadish	8863 Adjust Oddest	8864 Judaism Dadaism
8865 Dead-soul Deed-seal	8866 Dead-issue Dead-ass	8867 Add-sauce Audio-disc	8868 Odd-side Dead-seed	8869 Adds-up Odd-usage
8870 Judiciary Adducer	8871 Dud-coin Dead-keen	8872 Dead-cub Jade-cube	8873 Addict Dedicate	8874 Duodecimo Judo-cameo
8875 Judicial Dead-cool	8876 Judicious Odd-case	8877 Audio-jack Odd-cake	8878 Deduced Adduced	8879 Dud-copy Deed-copy
8880 Judder Doddery	8881 Added-on Duddon	8882 Jeddah Odd-job	8883 Dud-data Deed-audit	8884 Added-fee Dead-doom
8885 Diddle Doddle	8886 Daddies Odd-days	8887 Dead-decay Odd-joke	8888 Odd-deed Added-joy	8889 Adjudge Added-pay
8890 Dodger Judger	8891 Deadpan Dudgeon	8892 Dodgy-yob Odd-pub	8893 Dodipate Odd-gait	8894 Dodgem Jade-gem
8895 Eddy-pool Dead-ugly	8896 Judges Dodges	8897 Add-pace Dodgy-ice	8898 Dodged Judged	8899 Deed-page Dead-pig

8900 Day-prayer Deep-roar	8901 Deep-run Dog-iron	8902 Dog-rib Audio-probe	8903 Depart Deport	8904 Audiogram Diagram
8905 Deprave Deprive	8906 Degrees Jaguars	8907 Dog-race Jog-race	8908 Degrade Jeopardy	8909 Aid-group Dog-rope
8910 Edgware Deepener	8911 Digynian Dipnoan	8912 Japan-bay Dog-nob	8913 Dignity Dopant	8914 Dignify Dog-woof
8915 Diagonal Dag-wool	8916 Diagnose Edgewise	8917 Degunk Aid-agency	8918 Depend Dogwood	8919 Doping Dognap
8920 Dog-hair Ideaphoria	8921 Dogbane Idiophone	8922 Doughboy Ideophobia	8923 Doughty Dog-bite	8924 Dog-home Deopham
8925 Dupable Audiophile	8926 Doghouse Diphase	8927 Edaphic Jug-beak	8928 Doghood Dopehead	8929 Dog-bug Deep-bag
8930 Adapter Jupiter	8931 Adaption Adoption	8932 Depth Idiopathy	8933 Digitate Dupatta	8934 Dog-team Dope-time
8935 Digital Adaptive	8936 Digits Depots	8937 Diegetic Deep-quake	8938 Adapted Adopted	8939 Dog-tag Dig-top
8940 Deep-fry Dope-free	8941 Dopamine Dogman	8942 Dope-mob Dupe-fib	8943 Dogmata Dog-meat	8944 Dope-off Jagoff
8945 Dog-flea Dog-movie	8946 Digamous Dogmas	8947 Dogface Dab-face	8948 Deep-mud Dog-food	8949 Dope-mope Digimap
8950 Jugular Deplore	8951 Deplane Dayglow	8952 Dope-lab Deep-vibe	8953 Deplete Duplet	8954 Diploma Deplume
8955 Deep-love Deglove	8956 Duplex Douglas	8957 Doglike Deep-voice	8958 Diploid Deployed	8959 Diplopia Dogleg
8960 Deposer Adiposuria	8961 Jigsaw Digoxin	8962 Dap-shoe Deepish	8963 Deposit Digest	8964 Oedipism Deep-safe
8965 Deposal Dog-soul	8966 Degauss Gypsies	8967 Deep-soak Dip-sauce	8968 Deposed Deep-side	8969 Dog-spay Edge-sag
8970 Dog-care Deep-core	8971 Dogcow Deep-ocean	8972 Dog-cub Deep-echo	8973 Depict Adipocyte	8974 Digicam Deep-coma

8975	8976	8977	8978	8979
Deep-cave	Deep-cause	Daypack	Audio-paced	Dog-cage
Dig-coal	Dopey-cosy	Aid-pack	Dope-kid	Dog-cap
8980	8981	8982	8983	8984
Do-gooder	Dog-jaw	Dope-jab	Dig-data	Dogdom
Deep-dry	Dog-den	Dig-job	Dog-diet	Dope-doom
8985	8986	8987	8988	8989
Deepdale	Dog-days	Dogdyke	Deep-dyed	Dig-deep
Deep-dive	Aid-goods	Deep-dyke	Edgy-dad	Deep-edge
8990	8991	8992	8993	8994
Dagger	Deep-pain	Dog-pooh	Dope-pot	Dope-opium
Digger	Dog-paw	Dog-gooby	Deep-pit	Dupe-goofy
8995	8996	8997	8998	8999
Juggle	Dipygus	Deep-peace	Dipped	Deep-gap
Jiggle	Deep-pause	Dog-pace	Jagged	Dog-poop

ALPHA BETA 9000 – 9999

9000 Grazer Pizzeria	9001 Agrarian Parazoan	9002 Pyorrhea Pyrrho	9003 Parrot Priority	9004 Prearm Opera-room
9005 Guzzle Puzzle	9006 Prizes Prayers	9007 Prozac Prerace	9008 Prized Parried	9009 Prorogue Prurigo
9010 Granary Greenery	9011 Granny Prawn	9012 Piranha Green-hue	9013 Granite Parent	9014 Agronomy Perineum
9015 Growl Prowl	9016 Grains Greens	9017 Prince Prank	9018 Grand Ground	9019 Praying Preying
9020 Prober Grey-hair	9021 Grobian Pro-bono	9022 Grabby Grubby	9023 Preheat Probity	9024 Graham Poor-home
9025 Parable Agreeable	9026 Grubs Probes	9027 Pre-book Prebake	9028 Garbed Probed	9029 Garbage Grub-up
9030 Greater Porter	9031 Protein Portion	9032 Girth Perth	9033 Gritty Grotto	9034 Gratify Aperitif
9035 Partial Portal	9036 Ports Parts	9037 Partake Paretic	9038 Parotid Pirated	9039 Portage Protégé
9040 Prefer Primary	9041 Germany Profane	9042 Prefab Pure-fib	9043 Profit Primate	9044 Giraffe Perfume
9045 Profile Primal	9046 Promise Profuse	9047 Grimace Preface	9048 Pyramid Perfidy	9049 Grumpy Grampa
9050 Parlour Purveyor	9051 Preview Proven	9052 Gear-lube Guru-vibe	9053 Gravity Private	9054 Prelim Prolife
9055 Gravel Gorilla	9056 Girls Pearls	9057 Garlic Provoke	9058 Provide Prelude	9059 Prologue Agrology
9060 Greaser Grouser	9061 Person Prison	9062 Parish Perish	9063 Parasite Priest	9064 Prism Presume
9065 Perusal Parasol	9066 Grass Gross	9067 Prosaic Apraxic	9068 Preside Persuade	9069 Grasp Presage
9070 Grocery Procure	9071 Parkway Porcine	9072 Preach Perch	9073 Apricot Parakeet	9074 Pre-cum Pre-coma

9075 Parcel Perceive	9076 Gracious Precious	9077 Prick Precook	9078 Precede Proceed	9079 Precap Pork-pie
9080 Grader Perjury	9081 Garden Pardon	9082 Purdah Proud-boy	9083 Graduate Predate	9084 Peerdom Predoom
9085 Girdle Gradual	9086 Periods Paradise	9087 Produce Periodic	9088 Graded Guarded	9089 Grudge Prodigy
9090 Prepare Proper	9091 Paragon Progeny	9092 Graph Agraphia	9093 Parapet Garget	9094 Pure-gem Pro-game
9095 Purple Propel	9096 Grapes Groups	9097 Prepuce Priapic	9098 Grouped Purged	9099 Groupage Groggy
9100 Panzer Ignorer	9101 Gun-run Open-arena	9102 Ganzhou Pony-rib	9103 Generate Power-out	9104 Panorama Epineurium
9105 General Gnarl	9106 Powers Pioneers	9107 Generic Power-key	9108 Powered Upward	9109 Power-up Gonzaga
9110 Gunner Ginnery	9111 Pennine Pennon	9112 Pen-nib Pawn-bay	9113 Pinnate Punnet	9114 Pen-name Open-info
9115 Genuinely Gunnel	9116 Pennies Opinions	9117 Penance Pinnace	9118 Pinweed Upwind	9119 Opening Gaining
9120 Open-bar Gun-hero	9121 Pin-bone Gun-ban	9122 Gun-hub Puny-baby	9123 Gunboat Open-bite	9124 Gun-boom Open-home
9125 Ignoble Pinhole	9126 Open-house Agony-box	9127 Open-book Pen-hook	9128 Pinhead Geniohyoid	9129 Pin-hope Open-bag
9130 Punter Painter	9131 Ignition Pontine	9132 Open-tube Agnathia	9133 Point-out Peanutty	9134 Pentium Agent-fee
9135 Gentle Genital	9136 Pints Points	9137 Genetic Pontiac	9138 Painted Pointed	9139 Genotype Pent-up
9140 Pinafore Gunfire	9141 Gunman Ignominy	9142 Gun-mob Go-numb	9143 Pony-meat Puny-feet	9144 Gone-off Paw-off
9145 Painful Gainful	9146 Genomes Gnomes	9147 Genomic Gnomic	9148 Agony-mood Ganymede	9149 Gene-map Open-mug

9150 Penalize Open-layer	9151 Open-view Gun-law	9152 Gene-lab Gun-lube	9153 Penalty Geniality	9154 Open-leaf Pinealoma
9155 Genially Paywall	9156 Panels Penalise	9157 Open-look Gunlike	9158 Go-wild Open-lid	9159 Genealogy Penology
9160 Gainsayer Pin-size	9161 Pension Go-insane	9162 Punish Gnash	9163 Against Pianist	9164 Pianism Agonism
9165 Pensive Pensile	9166 Genesis Geniuses	9167 Open-sky Genius-key	9168 Agonised Open-side	9169 Pinesap Gun-usage
9170 Pincer Punker	9171 Pinecone Panacean	9172 Pinch Punch	9173 Gonocyte Open-cut	9174 Gynoecium Open-café
9175 Pencil Gawkily	9176 Agencies Eugenics	9177 Pancake Panicky	9178 Genocide Pounced	9179 Ginkgo Gene-copy
9180 Gender Powder	9181 Ugandan Iguanodon	9182 Gandhi Punjab	9183 Pundit Gun-jet	9184 Agendum Ependyma
9185 Panadol Gondola	9186 Pounds Ponds	9187 Pun-joke Gun-decoy	9188 Upended Pounded	9189 Poundage Gundog
9190 Ginger Ganger	9191 Penguin Pawpaw	9192 Gung-ho Gonoph	9193 Open-pot Gnu-goat	9194 Open-game Pongamia
9195 Pen-pal Gunplay	9196 Ganges Gangs	9197 Paw-poke Gain-pace	9198 Gun-guide Paw-pad	9199 Gang-up Guinea-pig
9200 Peaberry Aphorize	9201 Pea-brain Gaborone	9202 Pharaoh Euphorbia	9203 Puberty Yoghurt	9204 Ephraim Pharma
9205 Gabriel Gharial	9206 Phrase Pharisee	9207 Euphoric Phreak	9208 Upbraid Peabird	9209 Phrygia Phizog
9210 Euphonize Phoner	9211 Phone-in Gehenna	9212 Pubweb Phoney-yob	9213 Phonate Ghent	9214 Phoneme Euphonium
9215 Phenol Phonily	9216 Phones Phoenix	9217 Phonic Phoenicia	9218 Phoned Gabionade	9219 Gabionage Gybing
9220 Gibber Gabbro	9221 Gibbon Pub-ban	9222 Pooh-bah Pub-hub	9223 Gibbet Gobbet	9224 Poboy-beef Pooh-bum

9225 Pebble Gobble	9226 Phobias Gibbous	9227 Phobic Ephebic	9228 Gibbed Pub-bed	9229 Pub-hype Pooh-bug
9230 Pub-quiz Ghutra	9231 Photon Phyton	9232 Aphthae Eighth	9233 Ghetto Phytate	9234 Pubiotomy Pub-team
9235 Phytol Photo-lie	9236 Photos Ghats	9237 Photic Phatic	9238 Phytoid Photo-day	9239 Photopia Photo-op
9240 Ephemera Euphemize	9241 Pub-menu Pub-fun	9242 Gay-bomb Pub-fib	9243 Ghee-fat Pub-footy	9244 Pub-mafia Pooh-fume
9245 Poboy-meal Pub-movie	9246 Euphemise Pub-fix	9247 Aphemic Gooby-face	9248 Pubmed Pub-food	9249 Pay-homage Poboy-image
9250 Pabulary Phalera	9251 Goblin Aphelion	9252 Pub-vibe Ghoul-bay	9253 Goblet Giblet	9254 Phylum Phloem
9255 Upheaval Uphill	9256 Ghouls Phials	9257 Public Gibelike	9258 Piebald Uphold	9259 Philip Ophiology
9260 Phaser Physaria	9261 Gibson Phase-in	9262 Phish Gay-bash	9263 Ghost Aghast	9264 Ophism Orphism
9265 Pub-sale Physalia	9266 Phases Ephesus	9267 Phasic Aphasic	9268 Phased Pub-side	9269 Uphasp Pub-usage
9270 Pubic-area Pie-baker	9271 Phocine Ghee-can	9272 Gay-beach Gibe-echo	9273 Gib-cat Phuket	9274 Phakoma Pub-café
9275 Aphakial Phacelia	9276 Phooey-case Yoga-books	9277 Aphakic Pay-back	9278 Phacoid Aphicide	9279 Pub-cup Pub-cop
9280 Pub-door Pooh-odour	9281 Aphidian Ophidian	9282 Pub-job Gob-dab	9283 Pee-bidet Pub-date	9284 Pub-demo Gibe-deaf
9285 Age-badly Pooh-daily	9286 Aphids Pea-buds	9287 Pub-joke Gooby-juice	9288 Gay-buddy Pub-judo	9289 Pub-dope Pooh-dog
9290 Pub-goer Phooey-guru	9291 Iphigenia Pub-gin	9292 Pooh-pooh Pub-gab	9293 Pooh-pit Pub-patio	9294 Pub-game Gay-bigamy
9295 Pub-gala Pooh-pile	9296 Ephapse Euphagus	9297 Phagic Pub-peace	9298 Pub-guide Ape-biped	9299 Pub-gig Pooh-poop

9300 Patzer Petrary	9301 Patron Upturn	9302 Goat-rib Guitar-boy	9303 Patriot Peter-out	9304 Petrify Putrefy
9305 Patrol Petrol	9306 Guitars Peters	9307 Patricia Up-quark	9308 Putrid Petard	9309 Ego-trip Pterygia
9310 Agateware Potenza	9311 Uptown Patwin	9312 Gate-web Goat-whey	9313 Patent Potent	9314 Pet-name Putnam
9315 Optional Pet-wool	9316 Get-wise Goat-noose	9317 Patience Potency	9318 Goutweed Gatewood	9319 Gating Pouting
9320 Gather Pother	9321 Pathway Python	9322 Goat-baby Pet-bib	9323 Epithet Petabyte	9324 Apothem Pythium
9325 Pitiable Pothole	9326 Paths Gatehouse	9327 Gothic Pothook	9328 Pothead Goat-hide	9329 Gut-bug Peat-bog
9330 Gutter Pottery	9331 Agitation Petition	9332 Pay-tithe Gut-tube	9333 Guttate Gate-tout	9334 Petty-aim Get-time
9335 Putative Pettily	9336 Potatoes Puttees	9337 Pet-tyke Ptotic	9338 Agitated Aptitude	9339 Pottage Open-top
9340 Epitomize Optimize	9341 Gateman Pitman	9342 Gitmo-Bay Pitomba	9343 Optimate Goat-meat	9344 Optimum Put-off
9345 Optimal Potful	9346 Epitomes Optimise	9347 Epitomic Potomac	9348 Pet-food Get-mad	9349 Uptempo Gate-map
9350 Ptyalize Petiolar	9351 Ptyalin Petaline	9352 Opiate-lab Pet-vibe	9353 Petiolate Uptilt	9354 Ptolemy Petaluma
9355 Patella Agitolalia	9356 Petals Patulous	9357 Goatlike Pet-lice	9358 Pot-lid Petalody	9359 Putlog Gateleg
9360 Poetiser Pot-size	9361 Opaque-sin Gate-sway	9362 Potash Goatish	9363 Egotist Pietist	9364 Egotism Pietism
9365 Piteously Gutsily	9366 Geotaxis Ptosis	9367 Saucepot Gutsy-ace	9368 Put-aside Ptosed	9369 Pot-sip Gate-siege
9370 Pet-care Poeticize	9371 Optician Pitocin	9372 Patch Pitch	9373 Pituicyte Pet-cat	9374 Opiate-coma Poet-café

9375 Optical Poetical	9376 Optics Poetics	9377 Uptick Potcake	9378 Goat-kid Gut-acid	9379 Gate-keep Pet-cage
9380 Patio-door Pet-deer	9381 Get-done Goat-jaw	9382 Pet-job Gout-jab	9383 Gout-diet Gate-duty	9384 Gate-jam Put-dime
9385 Pet-dove Repeatedly	9386 Pet-ideas Pot-dose	9387 Peat-decay Pet-joke	9388 Pet-dad Piety-deed	9389 Pet-dog Pot-dope
9390 Pot-puree Potager	9391 Patagonia Pet-pony	9392 Epitaph Go-tough	9393 Pet-goat Opiate-pot	9394 Patagium Patio-gym
9395 Patagial Get-ugly	9396 Epitopes Pot-pies	9397 Gate-pike Gait-pace	9398 Put-paid Pet-guide	9399 Pet-pig Goat-poop
9400 Pfizer Pay-freeze	9401 Pomerania Game-zone	9402 Gym-robe Puma-rib	9403 Opium-root Gum-rot	9404 Game-room Pea-farm
9405 Game-rule Epimeral	9406 Gamers Pamirs	9407 Epimeric Pee-force	9408 Gym-ride Opium-yard	9409 Puma-rage Gym-rope
9410 Opium-war Game-ware	9411 Geminian Guamanian	9412 Game-noobie Puma-woobie	9413 Payment Augment	9414 Game-name Goofy-info
9415 Peafowl Geminal	9416 Gymnasia Pay-fines	9417 Egomaniac Geomancy	9418 Gumwood Gumweed	9419 Gaming Geminga
9420 Pembury Pea-fibre	9421 Gambian Game-ban	9422 Game-hub Puma-baby	9423 Gambit Gum-bite	9424 Game-boom Puma-home
9425 Gamble Gumboil	9426 Game-box Gym-house	9427 Game-book Gym-bike	9428 Gem-bead Goofy-head	9429 Gamboge Gym-bag
9430 Geometry Gumtree	9431 Gift-away Goofy-teen	9432 Ape-mouth Epimyth	9433 Gift-toy Game-quota	9434 Game-time Poem-tome
9435 Game-tool Puma-tail	9436 Gifts Gametes	9437 Gametic Geomatic	9438 Gifted Gift-aid	9439 Age-fatigue Ape-footage
9440 Gaffer Puffer	9441 Puffin Guffaw	9442 Puffy-bee Puma-fob	9443 Gemmate Gummite	9444 Goof-off Game-memo
9445 Pummel Piffle	9446 Gaffes Puffs	9447 Pay-office Game-face	9448 Gaffed Gummed	9449 Puff-up Puffy-ego

9450 Game-over Pea-flour	9451 Gumline Game-venue	9452 Opium-lab Age-flab	9453 Gimlet Upfault	9454 Opium-leaf Ego-flame
9455 Pay-fully Opium-vial	9456 Gay-males Goofy-lies	9457 Gemlike Pimlico	9458 Upfield Game-lead	9459 Pomology Gemology
9460 Gym-user Gum-size	9461 Pi-meson Game-sway	9462 Gumshoe Gym-shoe	9463 Upmost Agamist	9464 Gamesome Epimysium
9465 Gum-sole Gamesley	9466 Apomixis Opium-assay	9467 Ape-mask Yoga-music	9468 Opium-seed Games-day	9469 Gym-usage Opium-sap
9470 Game-cry Pie-maker	9471 Game-icon Puma-knee	9472 Game-cube Gum-ache	9473 Puma-cat Apomict	9474 Opium-coma Gym-café
9475 Pomace-oil Game-clue	9476 Pomaces Pumices	9477 Gum-acacia Ape-muck	9478 Pie-faced Po-faced	9479 Puma-cage Game-keep
9480 Gym-door Game-diary	9481 Puma-den Go-midway	9482 Gym-job Goofy-jibe	9483 Game-data Gym-date	9484 Game-demo Gum-edema
9485 Game-idol Gym-duel	9486 Gym-days Opium-dose	9487 Gum-decay Opium-juice	9488 Pomaded Gym-judo	9489 Goofy-dog Opium-dope
9490 Pamper Pumper	9491 Pompano Gamogony	9492 Puma-pooh Game-pub	9493 Pump-out Pimp-out	9494 Pompom Goofy-poem
9495 Pimple Pump-oil	9496 Pampas Pumps	9497 Puma-pace Game-peak	9498 Pumped Game-guide	9499 Pump-up Pumpage
9500 Glazier Polarize	9501 Govern Pelerine	9502 Gevurah Pale-orb	9503 Polarity Poverty	9504 Glorify Playroom
9505 Plural Pleural	9506 Glorious Players	9507 Pyloric Paleozoic	9508 Polaroid Glazed	9509 Glory-pea Glaze-up
9510 Plenary Glower	9511 Ugly-win Plow-on	9512 Plowboy Paulinho	9513 Plant Planet	9514 Plenum Polonium
9515 Plainly Planula	9516 Planes Plans	9517 Plank Glance	9518 Gland Poland	9519 Plunge Paving
9520 Goal-hero Gel-bra	9521 Globin Plebeian	9522 Ugly-baby Gay-lobby	9523 Globate Igloo-hut	9524 Pulham Pelham

9525 Global Pliable	9526 Globes Playhouse	9527 Playbook Eagle-beak	9528 Globoid Ugly-head	9529 Polybag Ugly-bug
9530 Paltry Poultry	9531 Gluten Platoon	9532 Goliath Epilith	9533 Palette Epaulette	9534 Playtime Goal-time
9535 Palatial Palatal	9536 Plates Pilots	9537 Politic Poultice	9538 Plated Pleated	9539 Pilotage Polytope
9540 Glamour Golfer	9541 Gleeman Palimony	9542 Aplomb Plumb	9543 Playmate Uplift	8544 Play-off Peel-off
9545 Gleeful Gloomily	9546 Plums Plumose	9547 Polemic Ugly-face	9548 Plumed Gleamed	9549 Plumage Plump
9550 Pillar Gallery	9551 Pollen Pillow	9552 Gullah Pallah	9553 Gullet Pellet	9554 Gallium Pallium
9555 Palilalia Pavlov	9556 Gloves Pelvis	9557 Pelvic Gallic	9558 Polled Pulled	9559 Gallop Pillage
9560 Pleasure Pulsar	9561 Pulsion Gloxinia	9562 Polish Peevish	9563 Pulsate Ugliest	9564 Plasma Gleesome
9565 Plausive Plosive	9566 Glass Gloss	9567 Pulaski Opalesce	9568 Pleased Palisade	9569 Gel-soap Goal-siege
9570 Glacier Placer	9571 Pelican Glycine	9572 Placebo Gulch	9573 Placate Plicate	9574 Glaucoma Pilcomayo
9575 Glacial Glycol	9576 Places Glucose	9577 Pluck Polack	9578 Placid Policed	9579 Goal-keep Pile-cap
9580 Glider Pleader	9581 Golden Paladin	9582 Play-Doh Payload-bay	9583 Plaudit Gelidity	9584 Pole-jam Ugly-dame
9585 Gladly Gelidly	9586 Uploads Glades	9587 Gold-key Guava-juice	9588 Glided Pleaded	9589 Pledge Plodge
9590 Apologize Gulper	9591 Playpen Polygon	9592 Plough Glyph	9593 Pulpit Palpate	9594 Polygamy Pulpify
9595 Plugola Pulpal	9596 Epilepsy Polyps	9597 Geologic Pelagic	9598 Plagued Polypoid	9599 Gloppy Plug-up

9600 Upsizer Ape-seizure	9601 Gas-zone Goose-run	9602 Gas-orb Guise-robe	9603 Geyserite Gas-route	9604 Gisarme Gas-room
9605 Pious-rule Apes-rave	9606 Posers Geysers	9607 Pay-source Gas-arc	9608 Pea-sized Pause-radio	9609 Upsurge Gas-rig
9610 Poisoner Opsonize	9611 Opsonin Pious-nun	9612 Gas-nub Goose-woobie	9613 Peasant Gas-unit	9614 Poise-wife Guise-name
9615 Poison-ivy Gas-wave	9616 Poisons Paxwax	9617 Poison-oak Psionic	9618 Poisoned Ape-sound	9619 Posing Pausing
9620 Pusher Gusher	9621 Pshaw Push-on	9622 Gas-hob Posh-boy	9623 Upshot Pushout	9624 Gooseham Pixham
9625 Apishly Gasohol	9626 Gashes Pushes	9627 Gas-book Goose-beak	9628 Gashed Pushed	9629 Gasbag Push-up
9630 Posture Poster	9631 Position Piston	9632 Postboy Go-south	9633 Apostate Post-it	9634 Pastime Episiotomy
9635 Apostle Epistle	9636 Posts Pests	9637 Egoistic Apositic	9638 Posted Posited	9639 Postage Gestapo
9640 Gas-fire Pismire	9641 Gasman Opsomania	9642 Pixie-fib Ugsome-yob	9643 Goosefoot Go-soft	9644 Gas-fume Epoxy-foam
9645 Gas-fuel Apes-movie	9646 Gas-fuse Orgasms	9647 Pox-face Orgasmic	9648 Gasified Guise-mode	9649 Gas-fog Apes-image
9650 Gas-layer Gasolier	9651 Epsilon Gasoline	9652 Gas-lab Pious-vibe	9653 Pixelate Pisolite	9654 Psalm Gay-asylum
9655 Yugoslavia Upsell	9656 Pixels Posy-vase	9657 Gooselike Gas-leak	9658 Pause-video Pea-salad	9659 Posology Upslope
9660 Pessary Guesser	9661 Passion Gossoon	9662 Pixyish Gassho	9663 Gusset Posset	9664 Opossum Passim
9665 Passive Piassava	9666 Pisses Pussies	9667 Passkey Passaic	9668 Passed Pissed	9669 Gossip Passage
9670 Piscary Pescara	9671 Piscean Gascony	9672 Psyche Pascha	9673 Gasket Gas-cut	9674 Gas-coma Pay-scam

9675￼Upscale￼Pascal	9676￼Pisces￼Psicose	9677￼Pea-sack￼Go-sick	9678￼Peasecod￼Psocidae	9679￼Geoscopy￼Episcope
9680￼Ipso-jure￼Pseudourea	9681￼Poseidon￼Pasadena	9682￼Apes-job￼Pox-jab	9683￼Gas-jet￼Pyxidate	9684￼Pyxidium￼Gas-doom
9685￼Apsidal￼Pseudova	9686￼Episodes￼Epoxides	9687￼Episodic￼Gas-decay	9688￼Age-seeded￼Pseudo-aid	9689￼Gas-dope￼Pseudo-gay
9690￼Gasper￼Pea-souper	9691￼Gas-gun￼Apes-gene	9692￼Pisgah￼Pasiphae	9693￼Gas-pit￼G-spot	9694￼Pause-game￼Epoxy-gum
9695￼Gospel￼Goose-pool	9696￼Gasps￼Gay-spouse	9697￼Geospace￼Apes-pace	9698￼Gasped￼Apes-guide	9699￼Goose-egg￼Gas-pipe
9700￼Go-crazy￼Epicurize	9701￼Epicurean￼Picaroon	9702￼Pea-crab￼Pay-curb	9703￼Go-kart￼Picrate	9704￼Pecorama￼Peace-room
9705￼Upcurl￼Peace-rule	9706￼Pacers￼Pokers	9707￼Pace-race￼Peakirk	9708￼Epicardia￼Picardy	9709￼Epicarp￼Epic-rage
9710￼Pecuniary￼Piacenza	9711￼Pacinian￼Pyocyanin	9712￼Poke-nib￼Peak-nub	9713￼Poke-into￼Piconet	9714￼Epic-name￼Apocynum
9715￼Peace-envoy￼Peace-wave	9716￼Pekinese￼Piecewise	9717￼Picnic￼Peacenik	9718￼Pokeweed￼Ape-kind	9719￼Pacing￼Poking
9720￼Poacher￼Peak-hour	9721￼Apachean￼Peace-boon	9722￼Peace-hub￼Peach-hue	9723￼Pachyotia￼Apachite	9724￼Pico-ohm￼Peak-boom
9725￼Peaceable￼Epochal	9726￼Peaches￼Pouches	9727￼Epic-book￼Poke-hook	9728￼Poached￼Pouched	9729￼Peace-hope￼Peace-hug
9730￼Picture￼Pectize	9731￼Pectin￼Peace-tone	9732￼Peace-oath￼Pacey-youth	9733￼Pectate￼Epic-quote	9734￼Peace-time￼Peak-time
9735￼Epicotyl￼Piketail	9736￼Picts￼Pay-cuts	9737￼Pectic￼Peaky-tyke	9738￼Peak-tide￼Pacated	9739￼Epic-tape￼Peace-tip
9740￼Pacifier￼Opacifier	9741￼Pokemon￼Paceman	9742￼Pyecombe￼Peace-mob	9743￼Poke-foot￼Epic-feat	9744￼Epic-fame￼Peace-memo
9745￼Peaceful￼Piecemeal	9746￼Epicomus￼Pacey-fox	9747￼Pacific￼Peace-make	9748￼Pacified￼Peak-mode	9749￼Pico-amp￼Gay-camp

9750 Peculiar Apicular	9751 Paceline Peak-view	9752 Gay-club Peace-vibe	9753 Pikelet Peculate	9754 G-clef Pay-claim
9755 Epically Apically	9756 Epicalyx Go-close	9757 Pikelike Geeky-look	9758 Go-cold Epic-video	9759 Pucelage Geoecology
9760 Epic-size Pay-Caesar	9761 Peak-sway Ape-cousin	9762 Pay-cash Geekish	9763 Epicist Upcast	9764 Epic-arm Peace-axiom
9765 Peak-sale Peace-seal	9766 Picasso Gay-kiss	9767 Peace-seek Epic-ski	9768 Poke-aside Guaiac-seed	9769 Epic-saga Peek-spy
9770 Pecker Picker	9771 Pack-away Peace-icon	9772 Geocache Pikachu	9773 Packet Pocket	9774 Epic-cameo Peace-café
9775 Pickle Upcycle	9776 Pickaxe Geckos	9777 Peacock Pick-key	9778 Packed Pocked	9779 Package Pick-up
9780 Picador Geocoder	9781 Apocodeine Epicedian	9782 Epic-job Poke-jab	9783 Piece-data Peace-date	9784 Epicedium Geekdom
9785 Epicedial Peace-deal	9786 Epicedes Picoides	9787 Poke-joke Epic-idiocy	9788 Peace-deed Poke-judo	9789 Poke-deep Puke-dope
9790 Peek-pry Epic-opera	9791 Pay-coupon Poke-open	9792 Ape-cough Peace-pub	9793 Apocopate Peace-gate	9794 Guaiac-gum Epic-poem
9795 Gay-couple Pike-pole	9796 Apocopes Pike-apex	9797 Pike-poke Peak-pace	9798 Peace-guide Gay-cupid	9799 Upkeep-pay Peace-gig
9800 Go-dizzy Apodizer	9801 Padrone Gadroon	9802 Pee-drib Good-robe	9803 Gujarati Good-art	9804 Pyoderma Pie-dream
9805 Epidural Pedrail	9806 Guiders Good-ears	9807 Go-dark Good-race	9808 Age-dread Good-read	9809 Guide-rope Pee-drop
9810 Guide-wire Pay-dowry	9811 Goodwin Go-down	9812 Guide-nob Pod-web	9813 Pedant Godwit	9814 Goodwife Good-name
9815 Guide-nail Ape-jowl	9816 Guide-noose Good-nose	9817 Guidance Podunk	9818 Pudenda Pedwood	9819 Guiding Goading
9820 Guide-bar Good-hair	9821 Upjohn Good-honey	9822 Pad-boob God-baby	9823 Gad-about Pay-debt	9824 Good-home Padiham

9825 Guidable Pay-double	9826 God-house Good-byes	9827 Guidebook Good-book	9828 Godhood Godhead	9829 Good-hope Goody-bag
9830 Podiatry Updater	9831 Guide-tone Good-tune	9832 Goad-youth Guide-tube	9833 Good-quote Paid-quota	9834 Good-time Guide-team
9835 Guide-tool Good-tale	9836 Updates Guide-taxi	9837 Geodetic Epidotic	9838 Updated Good-tide	9839 Good-tip Pod-tape
9840 Godfrey God-fury	9841 Goodman Aged-man	9842 Pad-moob Go-dumb	9843 Guide-feet Good-feat	9844 Paid-off Guide-memo
9845 Gadfly Good-move	9846 Pyjamas Podiums	9847 Epidemic Good-make	9848 Good-food Pyjama-day	9849 Good-image Guide-map
9850 Pedlar Godavari	9851 Guideline Good-view	9852 Guide-lab Good-vibe	9853 Good-lot Guide-vote	9854 Goodlife Pied-leaf
9855 Paid-leave Godlily	9856 Pedals Poodles	9857 Godlike Good-look	9858 Age-divide Good-lad	9859 Guadeloupe Podalgia
9860 Paid-user Good-size	9861 Godson Goodison	9862 Goodish Pie-dish	9863 Podesta Gaudiest	9864 Paid-sum Podosome
9865 Good-soul Pad-sole	9866 Apodosis Good-issue	9867 Geodesic Pay-desk	9868 Gods-day Good-side	9869 Aged-sage Good-soup
9870 Pedicure Good-care	9871 Good-icon Pad-knee	9872 Pedicab Paducah	9873 Podocyte Pudicity	9874 Good-café Paid-cameo
9875 Pedicle Pedicel	9876 Good-cause Paid-case	9877 Geoduck Good-cook	9878 Good-kid Guide-code	9879 Good-cop Guide-copy
9880 Gadder Pedder	9881 Pododynia Aged-doyen	9882 Good-job Paid-job	9883 Paid-duty Good-data	9884 Gaddafi Goddam
9885 Paddle Puddle	9886 Paddies Good-days	9887 Good-joke Guided-key	9888 Padded Good-deed	9889 Guide-dog Giddy-up
9890 Pedigree Podagra	9891 Pidgin Gudgeon	9892 Good-pub Pie-dough	9893 Gadget Goodput	9894 Good-game Gay-digamy
9895 Good-goal Go-deeply	9896 Good-guys Pod-peas	9897 Guide-pace Goad-pike	9898 Paid-guide Good-God	9899 Pedagogue Guide-page

9900 Apprize Pauperize	9901 Pea-green Pig-iron	9902 Paperboy Pay-probe	9903 Pop-art Paper-toy	9904 Pogrom Epigram
9905 Approve Apparel	9906 Papers Paupers	9907 Paprika Pay-price	9908 Upgrade Appeared	9909 Age-group Pay-garage
9910 Paganize Peignoir	9911 Pay-penny Appian-way	9912 Pigeon-bay Pagan-boy	9913 Appointee Pageant	9914 Epigenome Poop-enema
9915 Paganly Paginal	9916 Geognosy Paganise	9917 Pyogenic Geoponic	9918 Append Pigweed	9919 Piping Gaping
9920 Gopher Epiphora	9921 Epiphany Payphone	9922 Apiphobia Pig-baby	9923 Gigabyte Epiphyte	9924 Giga-ohm Pig-hoof
9925 Gaugeable Peephole	9926 Pageboys Gigabase	9927 Page-book Peg-hook	9928 Egghead Pagehood	9929 Apophyge Geophagia
9930 Appetize Peptize	9931 Egyptian Pupation	9932 Pig-taboo Age-apathy	9933 Appetite Pipette	9934 Gag-team Peep-time
9935 Pigtail Pipe-tool	9936 Ape-pets Pay-gates	9937 Peptic Pup-tyke	9938 Peptide Pupated	9939 Page-type Pup-tag
9940 Pogmoor Egg-fry	9941 Pygmean Gagman	9942 Pygmy-boy Pea-gumbo	9943 Pigfoot Pig-meat	9944 Pop-off Peg-off
9945 Pig-flu Agape-meal	9946 Pygmies Egg-mix	9947 Apogamic Epigamic	9948 Pygmoid Pig-food	9949 Giga-amp Pygmy-ape
9950 Popular Poplar	9951 Pipeline Pipevine	9952 Apple-bee Google-yahoo	9953 Piglet Populate	9954 Peplum Papaya-leaf
9955 Papilla Agape-love	9956 Apples Pupils	9957 Populace Egg-yolk	9958 Applaud Applied	9959 Apple-pie Apple-pay
9960 Appeaser Opposer	9961 Pepsin Pegasean	9962 Popish Uppish	9963 Opposite Apposite	9964 Gypsum Agapism
9965 Uppsala Gap-seal	9966 Pegasus Gypsies	9967 Egg-sac Egg-sauce	9968 Opposed Apposed	9969 Peep-spy Page-usage
9970 Pig-cry Pug-care	9971 Pope-icon Pipkin	9972 Pipe-echo Pee-pouch	9973 Pay-pact Pup-cot	9974 Egg-café Pig-coma

9975	9976	9977	9978	9979
Peep-clue	Age-peaks	Pay-pack	Peep-kid	Egg-cup
Pipe-cave	Egg-case	Pop-coke	Gauge-code	Pope-cap
9980	9981	9982	9983	9984
Pig-deer	Pig-jaw	Pope-job	Pagodite	Papadum
Gag-jury	Pug-den	Pug-jab	Age-update	Popedom
9985	9986	9987	9988	9989
Pop-idol	Pagodas	Papaya-juice	Age-guided	Pig-dog
Pug-duel	Pea-pods	Papa-doc	Go-giddy	Pipe-dope
9990	9991	9992	9993	9994
Pepper	Oppugn	Poppy-bee	Puppet	Pop-opium
Piggery	Popgun	Pig-pooh	Poppet	Gay-pygmy
9995	9996	9997	9998	9999
Giggle	Puppies	Apagogic	Pegged	Pug-pup
Goggle	Guppies	Epagogic	Gagged	Egg-pip

Printed in the United States
By Bookmasters